I0191850

Savage Economy

Savage Economy

The Returns of Middle English Romance

WALTER WADIAK

University of Notre Dame Press
Notre Dame, Indiana

University of Notre Dame Press
Notre Dame, Indiana 46556
www.undpress.nd.edu

Copyright © 2017 by the University of Notre Dame

All Rights Reserved

Published in the United States of America

Library of Congress Cataloging-in-Publication Data
Names: Wadiak, Walter, 1977– author.
Title: Savage economy : the returns of Middle English romance / Walter Wadiak.
Description: Notre Dame, Indiana : University of Notre Dame Press, 2016. |
    Includes bibliographical references and index.
Identifiers: LCCN 2016039532 (print) | LCCN 2016043020 (ebook) |
    ISBN 9780268101183 (hardcover : alk. paper) | ISBN 0268101183
    (hardcover : alk. paper) | ISBN 9780268101206 (pdf) |
    ISBN 9780268101213 (epub)
Subjects: LCSH: Romances, English—History and criticism. | English
    literature—Middle English, 1100–1500—History and criticism. | Violence
    in literature.
Classification: LCC PR327 .W33 2016 (print) | LCC PR327 (ebook) |
    DDC 821/.03309—dc23
LC record available at https://lccn.loc.gov/2016039532

∞ This paper meets the requirements of ANSI/NISO Z39.48-1992
(Permanence of Paper).

Contents

Preface   vii

Acknowledgments   xiii

CHAPTER 1
The Persistence of Romance   1

CHAPTER 2
The Gift and Its Returns   30

CHAPTER 3
Chaucerian Capital   63

CHAPTER 4
Gawain's "Nirt" and the Sign of Chivalry   88

CHAPTER 5
"What Shall These Bowes Do?"   119

Notes   151

Works Cited   173

Index   189

Preface

Romances, of course, should be read backwards. Only then does it become clear, for instance, what is wrong with Arthur's untimely nap at the beginning of Chretien de Troyes's *Yvain* or with the unfortunate Custom of the Stag in the same author's *Erec and Enide*. Or we might notice, looking back, that there is something just a little too precious about the Camelot depicted in the opening scene of *Sir Gawain and the Green Knight*—a complacency, we see in hindsight, that deserves a shock. Reading these stories retrospectively gives us access to the symbolic power of romance, the way in which *this* is like *that*, even as the genre resists the more strictly causal logic of a modern novel.[1] It might even be that a genre as disorganized and episodic as romance only makes sense in the ways that retrospective reading can reveal. The narrative structure of most romances consistently points us back to the beginning. The end is typically less an arrival someplace new than a confirmation of what the beginning already knows—less a resolution than a restatement of the initial problem.

This book asks what it would mean if the entire genre of romance could be understood in this way. What if, in other words, we thought about retrospection as ideological rather than simply narrative? It might turn out, in this case, that late romance could help us to read the genre's origins anew—that such romances could tell us what kind of thing romance really was all along. This book is about a group of these belated romances: the romances in Middle English, especially those of the fourteenth and fifteenth centuries. While a classic view of romance is to regard it as an "ideological imaginary" and a "structure of false consciousness" through which a feudal elite justified its power and privilege, this book argues for a more complicated model in which chivalry becomes the organizing principle of broader forms of community.[2] We will see that these communities, while not imagined fully until about the middle of the fifteenth century, can nevertheless be glimpsed in much earlier texts. Ultimately, I argue for reading the "reconstituted romances" of the fifteenth century and later as a mirror of the ways in which romance is in fact *always* reconstituting itself, returning compulsively to previous ideological needs even as the genre adapts itself to every new circumstance.

Savage Economy begins with the assumption that romance names a particular kind of chivalric fantasy to which violence is central, just as violence was instrumental to the formation and identity of the medieval warrior aristocracy as a distinct class. Violence—who got to use it and who was on the receiving end of it—is therefore the central question of this book. A traditional way of thinking about the violence of romance is to regard it as an expression of aristocratic privilege, of the unique *right* to violence wielded by a military caste in its relations with one another as well as with those lower down the social scale. Violence in this sense is the gift or *donum*—the asymmetrical gesture—that underwrites and reaffirms the feudal power of a privileged group. The analogy with the gift is important to my argument, insofar as aristocratic giving can perform the symbolic violence that romance also depends on more broadly in order to present itself as both a coded threat and an expression of chivalric values—at once a covering over and a revelation of the "truth" of a chivalry based on coercion and self-interest.

Broadly, the book charts a trajectory from violence aimed directly at securing feudal domination to the subtler and more diffuse modes of coercion that later English romances explore. The violence of these texts becomes less personal and direct in some of the ways that critical theory of the past decades has illuminated. Yet this story is ultimately one of persistence as much as change. The persistence of romance, as I refer to it throughout the book, is the persistence of an "archaic" past within the rapidly changing world that these texts illuminate. Gifts speak to the modernity of romance—its desire to insert itself into a late medieval commercial economy of increasing sophistication and volume—and at the same time to nostalgia, the characteristic desire of romance to return to the past. If anthropology tells us that the gift is by its very nature an ambiguous sign, this ambiguity speaks to an essential tension in the romances I read here, texts formed by a late medieval world that wants to go back even as it is driven ineluctably forward. While my argument does not deny the potential for romance to activate what Aranye Fradenburg calls "the *jouissance* of the encounter with the new," I suggest that a continuity of ideology and social function can be observed in spite of changing historical circumstances.[3]

This approach obviously has its limits. This study does not try to chart historical changes fully, but it does strive to illuminate the reasons and the particular contexts in which the persistence of romance is important. Ultimately, it suggests that the violence of chivalry—and the desire for violence that chivalry celebrates—is the central commitment of the Middle English romances. In many respects bourgeois and even "popular"—as many of the genre's readers have pointed out—English romances also dramatize how chivalric ideology persists as a residue in what might seem quite alien formations. In making this argument, I am keenly aware that I am all too often generalizing about texts whose precise social locations are remarkably diverse. This is probably unavoidable in a study that engages with multiple texts across a broad swath of time in making its claims.

A second limit of this approach—with resulting deficiencies that are somewhat harder to gauge—has to do with the kind of book this is not. For one could imagine a book that saw in the gift work of romance not an attempt at asymmetrical violence, but rather a way of imagining the gift as a truly radical gesture, along the lines of calls for us to "think the gift" as a means of going beyond our own restrictive economic and political regimes. Certainly many English romances do imagine gift giving as broadly constitutive of community. That should not be surprising: these texts have long been recognized to be speaking to a "larger community" than earlier Continental romances.[4] The "noble" gift, on such a reading, might be understood to be destructive not of others, but of self—a realization of Georges Bataille's arresting claim that "human beings are only united with each other through rents or wounds."[5] Such a reading is particularly intriguing as a way of accounting for those romances that could be said to subvert chivalric fantasies of possession, such as *The Awntyrs off Arthur* (discussed in chapter 2) and *Sir Gawain and the Green Knight* (discussed in chapter 4). This book takes a different view, however. I propose an understanding of romance as primarily interested in the preservation of an existing order, often precisely through the assimilation of what might seem at first glance to be revolutionary or novel. In this more conservative estimation of the genre, medieval romances—even those that qualify as in some sense "critical"—work more often than not to defend and reinscribe chivalry as a strategy of violent taking.[6] For me the interest of such texts lies partly in how they reveal the "archaic" roots of our own fantasies of ownership. This does not mean that there is nothing of ethical or human value in texts that so often conjure, in richly imaginative ways, alternatives to the world we inhabit, yet I do want to suggest that one undeniable function of romance is to perform a violence that continues to haunt us.

Chapter 1 begins by exploring how early English romance serves to affirm and express aristocratic identity and then shows how this basic purpose is tied to the classic function of the "noble" gift as described by modern anthropology. *Floris and Blancheflour* imagines the gift as a site of aristocratic distinction, sharply differentiating the gift from newer, commercial forms of exchange that this historically knowledgeable text also records. Yet the poem suggests that its gifts might activate a potentially universalizable desire for the objects of chivalry, a possibility that endangers the very distinction that *Floris* otherwise aims to secure. The second chapter shows that by the late fourteenth century, this threat was real enough to generate a response in the form of a group of "spendthrift" romances. The aggressivity of these heroes' reckless giving is arguably directed at a rising bourgeoisie, but such stories dramatize aristocratic impotence in a world that no longer seems to have a clear use for actual knightly violence. Violence, displaced onto noble exchange, becomes a symbolic gesture rather than a sustainable means of ensuring aristocratic power.

Chapter 3 considers Chaucer's *Knight's Tale* as a text in which violence becomes not just displaced but radically decentered, beyond the control and intention of any one actor. Yet precisely for that reason, the profits of violence can be appropriated by the community at large and known, by analogy, as the cultural value of the tale itself. *Sir Gawain and the Green Knight* (chapter 4) also suggests how violence becomes the sign of value that unites a community. Later romances of Gawain broaden their definition of the chivalric community to include non-nobles to the extent that they, too, can be seen to embody the potential for violence. The evolution of the Gawain story shows how romance, in becoming "popular," can rework chivalric ideology to suit new social needs without essentially transforming that ideology.

The final chapter explores how this process of adapting romance to new circumstances provides an imaginative basis for the emergently modern forms of social and economic life that late medieval outlaw tales depict. Stories like *A Gest of Robyn Hode* demonstrate the persistence of romance in the context of a literary tradition usually thought of as expressing romance's decline. If English romances have seemed to many readers to be marginally chivalric at best, outlaw tales are literally unchivalric in featuring heroes who are typically not knights. Yet stories like the *Gest* allow us to see in a new way the extent to which a nascent culture of capitalism remained at the same time a profoundly chivalric culture, invested in a violence that capitalism at once pretends to abjure and cannot do without.

Acknowledgments

This is a book about bad gifts—the kind that compel or seduce us into submission—but we know that life would be intolerable without real gifts: those that not only aid and nourish, but in doing so communicate some part of the giver's essence. In acknowledging my debts for the good gifts I have received, I hope in a modest way to say something about the people who have given them to me.

This book could not have been written without the support and dedicated mentorship of my graduate advisor, Elizabeth Allen, who mentioned after class one day—as if proposing a walk—that I might think about becoming a medievalist. From the moment I showed up in her office a week or so later, she has been the best of teachers. She has read some version of everything in this book—usually more than once—and offered endless encouragement while also asking the tough questions that sometimes needed to be asked. Two of my other teachers at the University of California, Irvine, Linda Georgianna and Robert Folkenflik, have read chapters and offered helpful suggestions, and both continue to be mentors as well as kind and wise friends. For their advice and insights at various points in the coming together of this book, I am also grateful to George Edmondson, John Ganim, Noah Guynn, William Kuskin, Kathy Lavezzo, Robert Meyer-Lee, Kevin Riordan, Elizabeth Scala, Ronald Schleifer, and George Shuffelton, among many others.

The Donald A. Strauss Foundation provided support in the form of a dissertation fellowship that helped me begin this project, and UC

Irvine gave additional support through its Summer Dissertation Fellowship program. Stephen Little at the University of Notre Dame Press was always quick in his replies and helped me negotiate a lengthy process. I am also most grateful to Andrew Galloway and the other anonymous reader of the manuscript, who suggested the inclusion of a coda and a preface, respectively, and were challenging in all the right ways. Beth Wright of Trio Bookworks provided excellent copyediting. *Philological Quarterly* and *Exemplaria* gave me permission to reprint material from previously published work that appears here in chapters 3 and 5, respectively. It was a stroke of luck for me that the anonymous readers and the editors at both journals were unusually helpful.

Some of my most profound debts are to the people who put up with me during the unnaturally long life of this project. My fellow graduate students at UC Irvine, especially R. Jacob McDonie, Megan Nowell, and Scott Eric Kaufman, were my close comrades as my ideas were first taking shape, and I am grateful for their conversation and friendship. Two of my colleagues in Singapore, Andrew Yerkes and Daniel Jernigan, alternately prodded and soothed until the thing was finally written, and both have since become cherished friends. Matthew Dudley was a source of loving support and companionship throughout the entirety of this book's making. Our closeness means more to me than I can begin to acknowledge here. My first debt, like all first debts, is to my parents: Ellen, who read to each of her children in turn, and Tommaso, who was there when we needed him most.

CHAPTER 1

The Persistence of Romance

This is a book about the meaning of gift giving in medieval romances, but it is more broadly about the kind of thing a medieval romance is. "Romance" is notoriously the vaguest of the categories by which we claim to be able to reduce medieval literature to some kind of order, and it was a category loosely employed by medieval writers and readers themselves. It originally signified no more than a text's vernacularity (anything written "en romanz"), only developing in time the associations with love, adventure, and courtliness that we think of as central to the form. Nor do all texts labeled as romances by medieval or modern readers fulfill even these basic criteria, leading one surveyist of the form to conclude that "it is practically impossible to generalize about the romances because they have so little in common."[1] Yet it is just as clear that we cannot do without some attempt to define the contours of the dominant genre of secular literature in the Middle Ages. "Romance" conjures a set of problems for literary history that seem intractable yet unavoidable.

Middle English romance has long been a kind of limit case for this set of problems. Minimalist in style, devoid for the most part of courtly interest, and typically unconcerned to delineate a complex psychology of love, many English romances look like anything but romances—a problem crystallized by a tendency in critical literature to summon up the names of other genres when describing what a given English romance is actually like: chronicle, epic, *exemplum*, saint's life, fabliau. In the readiness with which they blend into other genres, English romances dramatize with particular force the rule of thumb that medieval genres seem rarely to have "very sharp edges." Attempts to define English romance have also had to contend with a critical tradition that regards these texts as impoverished in relation to Continental exemplars, so that what the English poems seem to lack—"all the elements of chivalry and romance," in one reader's remarkable phrase—has been taken to signify a more general illegibility of form. Yet romance is central to the course of literary history in English, even perhaps to the extent of providing the "grounds for the English literature of later periods."[2] The problem of identifying with any certainty what the genre of English romance might amount to thus presents itself as a problem for the history of English literature in general. It is as if, having determined that virtually every post-Conquest literary text in English owes something to the legacy of romance, we have simultaneously decided that nothing really is one.

Such questions might initially seem remote from a book about gift giving, but in fact English romance imagines itself as a gift from its first lines. The very oldest of these texts in Middle English, *King Horn* (circa 1225), begins by promising us a gift in the form of a hero so exceptional and rare, so unlike anything or anyone else—"Nas non his iliche" (line 20)—that he quite literally lights up any room he enters, himself the bearer of charisma in the original sense of "a divine gift." Just hearing the story of such a man, the narrator assures us, will make us "blithe" (1).[3] If we are inclined to speak of the "spirit" of such texts—as the critical work on them has tended to do—this is in part because we recognize that, like the spirit or *hau* of the gift as first described by Marcel Mauss, the "spirit" of romance is what ensures that all the losses inflicted by the initial traumas of romance will be made good.[4] It is this spirit that allows us to recognize the earliest romances produced in post-Conquest England as stories especially obsessed with the returns they promise, so that even if "stories of departure and return are hardly unique to insular literature," there is still something highly symptomatic about the sheer number of such texts to appear in England from about 1200 to 1500—a fact that "connects these romances to their time and place."[5]

Such stories promise us implicitly (and often explicitly) that they will recoup the losses driving their protagonist into the world of action, so we can read the path from loss to recovery traced out by these romances as a literary economy. And it is not just any economy, moreover, but specifically that of the "noble" gift, since however confidently such stories promise that all losses will be recovered, their narrative space is precisely the interim between loss and recovery that differentiates such giving from the mere exchange of commodities.[6] Even when these romances seems in some broad sense popular, as opposed to aristocratic, they typically present themselves as authentic products of chivalric culture, despite and perhaps even because of so often being commodities in a growing late medieval marketplace for English writing.[7]

It is also characteristic of romance in medieval England that the informing spirit of these stories—grounded in the "rude vigor" that distinguishes them—is identifiable in their most characteristic excesses, even as this same spirit is also what ensures their knowability as romances. In this, too, romances of England perform the gift as an expression of what modern cultural studies, primarily through the work of gift theory itself, recognizes as "symbolic violence." On the one hand, then, scholars have long celebrated or lamented (according to taste) the considerable gore of these "pulp fictions"—their propensity for the "fierce and rough," "bloodthirsty," and "gruesome"—in short, for everything that makes "lethal chivalric violence . . . the genre's earliest and longest-lasting concern."[8] Yet most have accepted at the same time that "romance" might after all be the best word for a genre that also knows something about the symbolizing procedures through which brute force can be transformed into the value of chivalry. Scholarship implicitly recognizes, in other words, that even the so-called popular romances of medieval England are remarkably adept at the kinds of mystification that "spirit" names, just as the *hau* of the gift exerts its compelling force by virtue of its numinousness. We are beginning to recognize, in other words, that the romances of medieval England are remarkably chivalric in their concerns and values, precisely because they are also everything else: "bourgeois-gentry," "mercantile," "popular," "entirely and *essentially* middle-class," and in a few cases perhaps even "lower-class."[9] This book reads the scenes of aristocratic giving performed in English romances as a central metaphor for this complexity of social meaning. It argues that the paradoxes of the noble gift offer us an important way of understanding texts whose own paradoxical social location is becoming increasingly apparent. I explore how these stories enact, through their insistence on the gift, the persistence of a chivalric culture that will prove highly adaptable to new contexts.

Central to my analysis of this complexity is the question of violence in the English romances. What does it mean to say that violence becomes a gift in many of these stories? How, indeed, *can* violence become a gift? And how does this violence sustain a range of contexts which are, properly speaking, both chivalric and mercantile, medieval and emergently modern? By exploring the trajectory of English romance through time, this book suggests answers that are intended to shed new light on romance's longevity. Where we have traditionally understood romance as a mode of chivalric fantasy whose claims grow increasingly obsolete and absurd with the passage of the centuries, we might instead conceive of a mode whose violence is *always* available to reinforce a given order, including ultimately our own. "Chivalry" on my reading becomes, like romance itself, a term with immense travelling power. Specifically, the desire for chivalry that romance expresses can be understood, in my account, as a desire for forms of violence capable of regulating an evolving political economy.

This study contributes to a growing body of scholarship on aristocratic giving as a hermeneutic for understanding medieval literature. Much of this work has been focused on high-medieval epic, saga, and the *chanson de geste*, and Andrew Cowell in particular offers a reading of the gift's violence that has guided my own thinking.[10] Yet while this scholarship has been immensely valuable for its insights into the ways in which the noble gift helps to forge aristocratic identity in the Middle Ages, such work has tended on the whole to neglect and even marginalize romance, particularly that of the later medieval period. D. Vance Smith's *Arts of Possession* is a brilliant exception in its exploration of the "forms of surplus and exchange that continue to haunt us, forms whose persistence economic anthropology has not fully recognized." This book takes up Smith's invitation to trace that persistence more fully, especially in relation to Fredric Jameson's notion of romance as the literary genre whose unlikely persistence is an essential feature of modernity.[11] *Savage Economy* is in many ways an attempt to elaborate on Smith's analysis of an "ethics of possession" that continues to shape the economic logic of our own moment.

Smith's work also suggests a model for how gifts shape and manage the violent forms of desire central to romance. In this respect I have been inspired as well by more explicitly psychoanalytic accounts of the genre, especially by L. O. Aranye Fradenburg's *Sacrifice Your Love*, a meditation on sacrifice in the writing of Chaucer, and specifically by her understanding of how sacrifice structures "the militant European Christian subject." Similarly, Britton J. Harwood, in important articles on both Chaucerian romance and *Sir Gawain and the Green Knight*, has explored what it means for this subject to "submit to the demands of the gift." What matters most in such accounts, I suggest, is the central function of lack—the ways in which gifts become signifiers of the relations among desiring subjects. Often, as will become clear, those relations are forged in violence, tinged with the dangerous interplay between desire and death that romance so often depends on for its power.

Here it will suffice to say that psychoanalysis, the central modern account of desire, was from its beginnings interested in the symbolic power of the gift as this was known to late medieval chivalry. Jacques Lacan in particular relied on the anthropological work of Marcel Mauss and Claude Lévi-Strauss in formulating his theory that the symbolic order is constituted by a never-ending circulation of desire that begins with a gift: "the constituting gift of primitive exchange."[12] Bruce Holsinger provides a specifically medieval context for this theme in Lacan's work—one mediated, as Holsinger points out, by the psychoanalytic thinker's debt to his contemporary Georges Bataille's ethics of expenditure. Lacan gives a concrete form to this intellectual debt in *Seminar VII* when he speaks of "the piece of paper" on which he had quickly recorded (before he lost it) an account of a feudal potlatch held "somewhere in the region of Narbonne" during the Middle Ages. Despite having lost his lecture notes, Lacan nevertheless goes on to describe for his audience a medieval "festival" of giving in which desire takes a devastating form: "everything occurred," Lacan reports, "as if the foregrounding of the problematic of desire required as its necessary correlative the need for ostentatious forms of destruction, insofar as they are gratuitous." Echoing Bataille, Lacan ends his vignette by painting a picture of the medieval aristocracy as a class who (like Mauss's Kwakiutl chiefs) "rival each other in trying to destroy the most" through giving.[13] The gift, in this formulation, is a site where desire and violence converge. The early Middle English romance of *Floris and Blancheflour*, to which I will turn in the final section of this chapter, offers a basic model of the convergence that Lacan describes.

Lacan's reading of Mauss and Bataille perhaps begs the question, though, since the tradition from which he draws can by no means be characterized as uniform. The counterintuitive notion that the gift, particularly in its noble form, does perform violence has been broadly generative for contemporary cultural studies, beginning with Pierre Bourdieu's work on gift-giving practices among the Kabyle in Algeria—the initial germ of the French sociologist's grand theory of "symbolic violence" as what helps to ensure and reify social inequalities in all kinds of societies both premodern and modern.[14] Yet actually defining "symbolic violence" has proven no less frustrating than pinning down "romance," and this is one symptom of the ways in which the latter depends on the logic of the former. In laying the groundwork for a reading of romance in terms of the noble gift, I turn first to the question of what we mean when we speak of such gifts as symbolic violence, and how this meaning might be related in turn to the work of romance.

"A SORT OF SUBLIMATED WARFARE"

When the English king Richard II met Louis Duke of Orléans during a diplomatic visit to France in 1396, the two engaged in what one reader aptly calls a "duel of gifts":

Richard gave the duke a gold ewer and a *hanap* (a kind of ornate goblet), upon which the duke gave him a more precious ewer and *hanap*. Richard than gave him an *ouche*, an ornamental clasp, which he countered with a more beautiful one. Finally Richard stripped off his ruby ring and gave it to the duke, at which point the duke gave him a more valuable one, and left "with his head held high."[15]

The stakes of this metaphorical duel were real enough: a magnificent gift "could establish the recipient in a dependent relationship to the giver" by creating a bond of subservience based on obligation—an idea that extends back to Mauss's pioneering work on gift exchange in precapitalist societies.[16] The noble gift in this sense is "symbolic violence"—even, as we shall see, what Bourdieu dubs the "paradigm" of all such violence. The example of Richard's encounter with the French duke is apt in this respect, too, for it occurred as part of the peace negotiations at the close of the second phase of the Hundred Years' War. Read against this background, the duel takes on a specifically political character, as the central antagonists, standing in for their respective armies, trade gifts in place of blows. As in war, the logic of the encounter is one of steady escalation, from relatively cheap and commodified to more expensive and personal objects, culminating in Richard's gift of his own ring, a symbol of his personal authority, and the duke's aggressive reply.[17] The duke, brother to the French king, not only proves his "rank" (as Mauss would say) but—we might suppose in this context—also specifically works to refute Richard's claim of liege lordship over France and thus, by implication, over the duke's own territorial holdings. To come out behind in the gift-giving competition, by contrast, would have been to admit precisely the relationship of dependence with respect to Richard that the French monarchy had entered the Hundred Years' War to refute. By challenging Richard's right to give the superior gifts, the duke might be understood as also challenging Richard's right to give the all-important gift of France in exchange for vassalage.

But the story does not end there. Its continuation in Thomas Walsingham's *Chronica Maiora* rescues the gift from violence, as we might after all expect in the context of a diplomatic encounter. The violence of this remarkable exchange is, after all, merely symbolic, part of an elaborate process of negotiation in which not just material objects but kisses of peace will be exchanged among all present, culminating in the French king's gift of his daughter's hand in marriage, which Richard acknowledged aptly—according to Walsingham's account—as "an honourable and welcome gift" and "the good end and conclusion of a perpetual peace" between the warring kingdoms. The gift's power to secure peace was even to be given architectural form in a presentation to the church, a "Chapel of Peace and Our Lady" to be built on the spot of the peace negotiations "at [the two kings'] joint expense as an everlasting memorial."[18] Yet the fragility of the work done by these gifts is legible in the compulsion that they enact to keep giving more and more—from small objects to, finally, people and whole buildings. The need to give nobly in this fraught encounter seems almost like a confession that the intention of such gifts will always be open to question. Indeed, the violent meaning of the medieval noble gift—its latent aggressivity—depends in this example on all the ways in which that meaning is cloaked in elaborate declarations of the peaceful intentions of all parties, so that violence is both recognized and not. Such aggressivity is what Bourdieu calls the "the best-kept and worst-kept secret" of the gift.[19]

Among the more startling aspects of this account is the way in which it demonstrates the continuing centrality of aristocratic giving to a late medieval English scene that is at the same time emergently modern, the birthplace of a "culture of capitalism."[20] Against such a background, the picture of dueling gifts summoned by the English chronicler reminds us of what we might think of as the persistence of the medieval: here, the ways in which late medieval exchange continues to be fraught with all the violence and danger of Mauss's classic vision of the "primitive" economy. In his *Medieval Warrior Aristocracy* (2007), Cowell calls for us to move beyond the "false alterity" between a medieval economy of the gift and modern capitalist exchange to an appreciation of "a deeper alterity centered on the status of violence as enacted in the gift." He writes:

> In examining the medieval past, we must shift our focus from the opposition of gift and commodity to that of gift and violence. This is not to say that the former opposition did not exist; it is clear that markets existed essentially throughout the Middle Ages, and one axis of the gift's function was always in relation to the commodity. . . . Yet the other axis—of gift and socially destructive violence—was actually far more crucial for the warrior aristocracy of the late tenth through twelfth centuries. For this group, it is the contention that the strict gift/violence opposition seen by [anthropologists of the gift Marcel] Mauss and Lévi-Strauss must

be rejected, and that the gift itself must be examined much more closely as a form of aggression.[21]

I follow Cowell in attending to the violence of the medieval gift. Yet we might well ask, I propose, whether the two axes that he describes are not in fact related—that is, whether the violence of exchange is not also a question of the commodity *as well as* of the gift. For the notion that the commodity is innocent of violence is itself, of course, a fantasy of our own difference from the medieval. Recognizing this fact might be related, in turn, to the question of how a given form of exchange *can* be said to perform violence. This is not just to repeat the point that violence can be commodified—a fact as true of our own cultural forms as it is of medieval romances—but that, at a basic level, the commodity always contains a residue of the "archaic" violence that it would claim to disavow. And this in turn helps to show why a set of late medieval texts that actually know a great deal about commodities also fantasizes about a return to the mode of exchange that Cowell identifies with an earlier chivalric literature. The result of this complex interaction between overlapping regimes, I will suggest, is the complexity of a symbolic violence that is always shifting its meaning in relation to particular circumstances. This book proposes to examine such violence as a cultural phenomenon that is always evolving into something new.

If it is increasingly recognized that people "exchanged gifts even more exuberantly, in greater volume, and in more social arenas at the end of the Middle Ages than ever before," how might we talk about the persistence of these forms of exchange in the late medieval texts I explore here, even as those texts are profoundly marked by their engagement with mercantile culture?[22] The complexity that characterizes the economic imagination of English romances will force us to consider some difficult questions. What kind of violence can a gift do, and how might that violence be related, in turn, to our own most effective modes of domination? The answers are not self-evident, partly because the very possibility of there being a gift to begin with is tied to the idea of its opposite, the commodity "always," as Cowell puts it, already in circulation in the history of the medieval West. If there is no pure "time of the gift," there is also no pure form of the violence that such giving would realize (though Cowell admittedly comes close to finding one in the chronicle story of a clerk who, overwhelmed by the magnificence of a fine vase given him by Richard III of Normandy, "fell prostrate and died").[23] This is just to say that the violence of even "archaic" forms of exchange will always be "merely" symbolic. Symbolic violence, after all, is precisely *not* violence, however much we might fantasize about vases that are literally to die for. The history of gift theory suggests nothing so much as the radical ambiguity of the kind of violence at stake when we speak of the gift's ability to compel a return. As Walsingham's anecdote shows, the noble gift, too, cloaks the violent possessiveness at its heart. How then *can* we speak about such gifts?

The first person to do so was of course Mauss, whose *Essai sur le don* gave us the idea of the *kula* and especially the potlatch as specifically "noble" forms of giving. The term "noble" is used by both Mauss and many medieval texts to describe the gift-giving practices discussed throughout this book. Noble giving represents above all a struggle for rank among nobles or chiefs in the societies of Melanesia that serve as the essay's ethnographic point of focus.[24] The whole point of such giving—somewhat ironically, given Mauss's own commitment to a modern return to an ideal of "noble expenditure"—is rivalry and violence. The potlatch in particular for Mauss is a form of the gift that mimics the violence of war itself: a "struggle between nobles to establish a hierarchy amongst themselves," distinguished by "an extremely marked antagonistic character," reflecting "the principle of rivalry and hostility that prevails in all these practices."[25] Yet as though anxious about the specter he has raised, Mauss begins his account of the potlatch by assuring us that it is the exception, not the rule, of the societies whose gift-giving practices he documents, most of which he describes as systems for generating reciprocity as opposed to rivalry. Only as one reads the essay does it become clear that the potlatch is taking over, indeed, that it is coming to stand for the hidden role of violence in Mauss's accounts of what seem to be even the peaceful and reciprocal forms of gift exchange he wants to describe, until these, too, as Rodolphe Gasché remarks, "disclose . . . the rivalry that defines antagonistic prestations."[26] This mixing of gift types that Mauss initially wants to keep separate—the antagonistic potlatch and the reciprocal and peaceful *kula*—is evident by implication almost everywhere that Mauss subsequently refers to generosity and violence in the same breath, as when he describes the *mentalité* underlying premodern gift exchange as "a curious frame of mind, one of fear and exaggerated hostility, and of generosity that was likewise exaggerated."[27] Mauss's essay offers itself at least potentially as a deconstruction of the "strict gift/violence opposition" identified by Cowell, in which the gift always-already *is* violence, a "purely sumptuary destruction of wealth" in which "slaves are put to death, precious oils burnt, copper objects cast into the sea, and even the houses of princes set on fire."[28]

The question of what Mauss really means by "the gift" is fundamental to medieval studies in part because Mauss himself was fascinated by the medieval, beginning his essay with a quotation from the Scandinavian *Edda* and ending it with a vision of a modern return to "noble expenditure" as embodied by the court of King Arthur, whose knights, Mauss avers, sat down at the Round Table "around the common store of wealth." Mauss's medievalism colors his portrait of Germanic society as one that "developed to the extreme the entire system of *potlatch*, but in particular, the complete system of gifts"—a statement that frames in specifically medieval terms the problem of ambiguity that besets the essay as a whole, evident here in Mauss's confusing definition of the potlatch as not merely an aspect of a more "complete system of gifts" but as in fact an "entire system" unto itself.[29] Mauss thus gives us at least *two* versions of the Middle Ages: the era of shared wealth represented by the knights sitting in peace around Arthur's Round Table (which we should emulate) and the "entire system" of potlatch that at the essay's beginning was nothing more than an oddity but has become, by this point in the essay, potentially even more general than "the complete system of gifts" itself (reduced here to a particular instance of the larger system of the potlatch).

Part of the ambiguity has to do with Mauss's notion that even potlatch demands a return, so that what appears to be "purely sumptuary" expenditure actually *is* a "complete system of gifts"—an act of reciprocal exchange in which the winner of the potlatch gets something. This is precisely why the potlatch can be considered a form of violence. In a move that already anticipates Bourdieu's theory of symbolic violence,

Mauss implicitly suggests that the violence of the gift inheres in the way it demands a return while denying that it does so. The gift is "a polite fiction, formalism, and social deceit" motivated in reality by "obligation and economic self-interest."[30] Behind this false politesse lies the specter of aggression. While this is most evident in Mauss's description of the potlatch, it also determines in a more general way the distinction between gift and commodity in Mauss's writing. The noble gift does violence by refusing a certain and predictable return, throwing the receiver into uncertainty, placing her under an indeterminate obligation, even (in the case of potlatch) seeking to enslave. The gift's violence for Mauss is thus always partly a function of its status as a "not-commodity," a gesture that complicates, jeopardizes, or altogether refuses the predictable safety of exchange.

Mauss's essay, then, suggests both the instability of the opposition between gift and violence and also the fascination with the medieval that together characterize so much later gift theory. If Mauss himself does more to question than to uphold a gift-violence opposition, later writers are even more explicit about the violence inscribed in the noble gift. Important in this respect are Georges Bataille, who formulates the notion of aristocratic expenditure as "the need to destroy," and Marshall Sahlins, for whom gifts are "a sort of sublimated warfare" that function as "the primitive analogue of the social contract."[31] More explicitly than Mauss, these thinkers imagine generosity in precapitalist societies as an expression of violence in barely concealed terms, as in rituals of human sacrifice or in war itself (which Sahlins calls "the understructure of [precapitalist] society").[32] Bataille in particular was fascinated by the European Middle Ages as the paragon of gift culture, "a civilization of glorious wastefulness [whose] cathedrals, monasteries, castles, and fortresses embody the extravagant expenditures demanded by the medieval sovereign."[33] His work can be considered as a roughly cotemporaneous if more theoretical counterpart to the scholarship of academic medievalists like Georges Duby, who likewise viewed the basic impulse of the medieval gift economy in terms of a seemingly "senseless destruction" of wealth that was itself acquired violently.[34] Yet for all their explicitness about the violence of the gift, these later accounts do not so much resolve the ambiguity present in Mauss's account as simply reproduce it.

Sahlins's definition of the gift as both "a sort of sublimated warfare" as well as "a primitive analogue of the social contract" typifies this ambiguity, in which the gift is seen to defend against violence but at the same time to enact it ("sort of," as Sahlins aptly puts it).

I have lingered on the contradictory nature of much of this work because it suggests the complexity of what Bourdieu tries to do when he unites these disparate strands in his own work on symbolic violence—a term he invents—and its relation to the gift, which he sees as the paradigm of all such violence. When Bourdieu explores in systematic detail the paradox that gifts are both a replacement for violence and, at the same time, an expression of the violence supposedly displaced, he does so in response to the set of contradictions that we have been exploring. The gift, Bourdieu asserts, "is an attack on the freedom of the one who receives it" and even "a way to possess, by creating people obliged to reciprocate"—a claim that in one respect simply repeats Mauss's emphasis on the need to reciprocate the gift with a countergift. Yet Bourdieu departs from Mauss in his assertion that the gift functions as "symbolic" or, literally, "sweet" violence (*violence douce*) as opposed to overt violence (*violence ouvert*). Symbolic violence, for Bourdieu, is violence in which the goal of domination is misrecognized as such because it appears in euphemized form. As he somewhat opaquely puts it, "gift exchange is the paradigm of all the operations through which symbolic alchemy produces the reality-denying reality that the collective consciousness aims at as a collectively produced, sustained, and maintained misrecognition of the 'objective' truth" of domination.[35] Simply put, gifts are a more efficient way of establishing domination than can be achieved through overt violence, precisely because they depend on the participation of everybody (as an expression of "collective consciousness").

The notion of a "symbolic alchemy" might seem to hint at the medieval as the ultimate time of this "reality-denying reality" of symbolic violence, just as the gift is its "paradigm." In fact, however, Bourdieu's theory emphasizes the connections between premodern and modern societies. "Symbolic violence" is what persists in Bourdieu's account of how societies change. On the one hand, Bourdieu declares that "the precapitalist economy is the site *par excellence* of symbolic violence" because such euphemized violence is "the only way that relations of domination" can be disguised in the absence of modern institutions designed to uphold social distinctions.[36] The time of symbolic violence—the time of the gift—is premodern society. But if it seems to be banished, the gift nevertheless returns to haunt modernity in Bourdieu's account. In response to "the capacity for subversion and critique that the most brutal forms of 'economic' exploitation have aroused," there emerges

> a return to modes of accumulation based on the conversion of economic capital into symbolic capital, with all the forms of legitimizing redistribution, public ("social" policies) and private (financing of "disinterested" foundations, donations to hospitals, academic and cultural institutions, etc.), through which the dominant groups secure a capital of "credit" which seems to owe nothing to the logic of exploitation.[37]

The return of the gift in this narrative occurs as a result of "the capacity for subversion and critique," implying some vague, in-between time before the rise of this critical capacity and during which the gift had disappeared from history. Yet the indistinct nature of this account raises obvious questions of chronology and causality. When did the gift return, and in response to which specific threats? Why, suddenly, were the "objective mechanisms" that had replaced gift exchange no longer sufficient? It seems clear that such questions are far from Bourdieu's mind and that he speaks of "return" as a metaphor for what is really a kind of submerged continuity. Much of Bourdieu's work, especially in its focus on abstract forms of the gift such as the notion of "giftedness" in education (*The State Nobility*) or the ideal of disinterest so vital to modern theories of art (*The Rules of Art*, *Distinction*), attests to the continued need for symbolic violence in modern society. His work consistently reads the gift's persistence as part of a broader survival under modern capitalism of euphemizing strategies characteristic of earlier economic formations. More than mere residual ideology, the gift as symbolic violence is in Bourdieu's view what modernity continues to need.

Bourdieu's account nevertheless leaves unanswered some basic questions about how the gift's violence actually works. Specifically, he demands that we think about the nature of the relationship between the symbolic violence of the gift and "the most brutal forms" of real violence without ever precisely pinning down that relationship in his own work.[38] On the one hand, he suggests that "it would be wrong to see a contradiction in the fact that violence [in precapitalist societies] is both more present and more marked" than in societies that have developed more objective forms of domination.[39] Yet we have seen already that symbolic violence, like the gift itself, is also what continually returns for Bourdieu—what is always arising in response to an ever-resurgent *violence ouvert*, from which it can never be clearly separated. What seems clear is that symbolic violence is what persists in Bourdieu's account. Moreover, it evolves in ways that this book endeavors to trace. Symbolic violence is less a stable concept than a way of talking about the diverse ways in which communities experience the historically specific forms of violence that structure them. At the same time, Bourdieu's account is valuable in its insistence that there is continuity as well as change—that the logic of symbolic violence can be read across the divide that separates "precapitalist" cultures from modern ones.

If Bourdieu and others can help us to theorize the gift's persistence—its constant renewal as a cultural strategy in the context of widespread capitalist transformation—how might their ideas help us to think about the persistence of romance? To pose this question in the specific terms of my project here: If English romance is marked from the outset by historical belatedness, then how can we account for that belatedness as, in part, the strange persistence of a chivalric imaginary that was in many ways outmoded from the moment of its arrival on English soil? In what ways does English romance, like the gift described by modern theory, seek to negotiate the contradictions that inform its meaning as a cultural practice? Another way of putting this set of questions would be to ask simply: Why does romance, like Mauss's gift, keep coming back in late medieval England? In order to answer these questions, we first need to consider a tradition of thinking about the romances as texts whose violence is their most basic problem. Doing so will complicate our notion of how violence works in these texts, and by extension what these texts mean in their aspiration to be considered "romances" to begin with.

"WANTON WERKIS"

I have suggested that a tradition of thinking about the gift, as well as more broadly about the operations of symbolic violence, provides much of the inspiration for this study. Its textual focus, of course, is the Middle English romances. We know already that these romances represent the most important body of secular post-Conquest writing in English before Chaucer (and even Chaucer was heavily indebted to them—a fact that chapter 3 of this study takes as its point of departure). Whether or not these stories really were "pulp fictions" of medieval England, they were certainly available en masse to both medieval and early modern audiences. Helen Cooper, in a recent and magisterial survey of the impact exerted by English romance on the age of Shakespeare, lists in an appendix to her book no less than fifty-nine different story types—many encompassing multiple individual romances—still in circulation after 1500.[40] Cooper's study demonstrates that one of the primary reasons we should care about these fictions is that they are not, in fact, purely "medieval" at all but locatable at a momentous cultural turning point, where the late medieval and the early modern cease to be clearly distinguishable from each other.

But what are we to do with such "ugly ducklings"? Can literature so "crude" be recognized as romance at all?[41] The problem is not just with what Middle English romances seem to lack—"all the elements of chivalry and romance," quoted above—but with what they have in excess.[42] As the title of one recent article bluntly puts it, "Why Is Middle English Romance So Violent?"[43] The anxiety that English romances harbor a surplus of aggressivity is not confined to modern scholars, either. *The Wars of Alexander* (circa 1350–1450), itself an alliterative romance of late medieval England, begins with the narrator's assurance that his own story has nothing to do with the tales of senseless bloodshed or "wanton werkis" favored by "tha that ere wild-hedid" (12) but is intended by contrast for the wise (though, ironically, he proceeds to tell a story of wanton violence himself).[44]

Alexander is more explicit than most English romances about its structuring anxieties, but even the most gleefully gory of the romances can betray a telling ambivalence about their own excessive representations of chivalric (and sometimes not-so-chivalric) acts of violence. Thus, for instance, the narrator of *Havelok the Dane*, after describing in grisly detail the flaying and subsequent hanging of the story's villain as he cries out helplessly—"Merci! Merci!" (2501)—ends this description with a preemptive denunciation of any who might be inclined to pity the victim: "Datheit hwo recke: he was fals!" (2511).[45] Other romances attempt to draw a line between legitimate and excessive violence. Such is *Sir Gowther* (circa 1400), whose hero spends his teenage years slaying travelers at random, burning churches full of nuns, murdering priests, and setting widows aflame before discovering a useful outlet for his talents in the crusading business. While Gowther's actions are perhaps understandable in light of his demonic ancestry, the hero of *Libeaus Desconus* (circa 1375) can plead no such excuse. The son of that courtly paragon, Sir Gawain, the young Gyngeleyne nevertheless indulges a wild streak that earns him a comparison to "Sathan" (1180), until he acquires, like Gowther, the ability to see the difference between "acceptable" and "unacceptable" uses of force.[46] A further example is offered by *Sir Degaré* (circa 1330), a romance whose plot involves the hero in the near murder of both his father and grandfather in a rather remarkable doubling of the Oedipal stakes. This last poem raises the problem of knightly violence with particular force, since its story of loss and recovery is, as one reader comments, "not only provoked by transgression, but also, more revealingly, must itself deploy transgression."[47] Of course, even Degaré must renounce violence upon learning of his true lineage and knightly identity, as, for that matter, do Gowther and Gyngeleyne, Malory's Sir Gareth, and other heroes of the "fair unknown" tradition. In each of these romances, textual violence is legitimated in part by a strategic acknowledgment of potential moral objections, which are then either swept aside or answered by the subordination of violence to properly chivalric ends. Such stories suggest the extent to which violence is a problem not just for modern critics but for a genre that finds itself having to apologize continually for its most outrageous forms of desire.

Yet what of those moments that are less explicitly scandalous? If romance can be known in part by its ability to harness the magic of cultural concealment, can we see these stories as works of more subtlety than they have usually been given credit for being? I will argue that this is the case when it comes to the most notorious excesses of English romance. When I insist on the symbolic, highly mediated quality of violence in these texts, I have in mind an understandable stereotype of these stories as blood-soaked melodramas, evident in the notion that they are the "pulp fictions" of medieval England. Such a stereotype, while not without textual support, arguably prevents us from noticing this genre's most interesting work. That stereotype typically identifies violence with cultural debasement, reflected in what John Ganim—in an effort to account for the genre's frequent bloodletting—calls "a rather naïve fantasy world not unlike a modern cartoon or western."[48] To be sure, many of these stories do perform violence in explicit and memorable ways, a tendency that has been identified as a significant feature of English romance in work by Jeffrey Jerome Cohen, Geraldine Heng, Patricia Clare Ingham, and many others.[49] Yet the memorability of all those effusions of gore has tended to obscure the immensely complex attitude toward violence that so often characterizes this fiction, as much recent work on individual romances has also suggested. If part of what "chivalric" romance typically does is to aestheticize the violence that such stories also require, then the ostensibly pulpy and "middle-class" English romance is often surprisingly chivalric, as at least a few readers have suspected for some time.[50]

No surprise, then, that gifts should be everywhere in texts that think so much about their own violence. The scenes of giving that interest me enact romance as a thing grounded *in* violence, but they just as clearly do not reduce *to* violence in any simple sense, even when, as will often prove the case, they do involve a kind of injury—physical, emotional, or otherwise: a nick on the nape, a broken shoulder, a warning to behave, a trick that places one under an obligation, the sneer on the face of the giver. For what is remarkable about these stories is just how thoroughly and subtly they manage and measure their desire for bloodshed, so that the love of violence instantiates not simply horror but value. Central to this logic, I am arguing, is the noble gift as a similar kind of cultural practice that means and does symbolic violence, that in fact measures its own value precisely in terms of its power to do so. The gift is thus more than a thing that happens in many romances, or even a useful metaphor for describing the work of romance. Romance is rather itself a form of gift work, even—and in fact especially—in an era when literature in England begins to know "procedures of mass production."[51] The gift is the figure by means of which English romance comes to imagine itself as something paradoxical: wholly new in English literature yet, at the same time, oddly belated from the moment of its appearance, marked by the obsolescence of the chivalric forms that it celebrates.

The thirteenth-century *Floris and Blancheflour* offers one intriguing starting point for exploring the historical self-awareness of these texts. One of the very earliest English romances, *Floris* acknowledges in its basic plot the extent to which the time of romance has already passed. The narrative demands a return not just of its lost heroine but of romance itself as a time of the gift and, by extension, of a proper feudality. Insofar as all romance is nostalgic for an imaginary era marked by traditional relations and values, *Floris* is typical of romance in general. But the poem is exceptional in the extent to which it acknowledges the utter artificiality of its nostalgia. Another way of putting this is to say that *Floris* admits the impossibility of its own desire for the medieval, even as it coaxes us into sharing in that desire. The romance's self-conscious figure for this desire is, as we shall see, the possibility of the gift.

"THOURGH THI CATEL ICH AM BITRAID"

Floris well illustrates that English romance knows itself to be belated from the beginning. The Middle English version of the story, composed about 1250, is probably the second-oldest English romance (preceded only by *King Horn*, composed circa 1225). *Floris*, in turn, can be traced back to an Old French poem conventionally dated to the 1160s, the same period in which Marie de France and Chrétien de Troyes were writing their first romances. The story of *Floris* is thus arguably as old as romance itself, and it bears all the hallmarks of the genre, especially in the aristocratic version on which the English redactor depended. A tale of separated lovers reunited in an exotic setting, partly by the aid of magical means, *Floris* seems almost like an "ur-romance."[52] Yet what makes *Floris* so unusual—even as it speaks more broadly to the vexed situation of the earliest romances—is the readiness with which it confesses to that situation.

About halfway through the Middle English *Floris*, the hero has described for him the wonders of the Babylon to which he must journey in quest of his beloved Blancheflour. Among those wonders, we might be startled to encounter something at once entirely mundane and yet bizarrely threatening:

> Twente toures ther beth inne,
> That everich dai cheping is inne;
> Nis no dai thourg the yer
> That scheping nis therinne plener . . .
> That alderest feblest tour
> Wolde kepe an emperour
> To comen al ther withinne.

> [There are twenty towers within (this citadel) where there is trading every day. There is no day during the year when there is not trading in plenty. . . . The weakest tower would serve to keep out an emperor.][53]

On the one hand, there is nothing inherently unusual about this reminder of the modernity lurking within the medieval: here, the merchants in their fortified towers. *Floris* is a romance in which the hero himself "wends his very bourgeois way to Babylon" disguised as a merchant—a frequent enough disguise in English romances, and one that speaks to the historical knowledgeableness of these stories. On the other hand, this scene of merchants in towers, relentlessly buying and selling "everich dai," reminds us that, however knowledgeable a romance like *Floris* might be about its own historical moment, it experiences that knowledge as a weird form of trauma. Merchants are not knights, but their activities carry exactly the same aggressivity as if they were (as they are in the Old French source from which the episode is drawn).[54] Read in these terms, the scene evokes the commercial value system against which the hero must oppose himself as though it were an armed enemy, just as the hero's father in *King Horn* makes a fatal mistake when he assumes that the Saracens who have come to plunder his land must be merchants rather than conquerors.[55] The power of commerce in both stories is an implied antagonist in a displaced battle with cultural and religious others (even if, in the case of *Horn*, we might say that the father's mistake is to suppose himself to be in the emergently modern world described by a romance like *Floris*). English romance recognizes even from its first lines—as King Murray finds out the hard way—that the fall into romance has to happen *from* some historical place. But *Floris* admits that history is even more inescapable than *Horn* supposes, having already infiltrated the innermost recesses of aristocratic fantasy.

The story of *Floris* is broadly a story of what we might think of as a counterinfiltration of the citadel of commerce mounted by the powers of romance. Even the briefest plot synopsis shows the centrality of exchange to this project. Fearing that his son Floris will wed none but the daughter of a Christian slave, the king of Spain secretly sells the girl, Blancheflour, to a travelling merchant in exchange for gold and a marvelously wrought cup. When Floris learns the truth of Blancheflour's fate, he journeys to Babylon in the guise of a travelling merchant in order to seek her, carrying with him the cup for which Blancheflour was sold. Floris lodges at a succession of inns, each time giving his hosts a gold cup (though not the marvelous cup itself) in exchange for information about his beloved's whereabouts. In a speech already quoted, the final host, Darys, tells Floris that Blancheflour is being kept in the emir's fortified harem in the center of the city, and Darys encourages Floris to bribe the porter with the wonderful cup. Floris does so and arranges to have himself carried into Blancheflour's chambers by hiding in a basket of flowers. The lovers reunite but are discovered by the chamberlain. Brought before the emir and his barons to be judged, the lovers move the barons to compassion when each tries to press on the other the magic ring whose power might spare at least one of them. There is not a lord present who would not buy the lovers' freedom on the spot—"with grete garisoun hem begge" (1094)—if they only dared. Finally one of the barons convinces the emir that it would be "litel pris" (1152)—in a tellingly economic turn of phrase—if he were to slay the lovers. The emir at last relents and forgives the lovers on condition that Floris reveal how he managed to infiltrate the tower, and the romance ends with the now happily married couple returning to Spain to be crowned king and queen upon the death of Floris's father.

Even this bare outline reveals *Floris* to be a story that is not just about exchange but structured by it. As Kathleen Coyne Kelly remarks, the story amounts to the "bartering of Blauncheflur."[56] Likewise, Arthur Bahr suggests that Floris's "ingenuity in using mercantile tactics to triumph over [his] adversaries" would have made him an "attractive model" for the poem's likely audience of London merchants.[57] Christopher Cannon takes this reading of *Floris* as a "mercantile" text to its logical conclusion, arguing that *Floris* uses procedures of exchange to constitute itself as a cultural object. In a condensed but remarkably close reading, Cannon demonstrates that *Floris* imagines its own cultural value precisely in relation to the kinds of exchanges that the story depicts. His reading hinges on the notion that even information that ought to condemn the lovers—for instance, the story of how Floris got into the tower—turns out to have the opposite effect by evoking the sympathy of all who hear it. The story of *Floris* in this sense is the bearer of its own surplus value, so inherently great as to produce reliably an effect of wonder even in circumstances that would seem to preclude this. Merely to hear *Floris*, on his reading, is to recognize immediately the exceptional quality of the story itself, regardless of one's subject position in relation to the events narrated. *Floris* thus takes to its extreme a logic of commodified romance in which "any version of the excellence of its hero or heroine will do."[58]

Cannon's model of how English romance generates a sense of its value as a cultural object is vital to my own reading of this genre. Yet I want to complicate this picture by suggesting how keenly aware these fictions are of the simultaneous durability of what Mauss would call "archaic" economic and cultural formations. For it is curious that what *Floris* imagines is precisely the survival of those modes of value that its own logic of commodification seems to call radically into question. *Floris* illustrates the paradoxical way in which the increasing commercialization of English society after 1200 intensified, if anything, a cultural fascination with gifts and giving. As Andrew Galloway has suggested, the emphasis on gift exchange in even the earliest Middle English texts does not mean that thirteenth-century culture was a gift culture "in some ideal and totalized way."[59] *Floris*, I will argue, demonstrates how the notion of the gift "was perhaps more distinctly articulated and elaborated precisely as the 'commercialization' and professionalization of English society takes root" (725). The poem's most recent editor recognizes the centrality of the gift to its happy resolution.[60] Yet *Floris* dramatizes the extent to which its gifts are fraught with anxiety and this raises the question of how a story that knows so much about the circumstances of its own production can still prove itself to be a romance. Because this poem so keenly understands its own belatedness, that is, it also realizes that the gift cannot be conceived "in some ideal and totalized way" but must be actively imagined—brought into being by the desires that romance helps to activate and shape.

The poem's complex investment in the gift as an object of desire helps to explain the paradox that the violence in *Floris* seems (as Bourdieu would say) simultaneously more marked and more insistently repressed than in romances that reflect a more straightforwardly martial spirit. On the one hand, "the only sword that occurs in [the poem] is that of the Emir," who draws it only to forgive the couple after hearing their tale of mutual devotion.[61] At the same time, "the sword" is the entire foundation of this crusader romance. Although the first lines of the Middle English version are missing, a summary based on the Old French version begins with the burning and pillaging of the Galician countryside "until no trace of civilization remained," the slaughter of pilgrims on the way to the shrine of St. James, and the seizure of Blancheflour's mother as a slave. What follows is the first of many gifts, as the otherwise rapacious King Fenix "kindly" allows Blancheflour's mother to practice her own faith.[62] This act of lenience sets up a pattern in the story to come, culminating in the emir's decision to spare the lives of the hero and heroine.

Yet if the poem begins with a gift that displaces violence, the gift also reproduces that violence. Thus, even as she points to the poem's mercantile logic, Kelly remarks that the poem's heroine "epitomizes the ultimate gift . . . that can be given or received in a patriarchal society."[63] In her status as a gift object unable to control her own fate, Blancheflour recalls other heroines of Middle English romance, most notably Émaré and Chaucer's Custance, who are trapped within an economy that objectifies even as it idealizes them. Blancheflour's plight is also more broadly symptomatic, suggesting a problem not only with the exchange of women but with the ways in which romance, in order to defend against its own abjection as a commodified object, imagines the transactions that it records as consisting of animate forms—things with a certain spirit—including, of course, people. In the case of *Floris*, the gift of Blancheflour stands at the core of what might seem at first glance to be a thoroughly mercantile and even bourgeois poem. We might say that *Floris* knows itself as a romance precisely to the extent that it insists on the violence of these archaic forms of exchange.

Having reduced Blancheflour to the status of an object—albeit an animate, "gifted" one worth more than any other such object, as suggested by her equivalence with a cup so rare that "in al the world was non it lyche" (164)—the poem becomes predictably more interested in the relations between men. But men, too, end up being victims in this romance, especially in what I want to suggest is the poem's most erotically fraught transaction. This is the game of chess between Floris and the porter who guards the tower where Blancheflour is being held captive. As foretold by one of the helpers whom he meets along the way, Floris will encounter within the stronghold of the city a porter whose hostility and suspicion he will need to circumvent by stratagem. The helper, a sympathetic innkeeper named Darys, is the same figure who had earlier warned Floris that the "cheping" or exchange undertaken in Babylon is so formidable as to be absolutely secure from invasion or interruption. Darys now outlines a stratagem that itself depends on the weird power of exchange in this poem. In a speech rich with puns on the idea of "gynning" as both trickery and engineering, he instructs Floris to disguise himself as a "ginour" (701) or craftsman, which will deceive the porter by making him believe that Floris simply takes a professional interest in how the tower is constructed.

Yet the real "ginne" in this romance is not disguise but rather a form of strategic and deceitful exchange, as a frequent rhyming word—"winne"—implies in equating the winning of profit with the exercise of ingenuity.[64] The exchange proposed by Darys depends on the porter's love of playing chess for high stakes. Knowing that the porter will be "wel coveitous" (719) to win money of Floris, Darys suggests that Floris take advantage of the porter's greed by offering him a gift he literally can't refuse. For the first two days, Floris is to lose money to the porter with a strategically calculated air of carelessness ("Of thi moné tel thou no tale" [739]). In the slightly later Middle English *Sir Tristram*—which shares a manuscript with *Floris*—the point of this strategy is to win more money by seeming to lose. Yet Floris's career as a "chess hustler" takes a more complicated route from loss to profit—one that depends on the practice of noble giving.[65] If the chessboard or "scheker" evokes a space of rational calculation, perhaps the Exchequer itself—as Jenny Adams has glossed "scheker" in another context—Floris's gambling away of his substance evokes by contrast Mauss's association of gambling with reckless dispossession or "los," as Middle English texts critical of gambling were wont to call it.[66]

As Darys continues, Floris on the third day must bring with him his marvelous cup as bait in order to get the porter to offer even higher stakes. The cup, which Darys somehow knows is the same one for which Blancheflour was traded, will excite the porter's desire to such an extent that he will be helpless to resist Floris's designs:

> Wel yerne he thee wille bidde and praie
> That thou legge thi coupe to plaie.
> Thou schalt answeren him ate first
> No lenger plaie thou ne list.
> Wel moche he wil for thi coupe bede,
> Yif he mighte the better spede.
> Thou schalt bletheliche given hit him,
> Thai hit be gold pur and fin,
> And sai: "Me thinketh hit wel bisemeth te,
> Thai hit were worth swiche thre."
> Sai also thee ne faille non,
> Gold ne selver ne riche won.
> And he wil thanne so mochel love thee,
> That thou hit schalt bothe ihere and see
> That he wil falle to thi fot
> And bicome thi man, yif he mot.
> His manred thou schalt afonge,

And the trewthe of his honde.
Yif thou might thous his love winne,
He mai thee help with som ginne. (716–59)

[He will eagerly bid and pray you to put your cup at stake. Say at first that you don't wish to play any longer. He will then offer a large amount for the cup, hoping to speed the better. You shall blithely give it to him, even though it is of pure and fine gold, and say: 'I think it is fitting that you should have it, even if it were worth three times as much.' See that you don't run out of gold or silver or other rich things, and he will love you so much that you will hear and see him fall to your feet and become your man, if he may. You shall accept his fealty, along with his oath of loyalty. If you can win his love in this way, he may be able to help you with some stratagem.]

This remarkable scene imagines the giving of a noble gift as nothing less than a drama of seduction. Even as the chessboard evokes calculation and repressed violence, the exchanges that govern the transfer of the cup from Floris to the porter carry an almost erotic intensity, as Floris plays coy, exciting the porter's desire, in the lead-up to the moment when Floris will give the cup to the porter outright in a gesture fraught with implied same-sex attraction, thereby winning in return the porter's "love." Indeed, where the Old French source has Floire declare explicitly beforehand that he is giving the cup in exchange for help in his time of need (*mon besoing*), Floris by contrast makes no mention of conditions and instead launches into a panegyric on the porter, declaring him worthy of three such cups.[67] By these slight changes, the English composer alters the feel of the scene, turning an implied exchange into a drama of desire and betrayal.

Love is, of course, central to *Floris*, as the marvelous cup attests in its portrayal of the "love" (170) of Helen and Paris. Yet the cup—like the aristocratic game for which it is played—also carries an implied threat. If its lid portrays love, its sides are adorned with the real story—presumably painted onto the cup or engraved into it—of "how Paryse ledde awey the queene" (168). Paris's abduction and subsequent rape of Helen have clear parallels with Blancheflour's own status as a passive object of exchange, as has been noted.[68] But the cup in the Middle English poem, by contrast with its source, actively rewrites this story of rape. While the abduction itself is "purtrayd" (167) on the bottom half of the cup, we are told that over this—"on the covercle above" (169)— there stands a picture of "both her love," meaning the mutual love of Paris and Helen together, which is also "purtrayde" (170).[69] Even as the cup seems about to give the game away, a courtly *roman d'amour* quite literally puts a lid on things. A similar ambiguity attends the English version's revised account of the cup's history, which more explicitly interweaves desire and violence.[70] Initially the property of "Enneas the king, that nobel man" (177), who won it "in batayle" (178), the cup begins its economic life as a gift to that mythical hero's "lemman" (180). Passing by ill-defined means into the hands of Julius Caesar, it is then stolen by the same thief-turned-merchant who at the poem's beginning sells it to Floris's father in exchange for Blancheflour. The hero's father, in turn, having repented of his attempt to separate the lovers, gives it to Floris, who as we have seen offers it to the porter as a gift in exchange for homage and, as he only then reveals, for the porter's aid in securing Blancheflour.

The cup, then, does more than simply mean violence. It instantiates romance's power to transmute violence into the stuff of desire. Its appearance in the story as an alluring object is also, significantly, what allows Floris to resume his place in the feudal order, accepting the porter's "manred" (756) or homage. Yet almost in the same moment, the porter registers the treacherous character of the whole exchange in direct terms: "thourgh thi catel ich am bitraid [by means of your goods (i.e., the cup) I am betrayed]" (776). If this moment marks Floris's reentry into a feudal set of relationships, it does so at the cost of revealing the coercion that subtends those relationships. What seemed to be love is in reality constraint, even—as the porter recognizes—the likelihood of "deth" (767). Yet *Floris* enacts the power of romance to realize these violent possibilities as the satisfaction of a desire. Floris need not even ask the porter for the oath of homage explicitly. To do so, after all, would be to render the gift a mere exchange, as it is in other versions of the story. The scene rather enacts feudality in an ideal, primitive state: noble expenditure is so overwhelming in itself that the only possible response to it is self-enslavement on the part of the receiver. It is as classic a statement of the power of the noble gift to compel a return as any modern anthropologist could wish.

Yet *Floris* also testifies that even the earliest romances recognize the gift as a flexible symbolic procedure, one that might travel and be recruited for a variety of aims beyond the maintenance of aristocratic distinction. Insofar as the gift is a question of desire rather than pure violence, *Floris* is a story about the strange communities that desire can make. So, for instance, we might conclude that the transformation of violence into desire means that the long and bloody reconquest of Muslim Spain in the Middle Ages can be accounted for in terms of Floris's decision to adopt—in at least one manuscript—the Christian faith of his beloved Blancheflour.[71] The manuscript in question is the famous Auchinleck, which was produced in a London bookshop in the 1330s for urban readers most likely of the merchant class. That London merchants might be interested in a poem that represents merchants as a threat to aristocratic distinction is perhaps surprising. Nor does the poem, for all its emphasis on exchange, offer much hope of social advancement for the non-noble. As Bahr remarks, "a prince like Floris can slum it by playing a merchant when he needs to, but it is not at all clear how the poem's merchants—or [its] audience—could do the same."[72] Yet the poem clearly did appeal to Auchinleck's mercantile readers, and it is worth pausing to consider why this might be. One good reason is that Floris's heroism mostly boils down to his economic savvy, as Bahr suggests in pointing up Floris's "ingenuity in using mercantile tactics" throughout the poem.[73] Even the key scene of negotiation between Floris and the porter depends on Floris's ability to think like a merchant—to recognize that in giving a gift (the cup), he can secure a profit (Blancheflour). Seen this way, the whole story calls into question the distinction—between gifts and commodities—that the text also asks us to imagine as a site of aristocratic difference.

It is perhaps harder to see that the porter can potentially think like Floris, or at least *desire* like him. For the whole logic of their encounter depends on the possibility that a non-noble might desire the sublime object of chivalry—might in fact be more interested in *it* than in money. This is why the porter is willing to bid "wel moche" (744) for the hero's marvelous cup and also why neither "gold ne silver ne riche won" (750–51) can take its place as a means of securing the porter's loyalty. We might even say that Floris's ability to regain his aristocratic identity depends on the extent to which the desire for that identity is shared by his antagonist. The poem's logic here is that of an ideal that represents itself as *universally* desirable, able to appeal even to those whom it explicitly excludes. Thus one might at least question whether the poem's interest in merchants "serves ultimately to reinforce the distance between them and the hero," in spite of what my own reading has suggested so far about the poem's care to differentiate noble giving from mercantile bargaining.[74] For the broad appeal of the poem depends on its ability to bring merchants and knights together as part of a common imaginary, even if it does so only tacitly and provisionally. If the porter is the poem's victim, he is also a figure for the ways in which a non-noble audience will prove capable of valuing and (in the long run) adopting chivalric values to suit their own purposes. For all its anxiety about the preservation of aristocratic distinction, the overall shape of *Floris* already discerns what the subsequent history of English romance will bear out: that chivalry and its violence are destined to become the imaginative basis of regimes that seem on their face to have left these things behind.

CHAPTER 2

The Gift and Its Returns

Confronted by an accusing ghost who foretells the downfall of the
Round Table, Gawain asks an urgent question:

> "How shal we fare," quod the freke, "that fonden to fight,
> And thus defoulen the folke on fele kinges londes,
> And riches over reymes withouten eny right,
> Wynnen worshipp in werre thorgh wightnesse of hondes?" (261–64)
>
> ["What will we do," said the man, "whose business it is to fight,
> and thus to quell the people of many a king's lands, and enter into
> realms without any right, win worship in war through the strength
> of our hands?"][1]

What place does such a person have, Gawain wants to know, in a scheme
that makes "meeknesse and mercy" (250) the criteria for salvation?
Gawain's question is, as the poem's most recent editor notes, "astonish-
ing" in its bluntness, imagining "chivalry as a sponsor of violence, rather
than a protection against it."[2] But what is astonishing here is not that
Gawain celebrates chivalric violence, since, after all, this is what romance
always does. It is what this late fourteenth-century romance will itself
shortly proceed to do in its stylized, almost lapidary description of the
grueling and nearly fatal battle between Gawain and a challenger named
Galeron. If there is anything to astonish us here, it is Gawain representing

30

this violence as fundamentally self-interested, a matter of might ("wight-nesse") over "right." Indeed, the ghost will respond to Gawain's question with some bluntness of her own, labeling the Arthurian court "covetous" (265). Such an economy of violent self-interest, she warns, is unsustain-able. Disaster looms in the form of betrayal from within.

The Awntyrs off Arthur (before 1475) is one of a number of late medieval ghost stories about the future of romance, as this chapter demonstrates. To judge by the look of this particular ghost, that future is grim. The specter of Guinevere's dead mother is the picture of a chiv-alry shorn of its pride, food for worms, a "grisly goost" (111) indeed. Enumerating her many possessions in life, the ghost confronts Gawain with the reality of things that are always slipping away:

> Of al gamen or gle that on grounde growes
> Gretter then Dame Gaynour, of garson and golde,
> Of palaies, of parkes, of pondes, of plowes,
> Of townes, of toures, of tresour untolde,
> Of castelles, of contreyes, of cragges, of clowes.
> Now am I caught oute of kide to cares so colde;
> Into care am I caught and couched in clay. (146–52)

> [Of all the pleasure or joy that dwells in earth, (I had) greater than Dame Guinevere, of wealth and gold, of palaces, of parks, of ponds, of estates, of towns, of towers, of treasures untold, of castle, of counties, of mountains, of valleys. Now am I caught without kin in sorrows cold; caught in sorrow and buried in clay.]

The ghost presents a challenge to an acquisitive court in her insistence that such possession is transitory: "al the welth of the world . . . awey witis" (215), just as the hero of *Sir Launfal* will watch all that he thought was his melt away "as snow ayens the sunne" (740), or the knight of *Sir Amadace*, mortgaged and bankrupt, laments the loss of "his londus brode, / His castels hce, his townus made, / That were away evyrichon" (391–93).[3] The impossibility of full possession is more inescapable in the *Awntyrs* than in either of these other poems—a question of mor-tality rather than of feudal crisis—but the *Awntyrs* resembles other "spendthrift romances" in celebrating the very forms of surplus that it implicitly indicts.

This ambivalent attitude toward chivalric excess takes the form, in the *Awntyrs*, of a notoriously disjunctive movement within the poem. The story's first half, in which Gawain and Guinevere meet with the ghost of Guinevere's mother, would seem to sort ill with its second half, consisting of a seemingly unrelated episode in which the court, returned to Camelot, faces a challenger named Galeron, who accuses Arthur of having unjustly appropriated Galeron's lands and given them to Gawain. Though so different that the episodes were at one point read as entirely separate poems, more recent criticism has recognized the ways in which these episodes are linked by shared concerns.[4] Among them is the question of the gift, which is here transformed from an urgent call for charity toward the poor (and toward the ghost herself, in the form of prayers) into the violent consumption that marks the gift as specifically *noble*, the property of a distinct class.[5] The shape of the poem argues for the fundamental incompatibility of these models of the gift, so that the ghost's command to her aristocratic audience to give their substance away in acts of charity—"Gyf fast of thi goode / To folke that failen the fode / While thou art here" (232–34)—will be displaced by a largesse confined, in the poem's second half, to the aristocrats themselves.

In enjoining charity, the poem insists on reminding readers of the broader community that exists beyond the charmed circle of nobility: the community of all who are mortal. As the ghost warns Guinevere, "Muse on my mirrour; / For, king and emperour, / Thus dight shul ye be" (167–69). The ghost is herself now on the other side of that divide, a creature of dispossession—"anked and nedefull, naked on sight" (185)—who stands in stark contrast to her living daughter, lounging on an exalted "des" while surrounded "with riche dayntés" (183). Yet precisely because all that lives must die, the poem suggests, an economy of love can exist between the quick and the dead:

> "Thus dethe wil you dight, thare you not doute;
> Thereon hertly take hede while thou art here.
> Whan thou art richest arraied and ridest in thi route,
> Have pité on the poer—thou art of power . . .

The praier of poer may purchas the pes—
Of that thou yeves at the yete,
Whan thou art set in thi sete,
With al merthes at mete
And dayntés on des." (167–82)

Instead of securing aristocratic identity, on the model of the noble gift described by modern anthropology, the largesse demanded by the ghost offers the possibility that the giver "may purchas the pes" that binds together rich and poor, living and dead, in the community that exists among all those subject to death. Yet the limitless giving that would be required of the members of such a community is, in the end, too much for the poem to realize. For what this poem knows, finally, is that a gift so total would destroy chivalry itself as a mode of possession. The *Awntyrs* will consequently work to manage and measure its gifts, to conserve the gift's power to keep the aristocratic economy humming along, even as it celebrates the violence and waste that such interested giving realizes as the surplus value of noble life.

This careful work is legible in what A. C. Spearing has identified as "the special effect created by the poem's double emphasis on luxury and on violence."[6] That emphasis is most evident in the battle between Galeron and Gawain, the knight whose legendary courtesy repeatedly animates the gift in the history of English romance (as chapter 4 will explore in detail). It is thus Gawain, the knight of courtesy, who responds to the challenge posed by Galeron with typically lavish hospitality, yet also Gawain who will soon be hacking away at the latter's armor in a nearly fatal encounter whose entire point is its absolute waste—the noble eagerness with which a warrior elite gives itself over to violent destruction of both self and other:

Hardely then thes hathelese on helmes they hewe.
Thei beten downe beriles and bourdures bright;
Shildes on shildres that shene were to shewe,
Fretted were in fyne golde, thei failen in fight.
Stones of iral thay strenkel and strewe. (586–90)

[Fiercely then the warriors cut into helmets. They sheer away beryls and bright trim. The shields on their shoulders that bright were to look at, were adorned with fine gold, (but) they failed in that fight. Precious stones they scatter and strew.]

The moment, as Spearing remarks, "perfectly expresses the nature of the aristocratic life, which consists in a generous willingness to waste those material possessions that seem to be its essence."[7] The brutality of the scene, including the bloody decapitation of Gawain's favorite horse and not one but two impalements of the combatants, is balanced with a profound sense of the inherent value of such violent expenditure. For Carl Grey Martin, the scene responds to the ghost's demand for penance by encoding knightly violence as its own kind of penance, so that Gawain "internalizes the ghost's impassioned condition to perform his own intimate relation to bodily suffering, thereby disabling her rebuke of the court's moral lassitude and lofty self-regard."[8] Yet it matters to my argument that the form taken by such penance is that of the noble gift, for what is at issue here is finally not just payment for sin—or even the fantasy of violence that pays for itself—but the question of how such violence might be rendered meaningful, understood as a measure of the romance text's own value.

Thus for all the poem's loving focus on the sumptuousness of aristocratic waste, the noble gift will also finally be economized and thus rendered knowable as the currency of romance. Arthur will stop the fight at Guinevere's petitioning, displacing the exchange of blows—in all their "relentless reciprocity"—with an exchange of gifts.[9] Galeron, conceding defeat in the battle, will award Gawain de jure ownership in the lands of which he is already the de facto possessor, while Gawain, reciprocating, will immediately return some of the lands to Galeron and invite him to join the Round Table. In economizing the gift—making it into a trade that realizes a profit—the poem simultaneously economizes the violence it has just paid out for our enjoyment, reimagining the gift of violence as a symbolic act:

"Here I make the releyse, renke, by the Rode,
And, byfore thiese ryalle, resynge the my ryghte;

And sithen make the monraden with a mylde mode
As man of medlert makeles of might."
He talkes touard the King on hie ther he stode,
"Of rentes and richesse I make the releyse."
And bede that burly his bronde that burneshed was bright. (640–46)

["Here I release to you, sir, by the Cross, and before these royal (witnesses), I resign to you my right; and afterward will do you homage with a gentle will, as a man of Middle Earth matchless in might." He talks toward the king from where he stood, "Of rents and riches I resign my claim to you." And (with that) offered that stout man his brightly burnished sword.]

More than a feudal gesture of submission, Galeron's offer of his polished sword, so lately smeared with blood, transforms violence into the substance of noble giving, the destructive power of absolute waste into the symbolic wealth that drives the chivalric economy of honor. The frightening challenger, a dispossessed knight barred from the community, is transformed by the same stroke into "Sir Galeron the gay," an insider and knight of the Round Table, and promptly wedded to a wife "with giftes and garsons" (697). Just as the wounds of the combatants are "saned sonde" (699)—made whole—Camelot is itself rendered coherent once more.

Nor is this transformation any less effective for its failure to address the unlawfulness of Arthurian conquest, the sense that "the fundamental question of who justly owns the lands in dispute remains unresolved," for the point of the episode is less to justify violence then to render it symbolically valuable.[10] It is *because* the guilt lurking in the heart of the chivalric subject can never be fully allayed that chivalry will live on, just as—at the poem's end—the "mylion of Masses" (706) that Guinevere arranges for the soul of her dead mother will never really all be said—*could* never all be said. The monumental nature of chivalry's guilt is what marks the attempt to come to grips with it as an opportunity for "mynnynge" (706) or memorialization. Chivalry's persistence will be ensured, paradoxically, by the inadequacy of its attempts to pay its debts.

Yet the sleight of hand by which the *Awntyrs* achieves its romance ending cannot erase the sense of foreboding opened up by the ghost's earlier insistence on an end beyond this end—a time when the chivalric community of Camelot will be doomed precisely because of its inability to extend its gifts far enough, so that "al the rial rowte of the Rounde Table, / Thei shullen dye on a day" (304–5). In a move that ties her prophecy to the economic mismanagement of Arthur's court, it is specifically aristocratic excess—"appurtenaunce" (239)—that the ghost had earlier identified as the object of God's wrath. Despite the poem's attempt to recode the ghost's urgent call for a radical charity as the noble gift, we know that the destructive expenditure enacted within the confines of this community will prove insufficient to stave off that final disaster. In its closing reference to the provisions made for the ghost of Guinevere's mother, the poem reminds us that the community of the Round Table will live on only as a doomed island, separated from the broader community to which the ghost has tried in vain to draw its attention.

The ghost's indictment of Arthur's court might well stand as a gloss for an entire tradition of fifteenth-century English romance, the so-called Spendthrift Knight romances discussed in the remainder of this chapter. These stories take literally the problem of a chivalry unable to pay its debts in their portrayal of heroes who exhaust their wealth in a frenzied outpouring of noble largesse. If the *Awntyrs* ultimately brings itself back from the brink of the total gift, reclaiming the gift for aristocratic propriety, the spendthrift hero suggests what would happen if the demand to give were taken so seriously that it threatened to destroy the very self that such gifts are meant to affirm. Faced with an injunction to give that has become unrelenting, the spendthrift finds himself in danger of losing his very essence. He becomes a figure for a chivalry that seeks to perpetuate itself by imagining its own destruction in a final display of extravagant waste. Such a fate can only be averted, as in the *Awntyrs*, by means of the violent possessiveness that annuls the gift—by admitting, on some level, that chivalry takes with one hand what it seems to give with the other. For what these stories recognize is that the money has to come from somewhere. To Gawain's question about the fate of knighthood—"How shal we fare?"—these poems offer an answer based in a fantasy of the "noble" gift as both a giving and a taking, a realization of community that also allows for aristocratic self-assertion. So, as we shall see, Amadace gets "owte of dette full clene" (36), Launfal repays "all" that he "hadde borwyth" (418), and Cleges (in a likely pun) goes to heaven "clere" (575) not only of sins but of his outstanding balances.[11]

In fact, the need to get a profit is so pressing in these stories that the gift threatens to be erased from them altogether. Such stories arguably amount to what one reader bluntly calls "commercial romance" in their insistent focus on deriving a quite literal economic profit for their distressed heroes, however much these texts obviously want (in their emphasis on generosity) to be seen to position themselves against mercantile culture. Edward Foster's remark that *Sir Amadace* is finally "the story of a knight who gets out of debt" is entirely typical and well justified.[12] Yet it is remarkable that such precociously modern stories *do* imagine the returns of chivalry, even as the greater engagement of these late romances with mercantile culture has a number of consequences for their vision of how chivalry *could* return, and in what specific forms. One of those consequences is that the precise target of violence in these stories is often unclear. To say that mercantile culture is the target is partly true in at least two of the tales I explore here. Yet they are themselves as much a product of that culture as a reaction against it, and this is evidenced by the displaced and usually hidden nature of the violence that these texts imagine. *Amadace*—arguably the most commercial of the stories in this tradition—even goes so far as to imagine a magical violence that has no object at all.[13] This eerily disembodied violence takes the telling form of a ghost in *Amadace* especially—for like the *Awntyrs*, both *Amadace* and *Launfal* are (among other things) ghost stories. These particular ghosts speak to what Christopher Cannon has called the "spirit" of romance as one of commodification, but they simultaneously register the continuing dependence of a post-feudal world on a violence that can never be exorcised.[14] For like the revenant, violence is what always *will* return to haunt modern regimes that claim not to need it.

SPENDTHRIFT KNIGHTS AND THE DEATH OF CHIVALRY

The only text in this chapter that is not a ghost story, *Sir Cleges* nevertheless demonstrates how these stories imagine the return of a violence that cannot be fully erased from the post-feudal moment described by spendthrift romances. A former soldier for King Uther, Cleges has spent himself into poverty, but one Christmas day, while he is lamenting his fate in his garden, an angelic voice tells him to reach up and pick the unseasonable cherries that have miraculously appeared on a tree. Taking them to Uther's court, he is confronted by a series of courtiers who demand part of any reward that the king might give in return for the miraculous fruit. Realizing that nothing will be left over for him, he cleverly asks the king for "strokes twelve" (428) as his reward, which he then deals out to the greedy officials. The romance ends with Uther's recognition of Cleges as his former companion and the latter's promotion to the position of royal steward.

Cleges begins in the vein of other spendthrift knight stories with the wasting away of the hero's funds, but like everything about this poem, the actual cause of that wasting is overdetermined. Critics have tended to focus on the hero's giving of lavish Christmas feasts in honor of either the Virgin Mary or God (the intended recipient of the feast differs in the two extant versions of the poem). God is the ultimate gift giver in this romance, an inexhaustibly wealthy sovereign who, as Cleges remarks at several points in both versions, "off nought . . . madyst all thyng" (110, 275, 305). More than a mere pious tag, the fantasy of making something from nothing is central to the fantasy of plenitude that *Cleges* embraces; indeed, "no thyng" (351) is precisely what Cleges fears he will get after the greedy retainers at the king's court have each taken their share, even if the ability to transform this nothing back into something will reside as much with an earthly sovereign, King Uther, as it does with God. In fact, God will shortly absent himself from the story, though only after making his "presante" (304) of miraculous fruit in an implied return for Cleges's gift of honor to him in the form of feasts for his mother—gifts for which Cleges in fact already, like one of Mauss's islanders, expects a return, expressing a devout but also self-interested wish that "God wold hym quyte" (72) for his pains. If this language of exchange exemplifies what Dieter Mehl has called "the simple, almost calculating piety of some of these tales," that symbolic economy is also reflected more generally in the poem's initial description of Cleges, along with his wife, as "grete almusfolke" (31)—a term that evokes the central relationship in gift theory between status and liberality.[15] It is primarily thorough his liberality that Cleges is shown to be "a man of hy statoure" (10), a status that the minstrel who ultimately reveals his identity will later reaffirm in identical words (498).

But *Cleges* also explores a world in which this economy, increasingly under threat, does not translate easily or transparently from the divine to the human realm. For all his piety, Cleges comes in for some blunt criticism from the narrator, who reports that the knight frittered away his wealth unwisely—"Hys ryalty he forderyd ay" (73)—until his retainers, like his wealth, "weste awey onne every side" (80), leaving Cleges but one manor—"and that was of lytell valew" (76). In a world so rife with calculation that even the narrator seems to have a mercantile voice, people like Cleges are in trouble. The air of feudal crisis is evident in the pre-Arthurian setting of the poem in the reign of Uther Pendragon, a time "synonymous with hardship and turmoil" that might lend a certain poignancy to the hero's gifts to "squyres, that traveyled in lond of were / And wer fallyn in poverté bare" (16–17). This account of Cleges's generosity is "apt" (as Ad Putter remarks) insofar as it suggests a possible echo of the plight of former soldiers during the Hundred Years' War.

One might, going a bit further, even suggest a parallel to the aftermath of the second phase of that war, lasting from 1369 to 1389, which saw declining English fortunes, including economic strain for individual soldiers like those whom Cleges is eager to help.[16] The traditional dating of the poem to the closing decades of the fourteenth century might offer some support for this view. Yet even if there is no specific resonance to be found, the atmosphere is clearly one of despair. In setting up a story about a knight who helps others of his class before descending into poverty himself, *Cleges* speaks to the reality of aristocratic decline that Susan Crane has identified as a central concern of many Middle English romances, not just those that, like *Cleges*, dramatize this crisis in literal financial terms.[17] Such a crisis can only have a magical or miraculous solution since, like the other spendthrift knights discussed in this chapter, Cleges relieves distressed squires and knights only at the cost of his own ruin, a pattern that suggests the inevitability of the decline that this poem will struggle against.

Like the *Awntyrs*, *Cleges* finds its solution to this impasse in violence. The extent to which the poem will in fact come to depend on violence for its resolution is already evident from the opening lines, in the tone of almost deliberate self-restraint with which the narrator recounts the hero's reluctance to use force—"No man he wold buske ne bete" (20)—as well as the weird assurance that however much Cleges gave, no one was injured or lost anything because of it ("no man ought lore" [34]). This restraint ensures that Cleges, though "a man of mekyll might" (12), is at the same time "meke as meyd" (21), the embodiment of the ideal knight who toggles seamlessly between identities as lion of the battlefield and lamb of the hall. The hero's initial distance from his own violent potential will help to mark the moment in which he breaks as a kind of pleasurable release, as we shall see. Yet the sparse commentary on *Cleges* has tended to deny this pleasure, discreetly focusing its gaze instead on the Christian miracle that opens this story, described variously as "a particularly attractive combination of saint's life and popular fabliau" with a "pretty little miracle" at its center, a tale full of "simple and innocent manifestations of God's grace" and "a religious lesson about the importance of charity." By contrast, I want to pay close attention here to what Dinah Hazell has called the poem's "dark spots," even as I question her conclusion that such moments amount to a "disjuncture," born of the poem's status as a "generic *mélange*" of "modes [that] rest on very different moral standards."[18] The challenge of a poem like *Cleges*, we might rather conclude, is that it shows so clearly what the moral standard of romance is—how similar in effect to the naked self-interest of fabliau.

Whatever its debts to other genres, *Cleges* clearly wants to be thought of as a romance. The poem is thus concerned far more with the circulation of honor and shame than with fundamentally material issues of need and enjoyment. Even after his relative impoverishment, Cleges lives in a "palys" (181) and does not suffer the hardships of poverty that some other English romances chronicle, notably *Havelok the Dane*. Nor are we in the world of "hedonistic materialism" that Muscatine famously identified as the ethos of the fabliaux; Cleges is, if anything, among the more pious heroes of romance.[19] Yet like his spendthrift brethren Sir Amadace and Sir Launfal, Cleges's first thought upon recognizing that he cannot fully maintain his opulent lifestyle is for his chivalric reputation, as when the narrator recounts how the hero "wrong hys hondes and wepyd sore, / Fore fallyd was hys pride" (95–96). While excessive pride occasionally gets punished in English romance, particularly in penitential romances like *Sir Isumbras*, pride and its opposites— shame and scorn—are nonetheless central to the reputational economy of romance in ways that *Cleges* makes explicit.[20]

The importance of largesse to one's reputation is located specifically in generosity to minstrels, who function as the poem's "great merchants of symbolic capital."[21] Minstrels figure from the start among the diverse beneficiaries of the hero's largesse, receiving from him "hors and robys and rych rynges, / Gold and sylver and other thynges" (52–3), and minstrels will also be central to the poem's happy ending. Yet their role in the text is ambiguous in ways that the ending also makes clear. For now it is sufficient to observe that minstrelsy functions as a sort of metonymy for all that Cleges has lost by his fall into (relative) poverty. This is strikingly the point of the vision that the hero receives from heaven after he swoons from despair at his situation:

> And as he walkyd uppe and done
> Sore sygheng, he herd a sowne
> Off dyverse mynstralsy,
> Off trumpers, pypers, and nakerners,
> Off herpers notys and gytherners,
> Off sytall and of sautrey.
> Many carrals and grete dansyng
> In every syde herd he syng,
> In every place, treuly.
> He wrong hys hondes and wepyd sore;
> Mekyll mon he made ther,
> Sygheng full pytewysly. (97–108)

[And as he walked up and down, sighing sorely, he heard a sound of diverse kinds of minstrelsy, of trumpeters, pipers, and drummers, of the music of harp and cythern, of citole and psaltery. Many carols and much dancing on every side he heard, in every place, indeed. He wrung his hands and wept sorely. Great moaning he made there, sighing full piteously.]

That Cleges should only despair further upon hearing the heavenly music, as opposed to rejoicing, is a measure of the poem's willingness to admit that its own minstrelsy will have less to do with heavenly worship than with its earthly analogue: "worship" as the index of chivalric worth so familiar to readers of Malory. While he then proceeds duly to thank God for this miraculous "sonde" (111), Cleges sees it characteristically as a due return for his own worship of God in times past—"The myrth, that I was won to make / In this tyme fore Thi sake" (112–13)—rather than a sign of divine favor or cause for wonder. As an early indication of the extent to which even the miraculous is always already economized in this poem, Cleges's reaction to the "sonde" prefigures his wife's shrewd evaluation of the unseasonable fruit as a valuable commodity for which Cleges might receive a substantial reward from the king. Unlike the marvelous cherries, however, the vision of celestial mirth sent to Cleges seems by its very lack of substance only to drive the hero deeper into despair, causing him to dwell ruefully on his own lack of the material means to continue in his former largesse, the "rych metys and drynkes gode" (118) that constitute "manus fode" (119). At any rate, what Cleges says or does here hardly matters, since the privacy in which the scene occurs renders it superfluous to the plot, so that Cleges not only promptly forgets the miracle but never even bothers to tell his wife about it.[22] However much Cleges may want to economize the miracle by imagining it as a return gift from God, he does not recognize in the event any solution to his dilemma nor even, perhaps surprisingly, a sign of one.

Of course, this divine minstrelsy really is a sign, even if it does not itself possess the exchange value that drives this story forward at every turn. As Cleges's wife says of the cherries in the immediately following scene, they are a "tokenyng / Off mour godnes, that is coming"

(223–24), even as she follows up her hopeful interpretation with some practical advice about how to make her prophecy come true:

> "Tomorrow, when the dey do spryng,
> Ye schall to Cardyff to the Kyng,
> Full feyre hym to presente.
> Sych a gyft the may hafe ther,
> That we schall the beter fare." (232–36)

As a gift, in other words, the cherries will oblige the king to present Cleges with a countergift that could help relieve the latter's poverty. While there is nothing in this logic that would be out of place in Mauss's account of gift exchange, the wife's advice is problematic insofar as it unmasks such exchange as fundamentally self-interested, not all that different, in effect, from the exchange of commodities. The wife's calculating gaze already foreshadows the central problem of *Cleges*: the extent to which the miraculous fruit, as the central signifying object of the poem, is always-already a commodity and not in any simple sense the "present" (274) that Cleges asserts it to be.

It is no coincidence that this also marks the point in the narrative when God effectively drops out of the picture, having performed the strictly economic function for which Cleges constantly lauds him as the one who makes something from nothing. The point is worth stressing because the presence here of the motif of the "Miraculous Cherries" (also known as the "Unseasonable Growth" motif) is so often adduced as evidence of the influence of hagiography and religious drama on *Cleges*.[23] As in the case of the "biter bit" motif adopted from fabliau, however, the presence of a motif from devotional literature does not in itself argue for an essentially religious poem.[24] Even if one were to accept the elaborately Christological readings proposed for the cherries by some scholars of religious drama, we should be careful about attributing such meanings to the use of the cherry motif in *Cleges*, where its meaning is instead fundamentally economic. This is in fact suggested by the significance of cherries in a companion piece to the poem in at least one manuscript, Bodleian 6922.

As the romance's most recent editors note, the dramatized paternal narrator in *A Father's Instructions to His Son* likens cherries to the material world when counseling his son to "set nought by this world's weal, for it fares as a ripe cherry."[25] While the miraculous fruit of *Cleges* is sent by God and clearly not meant to suggest the temptations of the world, it does of course lead Cleges back to an enjoyment of "this world's weal" when Uther rewards him for his presentation of the fruit. Whatever its other associations, the unseasonable fruit in Cleges performs a resolutely material and even economic function. The cherries render the question of where they came from strangely irrelevant as soon as they appear, for the remainder of the poem is taken up wholly by the question of their (as it turns out, frustrated and problematic) exchange. What matters here is the fruit's surplus value as an exotic commodity, and this is the way the narrator refers to them—as a "nowylté" (217) or "newyng" (381).[26] As an object of exchange, the cherries are precisely the "manus fode" (119) that Cleges was lamenting his inability to provide when he first caught sight of them. Like so much else in this poem, then, the significance of the cherry motif is transformed by the "entirely original" context that the *Cleges* poet has imagined for it.[27] Where the cherry motif traditionally confirmed Mary's status as the mother of God, the poet, in transferring the miracle to a poor knight, gives it an economic meaning that may draw on the colloquial idea of life as a "cherry-fair."[28]

The subsumption of the poem's hagiographic potential by its economic plot is arguably complete by the time Cleges meets three greedy court officials. Following his wife's instructions, Cleges bears the fruit in a basket to Uther's court at "Cardyff" in hope of gaining a reward, where the first of the officials, a porter, stops him at the door. The porter's response to the cherries begins a pattern:

> The cherys he gan behold.
> Wele he wyst, fore his commyng,
> Fore hys present to the Kyng,
> Grete gyftes have he schuld. (279–82)

[He looked the cherries over. He knew very well that, for his visit, for his present to the king, he (i.e., Cleges) would have great gifts.]

While the language of gift exchange is evoked here in the narrator's allusion to the "grete gyftes" that Cleges can expect to receive in return for his present, the return gifts in this scenario are commodified when it becomes clear that their value can be calculated in advance. Like the cherries themselves, Uther's expected gifts fail as gifts because they *are* expected. The poem thus dramatizes the truism (exhaustively explored by Derrida) that a gift whose value can be anticipated is no gift at all.[29]

Yet it is striking that none of the actors in this drama of failed giving are merchants or even townspeople, and in this respect *Cleges*—like the other romances explored in this chapter—offers a critique of noble exchange as potentially similar to the kinds of economic activity that English romances more typically associate with threatening Others. Though they are of the hero's own class, the officials approach gift exchange in the same calculative spirit adopted by bourgeois characters like the mayor of Karlyeon (in *Launfal*) or the covetous merchant (in *Amadace*) in their economic dealings with the heroes of those romances.[30] The greedy officials are Others only in the general sense adumbrated by Frederic Jameson in his discussion of romance logic. That is, the officials' behavior simply mirrors the contradictions that beset the hero's own ideals (and by extension those of the society he champions), revealing these to be fundamentally self-interested.[31] In reminding us of the very reason for which Cleges himself has travelled to Uther's court, the officials' expectation of reward reproduces the hero's own motivation.

The introduction of violence at this point in the narrative suggests the stakes of this latent identification. Shrewdly aware that the division of his expected reward into three thirds (one for each official) will leave him with "no thyng . . . But if it be a melys mete" (350–53), Cleges resolves to ask the king for "strokes twelve" (428) with which to "pay" (430) his enemies rather than the "sylver our gold" they greedily anticipate (288). Although the "shared strokes" motif has widespread roots in folktale, George Shuffelton points out that *Cleges* "marks its originality" in its emphasis on the hero's own "unremitting charity," so that "the greed of the court officers appears in sharper contrast."[32] Yet it does not take much to see in this contrast a violent displacement of commercial desire. That the hero's violence is somewhat feeble, in relation to his own military past, is also part of its meaning as displacement. Precisely in its utter uselessness, the violence of the poem's ending gives more than justice; it gives the gift as that which defies calculation. As Uther points out to Cleges, the boon for which the latter has asked is of no use to an apparently poor man: "Thou had be better take gold our fe; / Mour nede therto thou hade" (437–38). Yet Cleges's insistence on the gift of violence, as opposed to "lond our lede / Or any gode" (425), is an insistence on the sublime surplus in which even the lowliest knight can claim ownership. Indeed, this insistence is what proves that he *is* a knight, and so the poem asks us to linger on the fact of violence, describing for us in detail the sharing of the strokes for which the motif is named. As he pursues his "adversarys" (431), we get a literally blow-by-blow account of Cleges's revenge, culminating in his attack on the usher, whose shoulder bone and right arm are both "brake atwo" (476). This is "as satisfying a dispensation of social justice as any dishonest middlemen might deserve," yet it is more significantly the mark of chivalry itself: the means by which Cleges reclaims his knightly identity.[33]

In order to see this as reclamation, it is necessary to recall the order of events in the poem's concluding scene. For it is not strictly true, as Putter asserts, that Cleges's identity is made known by a minstrel, even though it is a minstrel who first suggests the possibility that the man standing before the king is Cleges: "Somtyme men callyd hym Cleges / He was a knyght of youre" (494–95). Significantly, however, Uther does not believe the minstrel:

> The Kyng seyd: "This is not he in dede;
> It is long gon that he was dede,
> That I lovyd paramour.
> Wold God that he wer wyth me;
> I had hym lever than knyghtes thre:
> That knyght was styff in stoure." (499–504)

> [The King said: "This is not he, surely. It is a long time ago that he died, the one I loved so well. Would God he were with me; I'd rather have him than three other knights together. That knight was mighty in battle."]

Uther nevertheless expresses curiosity about the strange boon that his guest has requested ("The thre men that he strokes payd, / Wherefore it was and why" [509–10]). Cleges now explains the situation, causing Uther along with the rest of the court to laugh "so thei myght not sytte" (520) and to commend the ploy as "a nobull wytte" (521). Only after Cleges has told his story does Uther ask Cleges who he is, eliciting the response that marks the moment of recognition: "Som tyme men called me Sir Cleges; / I was your awne knight" (533–34). Though nearly identical to the minstrel's earlier statement (with the telling addition of the title "Sir"), Cleges's self-identification comes after he has proven that he is "styff in stoure," the powerful knight whom Uther once loved "paramour." It is Cleges's own performance, rather than the minstrel's information, that leads to Uther's recognition of his old companion.

This is why, as in the case of so many romances, it is idle to speculate on whether the various complications of the plot are particularly necessary: for instance, why Cleges does not appeal to Uther from the start, or at the very least when he has been victimized by the officials, or why—finally—he never acts to confirm or deny the minstrel's assertion about his identity, though all present are in a close-set "parlere" (481) rather than the hall, which would presumably have allowed Cleges himself to hear the minstrel identify him.[34] The futility of trying to account for such inconsistencies suggests that the connection between the hero's violent joke and his identity is central to the poem's meaning—so central that its composer was willing to sacrifice narrative coherence in order to achieve the needed link. The dramatic power of the poem's resolution depends on just this connection between Cleges's nobility of station and the "nobull wytte" that he displays in perceiving violence as the form of capital most appropriate to that station. Cleges is a knight because he performs like one.

That Cleges *must* perform his identity has significant implications in a poem that is all about performance, for it has long been noted that minstrels and minstrelsy play a vital role in *Cleges*, even more so than is usual for romances that self-consciously celebrate their (real or imagined) status as an orally transmitted form.[35] It is minstrels who "show us how the system works: if you give handsomely to minstrels, they will spread your good name, and that symbolic capital (honor, reputation) will in the end win you real capital (e.g., lucrative promotion to steward)."[36] But it should be clear by now that this account of the poem's economy is incomplete. It is not the poem's minstrels but rather Cleges himself who effectively performs and thereby makes known his identity. Far from relying on others to make good on the symbolic capital that attaches to his name, the hero in effect becomes his own minstrel.[37] By contrast, the failure of what we might call the poem's "professional" minstrels to affect the desired outcome is striking, especially in the version of the story preserved in the Advocates MS, in which the "geyst" (484) being recited to Uther upon Cleges's entrance is *about Cleges himself*.[38] The missing ingredient is the performance of violence as what effectively makes the story of *Cleges* legible to the court, for it is of course violence that is really the poem's "symbolic capital." As though uncomfortably aware of this, *Cleges* will also work to displace the violence that it performs, and it does so with a degree of self-consciousness that reveals a more sophisticated poem than *Cleges* is normally given credit for being.[39] Violence is what Cleges has left to give, and he does give it, though it is equally characteristic of the historical moment occupied by the poem that this violence should appear as after-dinner entertainment, safely contained by its location in the royal court.

The poem's setting is telling in this respect. As several readers have remarked, Uther's court is strangely Arthurian *avant la lettre* in at least one detail: its inexplicable possession of a "Ronde Tabull" (9).[40] But rather than regarding this is as a slip on the composer's part, we might instead take it as a symptom of a more general problem with history in *Cleges*. While it is surely true that Uther's court would have been known to the poem's audience as "synonymous with hardship and toil," *Cleges* nevertheless opens on a world in which wartime is located firmly if rather vaguely in the past, and vassals like Cleges himself are no longer needed for military service. Of a piece with the poem's tendency to gloss over the darker aspects of Uther's reign is the role of Igraine. Represented from Geoffrey of Monmouth's chronicle onward as the wife of a vassal whom Uther takes for his own in the first of his many wars, the Igraine of *Cleges* is merely an unnamed "lady gente" (386) to whom Uther sends some of Cleges's cherries as a love token. Far from being the tumultuous pre-Arthurian Britain we might expect, this is a world in which Cleges can expect to possess the reward given to him by the king at the poem's end, Cardiff castle, "with pes" (564), and there is no mention of further exploits on the hero's part, who pays his debts and proceeds to live "many yere / With joy and mery chere" (571–72). If the king's awarding of a "colere" (554) to Cleges's son evokes the "militarized world" of late medieval England, that world is not otherwise evident in the poem, whose entire problem, as the hero experiences, is its lack of opportunities for the exercise of prowess.[41]

Indeed, we have seen that, rather than celebrating feudal violence as a way of life, *Cleges* sublimates this violence, economizing it as noble exchange. Yet *Cleges* also envisions such exchange as incapable of sustaining itself as a distinctive practice in relation to the calculative mentality of the poem's antagonistically mercantile Others. Exiled from the uncannily post-feudal space of Uther's court, violence returns as the very substance of noble exchange itself. That return is also the turning point of *Cleges*, the moment at which it becomes possible for the hero to speak his proper name as "Sir Cleges." Yet it is equally significant that this moment of return can take place only as a kind of exception or, at best, a reminder of some dimly remembered past, exemplified by Uther's certainty that the hero must have died long ago. From the narrator's opening allusion to "ansytores, that before us were, / Bothe herdy and wyght" (2–3) to Uther's description of Cleges as once having been these things himself, the poem's tone is nostalgic. Chivalry returns, in the end, only *as* exchange—the very medium that does so much to threaten its survival. This is also the basic problem of two other spendthrift tales.

CHIVALRY'S RETURNS

Like *Cleges*, *Sir Launfal* and *Sir Amadace* envision the return of chivalry to an essentially post-feudal moment, and like the *Awntyrs* they envision this return of the past in the form of a ghost. The meaning of "gost" as what returns begins in Middle English, which in contrast to

Old English knows the ghost specifically as the revenant, the returned soul of a dead person as a visible form.[42] Many of the earliest such stories—like the Middle English *Gast of Gy* (circa 1350)—become occasions for expounding on the doctrine of Purgatory, yet romance, too, is a genre peopled by ghosts. Gawain, who sees a ghost in the *Awntyrs*, will become one in Malory's *Le Morte Darthur*. Seeing such ghosts as a return of the past—even as the return of chivalry itself—might already suggest what such phantoms have to do with the gift. For if the spendthrift hero literally spends himself out of the genre of romance, the ghost will be the return that such expenditure paradoxically ensures—a sign of the gift's power to endure, even to transform the material surpluses of the late medieval economy into something marvelous.

As a kind of visible return, the ghost offers itself as an opportunity for thinking about the work of romance as a particular way of seeing. The ghost is an appearing—an apparition—and its presence speaks to the peculiar optics of romance, its need for the kind of phantasmal capital that the ghost instantiates. Thus, for instance, Geoffrey of Monmouth's mid-twelfth-century *History of the Kings of Britain* can be called the "genesis" of English romance simply because "its metaphors . . . seem simultaneously to wish to express and also conceal," while, for yet another reader, the English romances as a whole recognize the "disturbing reality" of social conflict "in order to make valid their cultural concealment of it."[43] Such analyses point to the ways in which romance seems to waver between the impulse to confess all in one moment and to retract that confession the next, as one might expect of a genre whose plots themselves typically revolve around issues of secrecy, disguise, and (mis)recognition. Seen in this light, the romance ghost is not just a reminder of what persists *in* romance but of what romance itself does, the kind of seeing that this form makes possible.

It is significant, then, that both of these stories begin by admitting the extent to which they want to repress the truth, opening with what amounts to a plea for discretion. Launfal, having been denied royal largesse by Arthur's treacherous wife, makes up a lie about having to leave the court in order to inherit some lands; in reality he retreats in disgrace to a nearby town, where he spends his remaining goods so "savegelych" (130) that he is ultimately forced to relinquish his two remaining servants for lack of pay. As they prepare for their return to Arthur's court dressed in their rags, Launfal begs the servants not to reveal the true state of his affairs ("Tellyth no man of my poverté" [143]). Like Launfal, Amadace, too, must plead with a servant for discretion, telling his steward: "Lette nevyr mon wete my grete mischefe, / Butte hele hit us between" (29–30). As we will see, both plots depend from the beginning on the need for covering up. So while a certain lack of knowledge is the fundamental problem in *Cleges*—"Cleges" is not known as such—Launfal and Amadace can only embody their chivalric names to the extent that they are able to deceive others.

Given the conspicuous role of merchants in both *Launfal* and *Amadace*, one might be tempted to see this more urgent dislocation as evidence of a more intensely mercantile context for the two stories, in which the romances' heroes are themselves forced to behave *like* merchants, hiding their losses and advertising their gains in the manner of Chaucer's merchant, "sownynge alwey th' encrees of his wynnyng" (I. 275), or perhaps his shipman, another high liver who confesses that he would need to "goon out of the weye" (VII. 234)—on a pilgrimage, for instance—if his *pryvetee* were known.[44] But while Launfal and Amadace inhabit a more explicitly commercial world than Cleges, the need for secrecy in these stories cannot be explained purely in terms of the commercial imperative to conceal one's true worth, for the role of secrecy in both romances is ultimately about where money comes from to begin with. It is telling in this respect that the secret of poverty gets exchanged in both romances for its precise opposite—a secret about wealth.

The importance of secrecy in the case of *Launfal* is well known, even if it is not always appreciated that this secret (the secret, of course, of Launfal's affair with his fairy mistress) is also a secret about the origins of capital. Seen in this light, Launfal's secret possesses more general significance in a story that begins by identifying wealth as a defining characteristic of Arthur's court—with its "knyghtes that wer profitable" (10)—even as it leaves conspicuously open the question of where those profits come from. Yet violence is not absent from the story of *Launfal*, any more than it is from *Cleges*. In fact, the major additions made to *Launfal* by Thomas Chestre, the *armiger* who has been identified as the poem's likely composer, concern precisely the question that the poem refuses to answer. As several critics have noted, the episode of the hero's fight with Sir Valentyn appears to be strangely extraneous in light of the poem's overall design, so much so that Spearing labels it "absurd."[45] One possible reason for its inclusion has to do with the location of the fight. Sir Valentyn is from "Atalye" (561), glossed by A. J. Bliss as Atille, a city supposedly founded "by the 'pagans' in Lombardy, between two rivers."[46] The emphasis on Lombardy is probably not coincidental: the Lombards were the hated central bankers of the late Middle Ages.[47] Like the greedy court officials of *Cleges*, Sir Valentyn represents without precisely naming mercantile culture as a source of antagonism.

More importantly, as D. Vance Smith suggests, we can read the Valentyn episode as part of this poem's fascination with appearance and disappearance, the central tropes of a romance that concerns "the furtiveness of the very things that are most visible, extravagant, and seemingly gratuitous." Thus, when Launfal's invisible squire, Gefre, twice aids his master in the course of the battle with Valentyn—replacing Launfal's helmet and retrieving his fallen shield—we might infer that "Launfal's chivalric success depends upon a . . . failure of vision."[48] At the same time, the scene makes visible what it fantasizes about concealing: the origins of wealth as the poem knows these (in violence) rather than as it imagines them (in the form of a fairy mistress and the invisible minion who here aids Launfal). We might even say that while "chivalric success" in this poem depends on a *failure* of vision, it is equally significant that this success can claim as one of its apparent and visible proofs a slain giant "Gronyng wyth grysly wounde" (600) and, for good measure, "Alle the lordes of Atalye," whom the hero lays down with his sword "as lyght as dew" (601, 608).

If this performance of chivalric identity seems both more aggressive and more strangely hollow than in *Cleges*, this might be due in part to *Launfal's* more urgent portrayal of a world defined by the threat of chivalric obsolescence—of armor that is perpetually rusting away, as Sir Valentyn imagines it to be in his challenge to the hero when he tauntingly exhorts Launfal to "kepe his harneys from the ruste" (527) by agreeing to a battle.[49] For while chivalric performance is central to the poem's ideology, it is also characteristic of *Launfal* that this performance can only appear as a kind of surplus in relation to the romance's main plot—a surplus exchangeable, in fact, for the gifts that Launfal bestows on Sir Valentyn's messenger in return for his "tyding" about Sir Valentyn's challenge: "a noble courser, and a ring / And a robe of ray" (544–46). This is also why Launfal's deeds at the tournament—his "noblesse" (615), in the narrator's straight-faced account—can serve to remind Arthur of the hero's "cowthe of largesse" (624) in an associative movement that registers violence as just one more expression of the poem's symbolic capital. In a poem that codes wealth as a thing with no real origins and no apparent end, violence (or, more specifically, its seeming performance) is transformed from a means of extracting surplus into a form of capital in its own right.

So it is perhaps no coincidence that Chestre's second major addition to the poem—the tournament given by "the lordes of Karlyoun" (533) for the "love of Sir Launfal" (535)—follows directly on an extended description of the hero's largesse (421–32) and itself takes the form of an exchange in which "ech knyght leyd on other good dent" (446). Whether such moments "epicize" the hero's otherwise passive role—as one reader suggests—is perhaps less important than the way in which such moments contribute to the poem's overall fantasy of plenitude, in which acts of violence, like the poem's other commodities, exceed all attempts at calculation, so that the narrator is unable to say precisely, for instance, how many people were at the tournament ("The numbre y not how fale" [480]) but assures us that "many" (485) were injured before Launfal won the day.[50] The "absurd" quality of the scene is itself an index of the poem's commitment to surplus. By the same token, of course, these moments can *only* appear as surplus, thereby eluding any sense that violence and wealth might be connected in a more than incidental way. If the poem has the effect of expressing "the obligatory secrecy at the heart of capital," it is a secret that is hidden in plain sight, the origins of wealth written in precisely those episodes that can be identified as the narrative surplus of *Launfal* in relation to the poem's own sources.

In this drama of seeing and not seeing, the possibility of the chivalric is finally only knowable in the semitransparent form of a specter: the ghost of Launfal that returns from fairyland every year "upon a certayn day" (1024) in order to provide any knight who wishes "to kepe hys armes fro the rustus" (1028) with an opportunity for combat. Many readers have noted the ways in which this concluding scene, absent from the original story of Lanval as told by Marie de France, speaks to the English poem's more urgent anxiety about chivalry's future.[51] The image of rusting armor, already summoned by the poet when Sir Valentyn supposes that Launfal's "harneys" is in danger of "the ruste" (527), again poses the threat of "the chivalric economy's tendency toward inertia," suggesting the extent to which the hero's ghostly returns might be "more commemoration than fecund renewal," "memorial" as opposed to actual performance. Yet Launfal's returns are also a profit whose entire point is to be "largely inaccessible," safe from any sense that such returns might be connected to the violence that the poem works so hard to render invisible.[52] So it is one of this ghost's remarkable qualities to be both apparent—able to be grasped "wyth syght" (1026)—yet also invisible, as when we are assured just a few lines later that no man "saw hym yn thys lond" (1036) ever again after his disappearance. Like the forms of excess that he ambivalently embodies, Launfal himself becomes subject to the conflicting imperatives of a poem that demands from us, and from itself, a double commitment to both recognition and repression.

Amadace acts out this drama of concealment and revelation in even more literal terms. The poem resembles *Launfal* in being structured around a need for secrecy, and, as in *Launfal*, the real secret is not about poverty but its opposite. At the poem's opening, Amadace, having exhausted his resources through liberality, makes a final display of giving "full ryche giftus" (40) before mortgaging his lands and fleeing to the forest (with his remaining forty pounds of money in hand) in order to avoid detection as a bankrupt. He soon happens on a cottage in which he finds a woman weeping over a foul-smelling corpse. The woman explains that she is the wife of a merchant who spent all of his money in generosity toward others, leaving behind such vast debts that his creditor—a more conventionally greedy merchant—refuses to allow the generous merchant's burial until the debts are satisfied. In response, Amadace magnanimously pays the dead man's debts and uses his last shillings to ensure a proper funeral. Now totally bankrupt, the hero wanders once more into the forest, where he soon meets a ghost—the White Knight—who tells Amadace about an upcoming tournament whose prize is the hand of a princess in marriage. What Amadace himself does not yet know—but any reader familiar with the "Grateful Dead" motif will immediately suspect—is that the White Knight is the soul of the man whom the hero has recently buried and who now, by way of reward, offers to bring his benefactor "owte of kare" (471). Specifically, the ghost knight offers to help Amadace prevail in the tournament, instructing him to say that he is a castaway whose companions have all died in a shipwreck (with the implication that the truth of the hero's situation is too shameful to admit). The ghost's offer comes with an important catch, however: Amadace must agree to divide any winnings evenly with his supernatural ally when he has obtained the hand of the princess—an agreement that the White Knight returns years later to enforce by demanding that the hero *physically* divide his wife and young child in half so that the ghost can take half, only to relent when the hero actually agrees. The poem ends with the White Knight's commendation of Amadace's integrity.

Several readers have remarked on the way in which the White Knight's initial encounter with Amadace continues the theme of generosity with which the poem opens. The White Knight not only offers a return gift to the hero but does so while articulating the logic of the noble gift with a clarity that marks him as the story's anthropologist of exchange as well as its ghostly facilitator.[53] Reminding Amadace that no one can really claim to possess the gift—all material goods being "butte a lante lone" (454) from God—the White Knight sums up a view of the world in which generous actors can expect a good return both from others and from the Almighty himself, the ultimate giver (as in *Cleges*) who ensures the legitimacy of the entire economy:

> A mon that hase all way bynne kynde,
> Sum curtas mon yette may he fynde,
> That mekille may stonde in stalle;
> Repente the noghte that thu hase done,
> For He that schope bothe sunne and mone,
> Full wele may pay for alle. (463–68)

[A man who has always been kind to others may himself find a courteous man who might be of great help to him. Repent not for what you have done, for He that made both sun and moon is fully able to pay for all.]

As a way of driving home his point, the White Knight reminds Amadace of what the latter presumably already knows: that he should use his newfound wealth to be "large of feyce" (490), a phrase that neatly encapsulates the connection between liberality and reputation on which the chivalric economy depends. Indeed, one problem for readings that place undue stress on the poem's mercantile context is the extent to which *Amadace* imagines, in very specific terms, the transformation of symbolic capital into feudal wealth.[54] By being "large," the White Knight asserts, Amadace will obtain the human surplus that serves as an essential form of feudal wealth. In a process that is never clearly explained precisely because its reliability can be taken for granted, the "ten thowsand" (495) followers that comprise this surplus will help Amadace to "wynne full mekille honowre" (496), which will in turn be convertible into feudal lordship over "fild and frithe, towne and towre" (497). As is still true in a much later text like *The Merchant of Venice*, whose profligate and penniless young suitor cannot imagine travelling to Belmont without bearing "gifts of rich value," the question of whether the hero really needs to make such a grand show in order to win the lady (and thus the feudal lordship attached to her) is never answered simply because such a question would never be posed from within an economy that assumes a direct correlation between real capital and its symbolic equivalents.[55] Yet what *Amadace* also knows is that such an economy only works—or seems to—because its true basis lies elsewhere.

It is no coincidence, then, that violence is what *Amadace* explicitly forbids—an injunction that confesses how much this romance knows—for the poem in fact begins by admitting the simple fact that Amadace need not pay his debts at all. Like many a late medieval knight, he can live by intimidation. As Amadace himself puts it, he might "hold men in awe or threte, / That thay myghte noghte hor awne gud gete"

(22–23). While his words might recall the narrator's oblique assurance in *Cleges* that no man lost anything in his dealings with the hero, Amadace's statement is more direct in its evocation of a world in which social and economic struggle leads quite easily and naturally to violence, not as the exception but as the rule. Yet outright violence never actually occurs in the poem—to the extent that its *non*occurrence becomes the entire point.

The first instance of the poem's ambivalence on this score has already been mentioned: Amadace's encounter with the "dede cors" (131) of the spendthrift merchant for whose burial the hero generously offers to provide. In a scene that marks in a horrifying way the too-literal return of this gift, Amadace goes on to confront not just another corpse but an entire heap of them as, following the White Knight's instructions, he takes the way to a neighboring kingdom that lies along the shoreline:

> Now als Sir Amadace welke bi the se sonde,
> The broken schippus he ther fonde—
> Hit were mervayl to say.
> He fond wrekun amung the stones
> Knyghtes in menevere for the nones,
> Stedes quite and gray,
> With all kynne maner of richas
> That any mon myghte devise
> Castun uppe with waturs lay;
> Kistes and cofurs bothe ther stode,
> Was fulle of gold precius and gode,
> No mon bare noghte away. (517–28)

[Now as Sir Amadace walked by the shore, he found the broken ships there—it was a marvel to see. He found, wrecked among the rocks, knights in miniver, white and grey steeds, with all manner of rich things that a man might conceive, cast up and lying in the water. Both chests and coffers stood there, full of precious gold and goods that no man had borne away.]

Having clad himself in dead men's clothes—a sumptuous outfit of "gold webbe" (530)—and taken the best horse, Amadace makes his way to the tournament, where he promptly wins "full mecul honoure" (535) as well as the earlier promised "fild and frithe, toune and towre, / Castell and riche cite" (536–37). The episode brilliantly, if bizarrely, speaks to the meaning of the noble gift as a gesture that threatens the violence that it also works to displace. These corpses might not stink—in this, they are unlike the corpse of the merchant whom the hero has earlier buried—but they are corpses still.

A tableau that implies far more than it says, the moment evokes scenes of death that will be familiar to any reader of English romance, such as the "taas of bodyes ded" (I. 1005) in Chaucer *Knight's Tale* or—perhaps more aptly given the surrealism of this moment—the frozen and fragmentary bodies that populate the courtyard of the fairy king in *Sir Orfeo*.[56] As Karl Steel remarks, Amadace's strange encounter is typical of a romance in which the hero "does not create corpses; he simply comes across them." Instead of violence, we get "a kind of (unconscious) largesse of the dead."[57] At the same time, precisely because they *are* part of an economy, the shipwrecked bodies mark a return of what this romance cannot quite repress. If violence will not be performed openly, its traces will at least continue to haunt the poem. So the spectacle of the dead body returns, like a gift, to complete the exchange, a reminder that if largesse is what conceals social reality in the form of a stinking corpse, it is in the nature of such largesse not only to return that corpse with interest—multiplying death—but to do so openly, undoing the magic of concealment that the hero's initial gift of a decent burial seemed designed to ensure. And thus the entire scene is also a repetition with a precise logic. *Because* Amadace has buried the generous merchant, he may now take from the dead whatever he needs and leave them unburied. For Derek Brewer, this is simply "the non-naturalistic logic of folktale," but it is also the logic of noble exchange laid bare.[58] What the gift earns for itself in the poem, finally, is the right to declare its violence openly, in the grossly literal form of a mass of dead humanity that does not call for concealment but, on the contrary, demands display as a sumptuary object. If this return seems too literal, too commercial in its swapping of one corpse for others, its underlying logic instantiates noble expenditure not just in its excess but in its appearance as a phenomenon worthy of the hero's (and our) gaze: a "mervayl to say" (519).

The ultimate figure of such "marvelous" returning in the poem is, of course, the ghost, whose return in the form of a "quite knyghte" (445) is unique to *Amadace* among "grateful dead" stories. The composer evidently means for the merchant's posthumous promotion into the armigerous classes to be read as a reward for his generosity in life. The hero has already foreshadowed the ghost's social transformation from merchant to knight by acknowledging that the merchant, in behaving like Amadace himself, resembles him—that "he myghte full wele be of my kynne" (209).[59] Yet we might also conclude that the ghost of a merchant, as a member of the rising if not the newly dominant class in late medieval society, is impossible for this romance to imagine. To ask what a ghost merchant would do instead of riding around on a horse is to invite the kinds of questions that the composer of *Amadace* seems to have preferred not to answer. Instead he asserts that to become chivalric *is* to become a ghost.

Like Launfal's ghost, however, the White Knight brings with him more than simple obsolescence. He performs the violence that the poem must at once execute and disavow. It is a job he does well, and in doing it he provides the bodies with whose erstwhile trappings Amadace decks himself out. But the White Knight will go further even than Launfal in insisting upon the return of violence. This becomes clear when he demands not half of the hero's newfound wealth, as earlier agreed, but rather quite literally half of Amadace's wife and young child:

> He sayd, "Broke wele thi londus brode,
> Thi castels hee, thi townus made,
> Of hom kepe I righte none;
> Allso thi wuddus, thi waturs clere,
> Thi frithis, thi forestus, fer and nere,
> Thi ringus with riche stone,
> Allso thi silvyr, thi gold rede,
> For hit may stonde me in no stidde,
> I squere, bi Sayn John!

But, be my faythe, wothoutun stryve,
Half thi child, and halfe thi wyve,
And thay schall with me gone." (721–32)

[He said, "Enjoy your broad lands, your high castles, your towns, of which I take no account. Likewise your woods, your clear lakes, your forests, far and near, your rings set with rich jewels, likewise your silver, your bright gold, for these may do me no good, I swear, by Saint John! But, by my faith, without a fight, (give me) half your child and half your wife, and they shall come with me."]

What the ghost needs is not wealth—represented as all that feudal lordship affords—but blood. In a story where the primary business of actual knights seems to be to hand out charity and bury indigent merchants, it is a deceased merchant-turned-knight who embodies the fundamental violence of the chivalric economy: its profound dependence on suffering.

How can such a reading be reconciled with the frequent claim that *Amadace* represents romance at its most commercial—is even perhaps a text that knows itself to be a commodity in an emerging literary marketplace of manuscripts for sale? For it is undoubtedly true that the poem's gifts are always threatening to become, in the final analysis, mere commodities. Even the concluding encounter just described between the hero and the White Knight has been read as an expression of mercantile values. The ghost behaves like a penny-pinching merchant, insisting on the exact letter of the "forwart" (502) or contract by which Amadace has previously agreed to share exactly half of anything he gets with the ghost's help.[60] The moment suggests, at the very least, that "Amadace's ventures into the world outside the confines of the landowning class intimate a consciousness of alternatives," and at most that the romance is "bourgeois" or even "the most lower class of romances, celebrating money and its associated power from a vantage point near the bottom of the social scale."[61] What does it mean that the threatened eruption of *actual* violence into a text that has so far only fantasized about it should take the specific form of a potentially mercantile demand?

One answer would be to see this moment as the romance's fullest recognition of the hostile economic realities that the text's aristocratic hero needs to confront before he is able to enjoy restoration of his status.[62] But reading this ghostly encounter alongside the other texts explored in this chapter raises another possibility, for it suggests that the commodity itself has become a site of violence in *Amadace*. Violence, whose performance is difficult and largely forbidden in the post-chivalric world of these texts, simply disappears here into procedures of exchange. Violence becomes something that a knight and a merchant can agree on, and *this* is what allows one to be the other and vice versa.

Considered in this light, the White Knight's threatened challenge resembles the persistent demand of Launfal's specter that someone fight with him, as he returns every year to burnish the armor of a declining knighthood. Yet *Amadace* is the more unsettling text, its spirit a more unquiet one. What figures in *Launfal* as a safely contained and predictable ritual takes on more threatening proportions in *Amadace*. The ghost of chivalry, the poet seems to imply, is not so easily laid to rest, its relationship to a post-feudal moment less securely one of mere nostalgia. Of course, the White Knight, like the God of the Old Testament, will in the end relent, staying Amadace's hand as the blade is about to descend and assuring Amadace that "now is tyme of pees!" (804).[63] Yet in another sense the "tyme" of this poem is precisely what is at issue: the extent to which its historical moment is firmly of the present, safe from the return of the violence that it has promised cannot get to us in a world of merchants and money, a world in which a knight is no more than a figure of pity, knighthood at most a thing to be performed (as in *Launfal*) at yearly intervals. If *Cleges* and even *Launfal* seem ultimately to want to assure us of this—to keep us safe from the very returns they fantasize about—*Amadace* knows how difficult it is to measure the distance between war and peace, to stay on the right side of the line that divides an "archaic" past from our own moment.

No wonder English romances are haunted by ghosts. How could it be otherwise in a Middle English tradition that has always been known primarily in terms of its belatedness—in other words, as fertile territory for the ghosts of the past? Yet even a poet known primarily for (and defined by) his interest in the future—Geoffrey Chaucer—will have to contend with such phantoms, as I argue in the next chapter. This is more than a matter of literal ghosts, even if Chaucer does know something about such phenomena. For Chaucer explores, by means of the gift, the possibility of other sorts of appearances, especially the phantom forms of chivalric surplus that he identifies as the value of his own ambitiously literary writing. Chaucer, the poet of our own future, will also be interested in what persists.

CHAPTER 3

Chaucerian Capital

Chaucer was, though not himself a merchant, the son of one. He grew up in the Vintry Ward on the north bank of the Thames, at the point where England was most thoroughly penetrated by the forces of international commerce. "Born and bred of burgesses" as he was, the father of English poetry knew a great deal, we might suppose, about the "delusions and powers of capitalism." In the *General Prologue* to *The Canterbury Tales*, for instance, we see an "ethos of mercantile projection": a reminder, to Chaucer's aristocratic audience, that they were themselves engaged in the procedures of commerce that the "Chaucer" of the prologue invites that audience to deride. For Chaucer knows very well that the world of the court is not so different from the more candidly self-interested world of merchants and money into which he had been born—that many a knight at court was also a merchant, "worthy" in both senses of that word. It is no surprise, then, that literature itself will be commodified throughout *The Canterbury Tales*: in the Host's desire for a "thrifty" (II. 1165) tale, or the Man of Law's accommodating acknowledgment that "biheste is dette" (41), that he owes the Host a story and will tell it out promptly. The whole tale-telling game is in this sense an "ostentatiously nonaristocratic poetic project," a game begun for the tangible prize of a free dinner—a contest whose logic, as the Miller will assert, is one of "quiting" or paying back.[1]

Nor is it merely Chaucer's bourgeois "characters" who think about tale-telling in this way; Chaucer himself does. It is he who is really speaking, after all, when the Eagle reminds us in *The House of Fame* that this "Chaucer" is a shrewd auditor of import revenues as well as a poet:

> For when thy labour doon al ys,
> And hast mad alle thy rekenynges,
> In stede of reste and newe thynges,
> Thou goost hom to thy hous anoon;
> And, also domb as any stoon,
> Thou sittest at another book
> Tyl fully daswed ys thy look. (652–58)[2]

Chaucer's poetry is by his own admission a kind of accounting, legible as a book of "rekenynges": very like the books in which Chaucer recorded the values of the shipments of wool, sheepskins, and leather flowing out of the Port of London.[3] No wonder, then, that a poet who knew so much about the workings of commerce should also end up becoming the father of English literature, a figure whose name will be "synonymous with surplus value in English literature."[4]

Yet it is worth remembering that this same Chaucer also knew about another economy: that of the gift. For Chaucer's career as an esquire "en service" to three monarchs involved him deeply in the gift economies of court life, even as he probably owed his success at court in part to the kind of savvy that the son of a rich merchant could be depended on to display, for instance, in the negotiations that Chaucer may have conducted with one of the great Italian banking houses.[5] Certainly the nature of Chaucer's royal appointments—as controller of customs, clerk of the king's works, and so on—suggests that shrewdness, a keen eye for the value of things, was among the qualities that Chaucer himself was valued for. Yet if the location of this work was in some broad sense mercantile—the work of someone who dealt on a daily basis with merchants and bankers—Chaucer was paid for that work largely in gifts. It is not much of an overstatement to say that Chaucer's life, as preserved in the contemporary records, is for us largely a history of the gifts he received. He appears in his first definite shape to us in 1357, when he is granted a "paltock" or doublet, a pair of hose, and shoes to match by the countess of Ulster. Subsequent gifts provide us with vital information about the nature of Chaucer's employments and allegiances: in 1395–96, a fur-lined robe of scarlet; in 1374, a gallon pitcher of wine daily for life (commuted to an annuity of twenty marks in 1378—a gift of money now, but still a gift); also in 1374, an annuity for life from his powerful royal patron, John of Gaunt.[6]

Such gifts came in addition to Chaucer's regular wages. Sometimes—especially when the promised gifts were late in coming—he had to beg for them. Chaucer's *Complaint to His Purse* is, among other things, a poignant reminder that the relationship between the poet and the three monarchs whom he served was one of patronage as well as employment—a relationship, in other words, of total dependence. As David Carlson has noted of Chaucer's gifts from the crown, such gifts "reduced recipients to object-status." Dependent persons like Chaucer "were not persons from this respect but things, decorative objects, the purpose of which was to make a show of their patron's wealth and power."[7] If Chaucer was to become "synonymous with surplus value in literature," it is worth considering the extent to which he was himself a form of surplus in this scene of feudal magnificence. Dependent on gifts even for basic necessities like clothing and shelter—the second of which Chaucer enjoyed free from 1374 onward—Chaucer was, if in some ways privileged, also thoroughly *objectified*, a humble servant and occasional poet whose livelihood depended on his ability to give pleasure as well as to be useful, even if this meant knowing how to beg wittily.[8]

The House of Fame, insofar as it allows us to gauge the poet's self-awareness about such matters, gives us a picture not only of what such dependence felt like but also of Chaucer's fantasized response to what we might call his situation as an object in this aristocratic economy. If he is on the one hand a sort of literary accountant, as the Eagle suggests, "Chaucer" will later meet, in the House of Fame itself, with the minstrels whom he in so many ways resembled:

> Ther mette I cryinge many oon,
> "A larges, larges, hold up wel!
> God save the lady of thys pel,
> Our oune gentil lady Fame,
> And hem that wilnen to have name

Of us!" Thus herde y crien alle,
And faste comen out of halle
And shoken nobles and sterlynges.
And somme corouned were as kynges,
With corounes wroght ful of losenges;
And many ryban and many frenges
Were on her clothes trewely. (1308–19)

On the one hand, this picture speaks to Chaucer's anxiety that he, too, might be at root no more than a minstrel, the kind of begging poet whom Robert Meyer-Lee has identified as the laureate's uncanny double.[9] Chaucer was indeed one such beggar, and the picture of minstrels pleading for "larges" reminds us that however much Chaucer knew about the status of his writing as a cultural commodity, he also knew that the rewards of that writing would take the specific form of the gift.

Yet it is remarkable, given the ways in which this scene seems to describe the crippling dependence of minstrels on patrons, that minstrels, despite their dependence, are also "kynges," even if only in the sense of being "kings-of-arms" responsible for reciting the deeds of their noble patrons: "hem that wilnen to have name / Of us!" Even more striking is the fact that it is inexplicably the *minstrels*, not their aristocratic patrons, who actually show largesse in this scene. It is *they* who "faste comen out of halle / And shoken nobles and sterlynges," spilling coin onto the floor in what *The Riverside Chaucer* glosses as "a lavish display . . . of the sort associated with great nobles."[10] Minstrels, first seen here begging for largesse to "hold up wel"—literally, to hold out its personified hand in generosity—now transform weirdly into those who give it. However delusional the mock reign of these kings—things of ribbons and patches merely—they also exude a strange power as the givers of a phantasmal capital, a double of the very largesse for which these poets have just been importuning.

There is, I propose, something highly symptomatic about this moment of textual confusion. Chaucer's own dependence on the economy of the gift is well documented. He subsisted, as much as any minstrel and perhaps more, on marks of favor and material support from his aristocratic and royal patrons: gifts in the form of the clothing, shelter, and of course money he needed to maintain his place in the elite circles of Westminster and London. Yet what has been less well recognized is the extent to which this economy provides a model of value for his own writing and does so from the beginning of his career. If it is finally Chaucer who will be identified as the giver of gifts and father figure—a locus of "God's plenty" more gifted than any mere minstrel could ever hope to be—we should consider that behind this metaphor lurks a literal truth.[11] For Chaucer will remake dependence into a form of self-assertion, the noble gift into the substance of cultural value itself.[12]

Romance serves Chaucer as an overdetermined location for working out this poetics. Chaucer, who knows about the power of the gift firsthand, imagines his own poetic practice as a gifted one. And this also means that romance will persist in *The Canterbury Tales* despite everything that Chaucer knows, and invites us to see, about its outmodedness. If the "spendthrift knight" tales explored in the previous chapter foreshadow romance's future as a "popular" literature, this chapter explores the persistence of romance in the writing characteristic of another kind of future, the one represented by a self-consciously elite poet. Chaucer's gifts have been read very differently by literary history than the romances of the gift that we have been exploring so far. But Chaucerian surplus, too, performs the violence of noble giving in ways that will prove decisive for the future of romance.

CHAUCERIAN ROMANCE

What did Chaucer learn from romance? Was it, as Christopher Cannon has asserted, how to make things disappear? How, in effect, to transmute his own writing into the holographic forms of cultural value named by the commodity?[13] If so, there may be no more starkly literal realization of that lesson's fruits than the moment in *The Franklin's Tale* when romance itself is made to disappear. The squire Averagus, having sought the services of a magician to help him secure his reluctant beloved, gets a complimentary preview of what this magician can do for him, a taste of the sorts of illusions that a learned clerk can conjure up in exchange for money:

He shewed hym, er he wente to sopeer,
Forestes, parkes ful of wilde deer;
Ther saugh he hertes with hir hornes hye,
The gretteste that evere were seyn with ye.
He saugh of hem an hondred slayn with houndes,
And somme with arwes blede of bittre woundes.
He saugh, whan voyded were thise wilde deer,
Thise fauconers upon a fair ryver,
That with hir haukes han the heron slayn.
tho saugh he knyghtes justyng in a playn;
And after this he dide hym swich plesaunce
That he hym shewed his lady on a daunce,
On which hymself he daunced, as hym thoughte.
And whan this maister that this magyk wroughte
Saugh it was tyme, he clapte his handes two,
And farewel! al oure revel was ago. (V. 1190–1204)

In one sense a disappearing act, this moment is also of course a sudden appearing—an eruption of aristocratic lavishness and violence into a tale that has done so much to protect us from these things. In fact, I want to suggest that it is worth lingering over the simple fact that there *is* a gift here, even a noble one in the Maussian sense: a gift that signifies even as it displaces violence. As Britton J. Harwood remarks, this is a moment in which "God's own hecatomb" is opened to us to reveal the bloody corpses of animals slain with arrows or by other animals, knights contending for honor in a desolate "playn," and finally desire itself: the lady with whom a lover might dance for a moment, even if she belongs to another.[14]

In one sense, this scene of desire only reaffirms the logic of the commodity, of the tale's efforts at "safely framing and containing" the gift in the name of rational exchange.[15] The Franklin is after all a "contour" as well as a "vavasour" (I. 359–60)—an auditor who knows the precise value of what he is offering us, just like the hard-bargaining magician who will take no less than one thousand good English pounds before he will work his magic on the love-struck squire's behalf. The critical tradition that reads *The Franklin's Tale* as somehow a bit "bourgeois" is not therefore wrong, any more than reading English romances of less exalted pedigree in this way would be wrong.[16] We can even say that this tale is itself a commodity, however much the fake generosity of the tale's conclusion might want to protest otherwise. The magician will release the squire of his debt of one thousand pounds, prompting the squire to release the already-married object of his attentions from the promise that she has rashly made to sleep with him if he can perform a certain magic trick, which in turn relieves the woman's husband of the necessity of "generously" surrendering up his wife to the squire. At the end of it all, the squire can declare with satisfaction that it would be difficult to tell, and thus worth asking, who was the "most fre" (V. 1622) or generous of the characters. Readers who have seen this ending as a little too easy might be responding to the way in which it reproduces the magical economy of a fabliau like *The Shipman's Tale*, another story about a sum of money whose circulation somehow mysteriously generates a tidy profit for everyone.[17] Set in the time of romance—the time inhabited by "thise olde gentil Britouns" (709)—the Franklin's romance in fact evokes the emergently capitalist world of the fabliaux as the dominant time of *The Canterbury Tales*.

Yet this does not quite account for everything. It doesn't tell us why, when a fantasy is called for, it should take the specific form that it does: the very shapes of chivalric violence and desire that the Franklin has otherwise worked so hard to economize away.[18] In fact, let us suppose that this beguiling scene is really a trace, even perhaps a return of what *The Franklin's Tale* has tried to repress. For the Franklin has told us clearly that he has no interest in talking about such chivalric "labour" (V. 732), particularly in the form of jousts, tournaments, and so on. He sees all such work as unprofitable and pointless; he has, after all, just been listening to the chivalric fever dream that is *The Squire's Tale*. When the knight Averagus goes off "to seke in armes worshipe and honour" (811), the Franklin uses the same word—"labour"—to describe what such endeavors amount to: "for all his lust he sette in swich labour" (812). In a tale fraught with the perils of misdirected "lust," his comment warns about the potential of knightly pursuits to distract us from the profitable business of bourgeois romance. Hence it is remarkable that the abjected labor of chivalry is precisely what does return in the moment we are considering.

This return of the chivalric haunts the poem with the ghastly image of what it has refused and, indeed, *must* refuse in order to remain profitable: gifts more dangerous than those that will be proffered in the tale's pseudo-genteel denouement, and even more real, though they take the form of phantasm. One measure of the power of such shapes to compel is that they end up seducing even us, so that by the end of the scene it is specifically "*oure* revel" that is "ago" (1204, emphasis mine), as though we have for a moment entered the poem ourselves and done so, moreover, at the moment in which that poem is haunted by visions of a horrifying enjoyment it must otherwise reject. A similar thing has already occurred in *The Knight's Tale*, when the Knight seems to project himself into the temple of Mars, whose various scenes of destruction he is describing: "there saugh I" (I. 1995), "yet saugh I" (2011, 2017), "saugh I" (2028). The moment may speak to the Knight's personal investment in the kinds of destruction that he chronicles, but it also speaks to the sheer power of the images themselves, which will prove to be among the most compelling that *The Canterbury Tales* has to offer.[19]

It is to an exploration of *The Knight's Tale* that this chapter is devoted, for however different a Knight may be (and insist on being) from a Franklin, what both pilgrims understand is the power of a violence that neither will speak about openly. That Chaucer understands this, too, is crucial to an accurate sense of what the poet, in Cannon's neat formulation, "learned from romance." The logic of commodification was surely among those lessons. Indeed, *The Knight's Tale* will dramatize exactly how inescapable that logic is in its attempts to make all kinds of stuff vanish into thin air, from phantom sums of gold to dead bodies—to imagine, in other words, how such stuff might take on the sublime and ethereal form of the commodity itself. Such disappearances, in one sense, simply reproduce a familiar procedure for the manufacture of cultural capital, even if *The Knight's Tale*—simply because it is so much more ambitious than, say, *The Tale of Sir Thopas*—performs this work with a certain subtlety. I would not want to overstate the originality of my reading here, for in one sense it simply reinforces the extent of Chaucer's commitment to the kind of work that Cannon has so well described. And Chaucer's interest in making stuff disappear offers us one measure of his modernity—his desire for the form of the commodity.

But *The Knight's Tale* will simultaneously insist on what the tale itself calls the "encrees of chivalrye" (2184), a profit it identifies explicitly with the noble gift and its violence. The tale thus exemplifies, like *The Franklin's Tale*, the ways in which even very late romances imagine forms of excess that are primarily chivalric rather than mercantile or proto-capitalist. We already know, in fact, that these forms of excess are nowhere more spectacularly evident than in the Canterbury tale that does the most to repress and ignore them, for such forms are crucial to what Charles Muscatine long ago called the "general texture . . . of richness" in *The Knight's Tale*.[20] And this means that even as this tale marks a "crisis of chivalric identity"—in the apt phrase of a very different kind of reader[21]—the Knight's romance is at the same time the most successfully and even fiercely chivalric of all of the Canterbury stories, the founding gift that will set the economy of *The Canterbury Tales* in motion. How exactly this tale manages to transform the *failure* of chivalry into an expression of its continued survival is already suggested by the tale's surprising relationship to the kinds of romance we have been reading so far. For we will see that what Chaucer learned from romance was less a matter of innovation than of persistence, even if his ability to ensure that persistence would ultimately help to make him the father of English literature.

That romance will persist in and through Chaucer's writing is now well established. If it has taken us a while to recognize Chaucer's debts to the genre he was traditionally held to despise, our reluctance is probably due in part to our still powerful sense of Chaucer as a writer who rejects or at least transforms traditional genres: a writer who cares more about the future than he does about the past. The Knight, with his rusty armor, is on this reading a pathetic figure for a decayed chivalry, perhaps even himself a mercenary, whose tale repeatedly subjects knighthood to humiliating overthrow: Arcite, whose fated fall from his horse will kill him, as well as his rival Palamon, who will be dragged, against his will, to the stake by mere "knaves" (2728).[22] Though this tale will ultimately be devoted to what the Knight himself calls the "encrees of chivalrye" (2184), that increase will be realized in spite of what this tale understands to be its own obsolescence.

The time of romance certainly has passed in Chaucer's *Canterbury Tales*, as the Wife of Bath knows:

> In th' olde dayes of the Kyng Arthour,
> Of which that Britons speken greet honour,
> Al was this land fulfild of fayerye.
> The elf-queene, with hir joly compaignye,
> Daunced ful ofte in many a grene mede.
> This was the olde opinion, as I rede;
> I speke of manye hundred yeres ago.
> But now kan no man se none elves mo. (III. 857–64)

In fact, the Wife's romance will be invaded by the bourgeois teller herself, the magical hag who is really a gap-toothed weaver of English cloth. If *The Wife of Bath's Tale* shows how Chaucer "took his distance" from an "outmoded" genre, that distance is registered by this romance's narrator, an old woman who knows quite well that her tale is unbelievable and who thus helps us to measure the extent to which Chaucerian romance constitutes a self-consciously "late adaptation of the form."[23]

The Wife of Bath is not the only pilgrim to run up against the irretrievable pastness of romance in the process of trying to narrate one. *The Squire's Tale*, long recognized for what it has to tell us about "the decline of chivalry," is about the impossibility of even mourning for that decline.[24] The Squire muses fatuously that if Gawain himself were to come back from fairyland, even he would not be able to speak as well as the "strange knyght" (V. 59), who at that moment enters the tale bearing exotic gifts. Similarly, the Squire will later imagine recruiting the shade of Lancelot to describe, in something like the style of a fashion columnist, the decadent splendors of the court of Genghis Khan:

> Who koude telle yow the forme of daunces
> So unkouthe, and swiche fresshe contenaunces,
> Swich subtil lookyng and dissymulynges
> For drede of jalouse mennes aperceyvynges?
> No man but Launcelot, and he is deed. (V. 283–87)

Such mourning, more aware of itself than of its object, bears the imprint of the very loss it mourns.

Yet precisely because the work of chivalric mourning will never be complete in *The Canterbury Tales*, it will also continue to return. From the very moment when the Miller offers to "quite" (3127) *The Knight's Tale*—to offer a return, but also to contain its power by economizing it—the *Tales* will struggle with the pure loss that stands at the core of the Knight's vision.[25] The Miller will ask us to laugh. His tale's anti-courtly hero, randy young Nicholas, will be "allone, withouten any compaignye" (I. 3204) in his bedroom, just as Arcite, the doomed young lover of the Knight's tragic romance, was left "allone, withouten any compaignye" (2779) in his cold grave, and this equivalence will encourage us to stop shedding tears, to replace *thanatos* with *eros*, and, in doing so, to recognize the power of satire to turn "harm" into "jape" (3842)—suffering and loss into the profit of an amused chuckle. But the haste with which mourning is averted in *The Canterbury Tales* should make us suspicious, especially in the case of a poem whose entire movement is directed toward an act of veneration—the worship of a relic or remainder—that is also a ritual of mourning. What can we say about such mourning and the relics and traces it produces for our adoration?

THESEAN "DISPENCE"

Let us begin, as *The Knight's Tale* does, with a gift. This tale understands that in order to make a gift of itself, it has to put a stop to circulation, and circulation does frequently come to a halt in the course of the story, most memorably in the narrator's description of Arcite's death wound as "clothered blood" (2745), the "massified liquid that cannot circulate, can't be emptied or moved."[26] The tale's need to destroy will in fact be expressed as a refusal of circulation, but it matters to my reading that the initial form of this refusal is specifically economic: the Theban cousins, taken in war by Theseus, will not be exchanged for ransom. "Ther may no gold hem quite" (I. 1032), as the Knight tells us, and the inability to pay for or redeem (*quiten*) the cousins is also the extent to which they become infinitely valuable, sublime objects whose price can only be adequately calculated by means of the gift's sacrificial logic (however much the Miller will beg to differ). Arcite in particular will become the tale's central gift, first when he is given by Theseus to his eternal friend Perotheus, "withouten any raunsoun . . . Frely to goon" (1203–7), and then again when he is sacrificed, given up as human surplus, by the poem itself.

Before turning to what exactly this poem gives, though, it is worth paying attention to who does the giving, for Theseus's work as a "noble" giver provides a useful if also partial model for the poem's own rather more secret economies. It is a commonplace to notice that Theseus gives—and gives way—repeatedly in the tale, from the moment of his introduction as a compassionate ruler who will take pity on the Theban women, granting their request for vengeance against Creon and restoring to them, giftlike, the "bones of hir frendes" (992) to be buried. That such gifts depend from the outset on the destruction of war is a measure of the extent to which Theseus's giving will be "noble," an expression of the violence it also displaces, and as such the primary gesture by which Theseus makes his ordering power felt in the tale.

The most famous expression of what we might call Thesean "dispence" (1822) is the amphitheater that the duke has constructed to house the tournament in which the cousins, enemies because of their mutual love of Theseus's ward Emilye, will fight to determine which of them will have her. The amphitheater, in its function as a noble gift to the duke's subjects, will work both to express and to contain violence: substituting the orderly space of a chivalric tournament for the primal scene in which the cousins, knee deep in blood, are found by Theseus locked in murderous combat, yet ironically expressing violence in its very architecture. Robert Epstein calls the amphitheater "a gargantuan act of symbolic violence."[27] Thus the statue of Mars in the amphitheater's adjoining temple to that god is described in terms that conjoin the horror of violence with chilling admiration for the subtlety with which violence is portrayed:

This god of armes was arrayed thus.
A wolf ther stood biforn hym at his feet

With eyen rede, and of a man he eet;
With soutil pencel was depeynted this storie
In redoutynge of Mars and of his glorie. (2046–50)

The "soutil" narration of a horrifying "storie" would also be a
good way to describe *The Knight's Tale*, and such subtlety is one way
in which the tale imagines its value as specifically cultural. As Epstein
remarks, the symbolic value that this tale knows itself to possess finds
expression in the economic capital that Theseus is willing to spend on
the amphitheater's construction: "With many a floryn he the hewes
boghte" (2088).[28] Yet it is important to my reading here that Thesean
expenditure takes the specific form of the gift, of lordly "dispence," for
the logic of the gift is precisely what the amphitheater concretizes as
the place in which Theseus intends "for to doon his ryte and sacrifise"
(1902), as well as the place in which the poem will sacrifice one of its
two young lovers, Arcite, who will die at the whim of the gods. If the
amphitheater, as symbolic violence, euphemizes and covers over its own
real function—inviting us to deny, like "the ironic Chaucerian observer,"
the "violence before our eyes"—it also expresses the extent to which the
tale will locate the sublime value of romance *in* violence.[29] Indeed, the
question of how the violence of cultural production actually works will
prove to be central to this tale.

For now, it is worth simply noting that Thesean "dispence" serves
throughout this entire section of the tale—from the building of the
amphitheater to the description of the ensuing tournament and its
aftermath—to contain violence in precisely the ambiguous ways that
the amphitheater literalizes at the level of architecture. This is clearest
in the case of the "yiftes" that Theseus distributes to the tournament's
participants after Arcite has won the tournament, angering the knights
fighting for Palamon:

For which anon duc Theseus leet crye,
To stynten alle rancour and envye,
The gree as wel of o syde as of oother,
And eyther syde ylik as ootheres brother;
And yaf hem yiftes after hir degree,

And fully heeld a feeste dayes three,
And conveyed the kynges worthily
Out of his toun a journee largely. (2731–38)

Theseus's largesse defends against violence by reestablishing the delicate balance of prestige—"eyther syde ylik as ootheres brother" (2734)—that has been disturbed by Arcite's victory, reaffirming the social order based on rank central to Mauss's analysis of the gift (when Theseus gives the gifts to the participants "after hir degree"). More urgently, the "yiftes" also substitute generosity for the outright war that might arise from "rancor and envye." And Theseus will follow these gifts with still others, when he gives a grand funeral for Arcite (who will soon die of wounds sustained during the tournament), and when he gives the anthropologically exemplary gift of a woman, Emilye, to the cousin who survives.[30] At every turn, Thesean "dispence" works to order a world otherwise ready to come apart at the seams, prey to the "chaos" that an influential strand of criticism has identified as this tale's central anxiety. Nor is it surprising that it should be Theseus, whose "noble designs" are identified with the impulse toward order in this tradition, whose gifts keep the looming threats of war and disorder at bay.[31]

The gift's ordering power could be adduced in support of readings of the tale that stress the civilizing potential of chivalric life, yet it could equally be taken as evidence in favor of an opposed set of readings that see violence and power at the root of this tale's interest in chivalry.[32] Indeed, the gift is the place where these two strands of the critical tradition might be said to meet, since the noble gift imposes order precisely by means of violence. The gifts of this tale will suggest that the distinction drawn by the entire debate is misguided insofar as chivalry just *is* the violence that it pretends to defend against. We have already seen a hint of this underlying truth in the notion that one of Theseus's many gifts, the amphitheater, performs the violence it is ostensibly built to contain. In the tale's famous climax, even this ambiguous containment will fail spectacularly when a vengeful Saturn sends from "out of the ground a furie infernal" (2684) with a suddenness that seems to pierce the amphitheater's carefully constructed membrane—the boundary line that marks off the symbolic from the Real—toppling the victorious

Arcite from his horse and plunging him into a delirium from which he will never rise. The suspicion of some readers that Theseus may be no better than Saturn is instructive here, for the effect of the episode is to perform exactly the violence that Theseus has earlier tried to forestall by proclaiming that the tournament will not be fought "in the gyse / Of mortal bataille" (2539–40) but rather in a way that limits "destruccion of blood" (2564).[33]

Blood is exactly what does now pour out freely, both in the inexplicably violent tournament itself—where blood bursts forth in "stierne stremes rede" (2610) in spite of Theseus's commandment—and, even more memorably, after Arcite's fall leaves him as shriveled and black "as any cole or crowe, / So was the blood yronnen in his face" (2692–93). Later, it is again blood, now "clothered," that will swell Arcite's heart past the point of human endurance. Such moments suggest the extent to which the tale as a whole expresses an economy of blood, of instances of pouring out and keeping back that collectively determine this tale's value. To say that Theseus in the end lacks full control over this blood economy is to recognize this economy as truly total, an aspect of the divine order itself—a recognition that underlies Palamon's earlier complaint against the gods "that hath destroyed wel ny al the blood / Of Thebes with his waste walles wyde" (1330–31). Walls have failed to keep blood from flowing outward: the boundary has been and will be pierced again, laid waste in acts of sacrifice, even as the poem also works to hold blood back, to capture and treasure blood— "gentil blood" (2539) in particular—as the stuff out of which chivalric value is made. Far from marking a failure or critique of chivalry—as many have suggested—such destruction is actually central to the Knight's vision of the pleasures of chivalric life, as psychoanalytic readings of his tale have been telling us for some time.

Even as the tale offers its destructiveness as a gift, it registers the difficulty of any attempt to calculate the gift's true value. Theseus's amphitheater is the best-known example of the tale's attempt to respond to this problem of measurement by economizing, and thus containing and possessing, the value of chivalric destruction as a form of symbolic capital. One problem is that to calculate too blatantly leaves one open to the charge of being a mere merchant, like the women of the town who fail to understand why Arcite must die: "'Why woldestow be deed,' thise wommen crye, / 'And haddest gold ynough, and Emelye?'" (2835–36). Gold is certainly central to this tale's calculation of its own value. But it is also characteristic of the dilemma I am describing that the value of this gold must be a kind of secret, a thing that disappears in the act of being mentioned, like the precious jewels cast into the fire that consumes Arcite's body (2945). More than another instance of the Knight's well-known penchant for the trope of *occupatio*, the tale's most telling gift will be one that seeks to economize, even as it expresses, the value of this tale's destruction.

VANISHING SURPLUS

To see how, it is to yet another of Theseus's gifts that we must turn. This will be a gift given, ironically, to Arcite, the figure who is himself in so many ways this poem's ultimate gift, "fully *destined*" for sacrifice.[34] By the time he has fled from Athens back to Thebes, Arcite is a ghost remarkably like those we met in the last chapter: unrecognizable, hollowed out, and pale, in this case by the extreme mourning of courtly love:

> So muche sorwe hadde nevere creature
> That is, or shal, whil that the world may dure.
> His slep, his mete, his drynke, is hym biraft,
> That lene he wex and drye as is a shaft;
> His eyen holwe and grisly to biholde,
> His hewe falow and pale as asshen colde. (1359–64)

Arcite's transformation into a penitential ghost even drives the plot forward since it equips him with a ready-made disguise as one so transformed "of maladye the which he hadde endured, / He myghte wel, if that he bar hym lowe, / Lyve in Atthenes everemoore unknowe" (1403–6). Already a shadow of his former self, Arcite will later imagine himself on the threshold of becoming a ghost in his deathbed promise to haunt Emilye in perpetual service—"To yow, my lady . . . I biquethe

the servyce of my goost" (2767–68)—just as he begins the episode that interests me here by taking literal "servyse" as a lowly page "of the chambre of Emelye the brighte" (1426–27).[35] Arcite is a phantom whose surplus meaning haunts this tale well before he dies.

He is also the possessor of this tale's phantom surplus in strictly economic terms. For it is remarkable that the value of Arcite's sacrifice— his already determined ghostliness—will be known not just through his own spectacular suffering, with all its "peynes stronge" (2771), but in the form of actual capital. The relevant episode occurs in Chaucer's source for the tale as a mere aside, when Boccaccio describes how Arcita, having been banished from Teseo's Athens but determined to be near his beloved Emilia at all costs, insinuates himself into Teseo's household in the disguise of a servant. In Chaucer's greatly expanded account of this moment, Arcite's career at Theseus's court will be an opportunity to sketch out an economy of sacrifice that mirrors that of the tale as a whole. Arcite, having gained the trust and love of all at Theseus's court in his disguise as one Philostrate, rises in meteoric fashion from lowly page to become a squire of Theseus's own bedchamber, a trajectory of social advancement that, as Richard Firth Green argues, bears striking similarities to analogous episodes in English metrical romances such as *Havelok the Dane*.[36]

We shall see that the parallel is significant, but the primary interest of this episode for my argument lies in the way this moment generates a surplus that must be expelled from the text. Arcite himself will of course be another such surplus, so that to attend to this moment of the gift is to recognize a calculation of what will later be so hard to reckon up. The problem here is simply that the disguised Arcite is given a lot more gold by Theseus than he knows what to do with, so he does what his aristocratic nature tells him he should and spends it as quickly as possible:

Of his chambre he [Theseus] made him [Arcite] a squier,
And gaf hym gold to mayntayne his degree.
And eek men broghte hym out of his contree,
From yeer to yeer, ful pryvely his rente;
But honestly and slyly he it spente,
That no man wondred how that he it hadde. (1440–45)

Perhaps the most striking thing about this passage is that it is there at all. Why do we need to know about gold that disappears as soon as it is mentioned? The answer, at the level of plot, is that we don't. Yet precisely because this gold *is* surplus to anything that actually happens in the tale, its appearance as yet another manifestation of Thesean "dispence" expresses the logic of a romance in which, as one reader dryly notes, "the knight does *not* go forth."[37] The utter uselessness of Theseus's gold is legible in the way it vanishes into the recesses of the narrative, by means that are themselves literally unimaginable (for how might one spend such a windfall both "honestly" and yet also "slyly"?).[38] That Arcite has his own "rente" (1443) secretly ferried from Thebes to Athens as well only raises more urgently this problem of surplus while hinting at questions that neither the Knight nor Chaucer has any intention of answering, such as why Arcite would risk by means of this arrangement the exposure that he fears.

This vanishing act drives home the force of Cannon's remark that what Chaucer learned from romance was "how to *de*-materialize things"—how to make them, in essence, "immaterialities luminescent enough to seem even more solid than things themselves." Like the wondrous "book" of romance that seems to vanish before our eyes in Cannon's reading of *The Book of the Duchess*, the value of Arcite's phantom gold lies in its ability to be abstract "capital" in the full sense of that term—to be both there and somehow not there. So it is worth lingering on Arcite's gold as an example of what vanishes, if only as an indication of Chaucer's more general interest, throughout his romance writing, in making things disappear. Books of romance are one of those things, and we might add dancing fairies, wondrous steeds, even mere rocks.[39] Doesn't the disappearance of money—so offhandedly as to seem almost incidental—simply show that what underlies these various disappearances is a desire for the most sublime form that any such disappearance might take: capital itself? In one sense, this is undeniable. Yet if the last chapter suggested how even a procedure of abstraction can also mark a return—in the form of the ghost—this one argues for Chaucer's interest in the remains of all such vanishings.

In fact, I now want to suggest how these traces will become the tale's gifts—the sites of its imagined value as an enactment of the chivalric logic of sacrifice. Here it is relevant that the textual moment of Arcite's romance career contains echoes of more "popular" productions like *Havelok*. The possibility that Arcite might have been a hero like Havelok, winning wife and kingdom, weighs heavily on this tale, helping us to measure the value of its sacrifices. The pressure of this shadow romance is such that even Palamon wonders why Arcite, since he has been set at liberty, does not take to arms and win both kingdom and lady:

> Thou mayst, syn thou hast wisdom and manhede,
> Assemblen alle the folk of oure kynrede,
> And make a werre so sharp on this citee,
> That by som aventure or some tretee
> Thow mayst have hire to lady and to wyf
> For whom that I moste nedes lese my lyf.
> For, as by wey of possibilitee,
> Sith thou art at thy large, of prisoun free,
> And art a lord, greet is thyn avauntage. (I. 1285–93)

While the "wey of possibilitee" afforded by this familiar scenario of English metrical romance is what must be forbidden, it is also what must be raised. Chaucer raises it quite independently of his source, which instead has Palemone comment here (with characteristic Boccaccian insouciance) that Arcita will at least be able to get his mind off Emelia. The latter statement carries a whiff perhaps of those "cynical Latin gallantries" that Chaucer supposedly rejected in his "medievalizing" of another of Boccaccio's stories.[40] Yet the question of why Chaucer's Arcite will not look to his own "avauntage" suggests as well the extent to which Chaucer is writing *against* the pressure of a native romance tradition particular to his own literary context, even as the refusal to tread that familiar path signals yet another way in which this tale will enact the gift as that which leaves traces, whether material or textual, of what it wants credit for refusing.

We might even give a name to the logic by which the tale generates such traces, for in the middle of Theseus's temple of Mars, arguably the very ekphrastic center of this tale, there reposes a figure whose power is that of Saturn the destroyer:

Amyddes of the temple sat Meschaunce,
With disconfort and sory contenaunce. (2009–10)

Meschaunce evokes a logic of refusal, the threat that the knightly
chance or "aventure" will end not in triumph but in death. Etymologi-
cally just "what happens," "aventure" is of course intimately bound up
with the plots of romance, where it typically indicates the assurance
that the knight's adventure will be a happy one, a "venture" issuing in
profit. "Aventure" summons for Chaucer just this possibility of profit,
being "the term that merchants came to appropriate by way of sug-
gesting the resemblance between their particular form of professional
activity and the time-honoured values of the knightly class."[41] The fig-
ure for such adventure in Chaucer's writing is of course that "knyght
auntrous" (VII. 909) Sir Thopas, the topaz knight whose name adver-
tises his value, just like those "romances of prys" (207) that wear their
cultural "price" on their very faces, stamped as debased objects that are
in reality—as the Host will soon opine of *Thopas* itself—"nat worth a
toord" (240).[42]

Adventure in this emergently mercantile (and thus always already
debased) sense is of course exactly what does *not* happen to Arcite,
despite Palamon's rueful prediction that Arcite will be blessed with "som
aventure" (I. 1286). Adventure is what might reveal the gifts of romance
to be counterfeit, as Chaucer knows. The only blood spilled in *Sir Tho-
pas*, one recalls, is the horse's, whose "sydes were al blood" (VII. 777).
Such fake adventures betray the desire to take back what you give, and
in this sense even *The Franklin's Tale* is a tale of "aventures" (V. 710).[43]
Chaucer, unlike either the Franklin or his minstrel double "Chaucer,"
will not be caught out so easily. The poet, too, fantasizes about having a
"sovereyn prys" (I. 67)—one not dependent on the fluctuations of the
marketplace.[44] And so "aventure" turns out to be a kind of nonevent in
this tale: the riding accident that is, for all its tragedy, "*nat but* an even-
ture" (2722, emphasis mine).

"Aventure" in this tricky sense is not chance at all but predestina-
tion guided by the hand of "Saturnus the colde / that knew so manye
of aventures olde" (2443–44). If Arcite is here the plaything of fate—a

figure who might point forward to the early modern scene of what Chaucer will precociously recognize elsewhere to be "tragedye"—it nevertheless matters to my argument that he can only apprehend the value of that form through a logic of negation, a refusal of the profit that popularized adventure stories promise (even as he deliberately obscures the possibility that this literature, too, might ground its profits to a surprising extent in loss).[45] What the Knight tellingly glosses as the "encrees of chivalrye" (2184) will be assured precisely by this negation, as we have seen by now. The trace of what is forgone will persist, even at the lexical level. As I have argued, such traces are vital to the ways in which this tale imagines romance's persistence. *The Knight's Tale* offers itself as a form of this persistence—an assertion of the power of chivalric mourning legible in traces both material and textual. We have seen that Arcite himself is the most spectacular such trace, one that lies, by the tale's end, spent "as any cole" (2692), the ultimate figure of consumption.[46] We might now be able to see, too, that Arcite's persistent if marginally living body is a fit emblem for a poem that is itself a mere trace, from its start a "remenant" (888), a ghost of previous, much fuller tellings that would take too long to repeat, as the Knight confesses: "But al that thyng I moot as now forbere" (885).

This might cast a new light on the old notion that Chaucer composed *The Knight's Tale* during his tenure as clerk of the king's works from 1389 to 1391. Usually, this is taken to mean that Chaucer learned from this work how to make a grand show of things: to summon a spectacle of magnificence such as the tale itself offers us in its vision of what "noble life" is like.[47] The reality of his job was of course somewhat different: endless haggling over prices and wages, careful auditing of the kind that he had already performed as a comptroller of taxes—in a word, accounting.[48] Yet also, interestingly, scavenging: one of his jobs was to survey the dead stock left over from previous works, scanning the heap for anything valuable. Listed as "dead stock" in the long document that describes Chaucer's inventory of this stock, in entering his office, we find "various 'machines,' three completely broken wheels, a pair of andirons, a windlass with a worn rod," along with such treasures as a frying pan, a rake, and an instrument for plumbing—what amounts to "a real junkyard."[49] A heap of stuff suggestive, perhaps, in its resemblance to the "taas of bodyes dede" (1005) from which the tale's heroes, themselves all but dead stuff—"Nat fully quyke, ne fully dede" (1015)—are plucked by the nameless scavengers at the tale's beginning. They are modest, even slightly pathetic remainders whose value it was nevertheless Chaucer's job to assess. It is perhaps in this way that we can best understand the raw materials of the tale's "vision."

One thing Chaucer learned from romance, we might conclude, was how to imagine this rather ghoulish persistence as the basis for his own claim to distinction. For the gifts he gives us are in fact not just pathetic but dead remainders, and as such they exemplify the future of chivalry as in part a ritual of mourning. Yet Chaucer's peculiar genius is to make these gifts into the very stuff of literary value, in which he would show himself to be somehow both more than and yet also comparable to the minstrels whose ambiguous largesse he imagines in *The House of Fame*, that first document of his emerging sense of what poetry might be worth. And this means that Chaucer will insist on the surplus value of chivalric life with a commitment that defies all attempts to economize it, even as he does in fact—slyly, discreetly—offer us a way of measuring the value of chivalry's destruction. In this he resembles the tale's narrator, who in a famous moment of *occupatio* catalogues the procession of noble goods that the mourners at Arcite's funeral cast into the fire that consumes the hero's body. The narrator will not mention the "richesse" that "about his body is" (2940)—the jewels, the shields and spears, the precious vestments, the "cuppes ful of wyn, and milk, and blood" (2949)—because he knows that his pretended renunciation of all these goods has the power to sublimate, like a purifying flame, the value of whatever it touches.

This is yet another disappearance, but its difference from the kind of sublimation performed by Marx's commodity fetish is suggested by its work as a sacrifice that might be mourned. In fact, it is only by being mourned that Arcite *does* become sublime. Arcite was—until his sudden death—"an enemy, an unwanted suitor, and a prisoner of war"—yet simply by dying, he is transformed into an object of veneration, so that even "his sworn brother-enemy howls with grief and then dons black mourning clothes and ashes" while Emelye—who never wanted to marry either of the cousins—"shrieks with grief." And their mourning becomes general: "Infinite been the sorwes and the teeres, / Of olde folk, and folk of tendre yeeres, / In al the toun for the deeth of this Theban" (2827–29).[50] One might read this, as Anne McTaggart does, in terms of a Girardian model of sacrifice as what galvanizes the community, so that the tale performs "an underlying narrative movement from competition to consensus and unity through violence."[51] The possible limits of such a reading are apparent in the fact that neither Theseus nor the Athenian community at large can be said to arrange the scapegoating and consequent death of Arcite in any meaningful way. Yet it is true that the tale, simply because it gives us a world in which violence is the basic condition of life, does suggest how violence may become central to community formation in some of the ways found in the Girardian model.

In fact, it is arguably *because* the tale enacts its violence as perfectly objective, so to speak—that is, both arbitrary and inevitable—that it demonstrates how communities constitute themselves by means of violence even when they cannot be said to do so consciously. Here it could even be said that the tale's violence occurs virtually without agency, insofar as what Saturn personifies and the amphitheater records are essentially the same thing: a catalogue of (almost) every possible way in which a medieval person might die. That both Saturn's famously chilling speech (2453–78) and the amphitheater's grisly details are Chaucer's additions to the story is, in this respect, no coincidence, for *The Knight's Tale* describes a world so permeated with violence that the question of agency is beside the point. The violence of the tale does not belong *to* anyone at all and is directed at no one in particular, even if Arcite becomes its unwitting target. This is why violence can become, in a sense, community property, even the basic property *of* the community. What Roberto Esposito calls "the reversal of protection into persecution" occurs in *The Knight's Tale* despite, not because of, the intentions of an ordering Theseus.[52]

Theseus does, however, articulate this vision in terms that allow arbitrary violence to be reckoned as the good of chivalry—what Palamon, mourning the death of his erstwhile rival, has already called "fredom, and al that longeth to that art" (2791). Theseus will now go on to envision Arcite's gift of death as the basis not just of the fallen warrior's own claim to prestige—his chivalric "name" (3056)—but also as the very basis of the community who will mourn his loss. Even before he speaks, the mourning of this community has resulted in its solidarity, as the Athenians agree—by "oon general assent"—to cast aside their black garments and hold a "parlement" (2969). As Aranye Fradenburg notes, this impossibly synchronized end of group mourning is "a figure for the unanimity of community and *assent*," and it is Theseus who gives voice to the political consensus that results.[53] But his articulation of that consensus—despite its conventional Boethian touches—says no more than Saturn already has: that everyone, eventually, "moot by ded" (3030). Indeed, Theseus's ensuing list of the ways in which death comes to us all—"som in his bed, som in the depe see, / som in the large feeld" (3031–32)—quickly threatens to remind us of Saturn's malevolent omnipresence. The duke's reassuring picture of a universe bound together by a "faire cheyne of love" (2991) gives way to the reality that this community is also, and perhaps more urgently in this tale, bound together by a common mortality.

The Canterbury pilgrims, for their part, will largely mirror this community of those who mourn, judging the tale to be "a noble storie, / worthy for to drawen to memorie" (3111–12), even if the Miller will aver that he at least has something equally good up his sleeve. The positive reception suggests how romance will come to speak to the aspirations of a broad and socially diverse audience while nevertheless retaining something of its elite flavor in the century to come. In fact, the tale demonstrates that the power of romance lies precisely in its ability to make chivalry and its violence the imaginative basis for communal desire and nostalgia. *The Knight's Tale* suggests how even a story that is in many ways about the death of chivalry still manages to ensure the "encrees of chivalrye" (2184). Chaucer's contemporary, the *Gawain* poet, will imagine the persistence of chivalry in a different way: as a wound on the body whose trace can be read long after the event. But *Sir Gawain and the Green Knight* will come to envision this persistence as the basis for much broader affinities than those that Chaucer's Knight is able to imagine in his anxious tale—eager to distance itself from the taint of popularity—or in his mocking portrait of the townswomen of

Athens, who fail to see why Arcite should want to die when he had so much gold and a pretty girl (2835–36). By contrast, *Gawain*-romance shows in its later development how chivalry would become, by the fifteenth century, the imaginative basis for a community that explicitly includes the non-noble, even as this tradition locates the possibility of such a community in the violence that holds it together.

CHAPTER 4

Gawain's "Nirt" and the Sign of Chivalry

To say that the preeminent romance of the Ricardian age will imagine the persistence of chivalry is, in one sense, simply to restate the critical commonplace that *Sir Gawain and the Green Knight* is a poem whose time is cyclical rather than linear.[1] Chivalry, like the ripeness of late summer or the grandeur of Troy, is both what is always decaying in this poem and what will always rise again, transformed. Cyclicity, as the poem's narrator tells us right away, is the foundation on which Arthur's reign rests, the imagined historical result of Troy's having been burnt "to bronde3 and askez" (2) and the latest culmination of an insular history that is itself represented as cyclical, endlessly alternating between "blysse and blunder" (18).[2] Gawain's personal story is likewise marked by circularity, the passage of the seasons that brings both death and renewal as the year passes from today on into "3isterdayez mony" (529), just as Gawain will himself be reborn, washed as clean as if he had never once transgressed: "pured as clene / as þou hadez neuer forfeted syþen þou watz fyrst borne" (2393–94). Chivalry will find renewal in the figure of the poem's green girdle, transformed from the sign of death—the sign that mortifies Gawain's flesh as a stubborn reminder of his fault—into an emblem of chivalry's rebirth, adopted by Arthur's court as the common symbol of knighthood.

Even though we already know all this, it matters that the returns of this poem will be realized specifically as a gift, indeed as an entire tradition of English romance: the fourteenth- and fifteenth-century stories that cluster around the figure of Gawain. Collectively, these romances dramatize the meaning of the noble gift as a symbolic act that both signifies and displaces violence in ways that we have been exploring throughout this book.[3] It will not be surprising, then, to find that Gawain in his English manifestation is the most courteous and even submissive of knights, yet that the stories about him also revolve, almost without exception, around problems of violence. These romances organize themselves around a specific gesture of violence: the glancing "tappe" (2357) that the Green Knight bestows upon Gawain at the end of the fourteenth-century masterpiece that inaugurates this literary tradition. Nor is this the only *Gawain*-romance to make a gift of its violence, as the second half of this chapter makes clear in its discussion of the later tradition. At least two of these poems are themselves gifts: responses to the original poem that makes Gawain the giver, rather than the recipient, of the potentially deadly blow. This literary return suggests the extent to which the tradition of *Gawain*-romance treats violence as inseparable from the exchanges that it records, both within and between the romances that it gathers together.

Yet how exactly does an act of violence become a gift? How does the violence of romance know itself as a thing to be cherished, even treasured up in the storehouse of cultural memory, while also knowing itself as a potential source of shame, needful of concealment? *Gawain*-romance is fertile ground for these questions because, like the other romances we have been reading, it performs the work of memory—a memorializing of knightly violence—at a historical moment when the uses of that violence were becoming unclear. And this work of memory will also prove to be the work of the gift. In these stories the gift *is* what ensures memory, whether in the form of a scar or, as Gawain himself says, as the "sygne" (2433) of an excess that enjoins our remembrance in the very act of being atoned for. The gift does more than substitute for violence. It also expresses (as so much gift theory tells us) the very aggressivity whose full force the gift wards off. This is why readings of *Gawain*-romance in terms of either mercantile or chivalric culture miss an essential dimension of this tradition. The gift in *Gawain*-romance expresses a longing not just for the value of chivalry in general but specifically for chivalry's potential to recruit violence as a basis for mastery.

At the same time, stories of Gawain dramatize why sociopoliti-
cal mastery needs to be reconfigured by the late fourteenth century
as cultural mastery. The previous chapter suggested that Chaucerian
romance performs a similar kind of work around the same time, and
we will see that *Gawain*-romance extends that work in a variety of
ways. In a broad sense, this is of course what every romance tries
to do when it reimagines feudal domination as cultural eliteness. Yet
Gawain-romance marks an intensification of romance's desire to real-
ize the coercive potential of chivalry as the value of literature itself—
its desire, in effect, to take the measure of its own worth by means of
specific rituals that code violence as a form of exchange and vice versa.
This desire can in turn help us to account for Gawain's popularity
as a hero of English romance. "Gawain" in this sense is more than a
Welsh name with insular, metonymically English associations. The
name "Gawain" was also synonymous for readers of English romance
(despite and often *because* of their divergent class interests) with the
profits of the chivalric economy.

WHAT'S IN A "TAPPE"?

Sir Gawain and the Green Knight is a poem born out of crisis, as
Charles Muscatine argued in his classic interpretation of the poem as a
response to chivalric decline. For many subsequent critics, the roots of
this crisis were to be found in the growth of a commercial economy in
the late Middle Ages—a development that brought into question many
of the chivalric values to which the poet, on this reading, was so deeply
committed. The Marxist view that what the poem is really about is
commerce—inaugurated by P. B. Taylor in his aptly titled "Commerce
and Comedy in *Sir Gawain and the Green Knight*"—was refined by Jill
Mann, who saw the poem's focus on the value of *trewthe* as directed
toward a mercantile audience concerned with that virtue's role in
underwriting financial transactions. The celebrated girdle itself, on one
obvious level a gift, becomes for R. A. Shoaf a sign of the relativity and
arbitrariness that attaches to any kind of value in a commercial world:
like money, the girdle is "a sign and no more."[4]

Yet for all its obvious interest in the mercantile—in fact, precisely because of it—*Sir Gawain* is also a romance of the gift, as critics have increasingly come to recognize. For Felicity Riddy, the gifts in *Gawain* "seem to be emblems of the aristocratic value system," even if they are also simultaneously "a point at which the city and the court come together" in pursuit of shared values, especially the economically charged virtue of *trewthe*.[5] David Aers has argued more sharply for the poem's insistence on the giftedness of its exchanges, declaring that "the poem carefully occludes all contemporary conflicts over the extraction and distribution of 'lucrum'" so that "exchanges (of clothing, food, kisses, or blows) are exchanges of gifts, not, carefully and precisely not, exchanges of commodities in fourteenth-century commerce."[6] But the most sustained analysis to date of the poem's gifts is Britton Harwood's reading of them in theological terms as expressions of an ultimately Christian economy of salvation. While admitting that the poem "raises questions about the fate of the gift within late feudalism," Harwood goes on to argue that the *Gawain* poet "appropriates gift-exchange for a wholly Christian purpose"—the purpose of dramatizing (in Harwood's evocative phrase) "fallen humanity's inability to make a gift of itself."[7]

While my reading will differ from Harwood's, it is worth taking seriously the notion that the central problem of this text is Gawain's own failure to give properly. This is, after all, precisely the point on which the hero accuses himself near the poem's end:

> For care of thy knokke cowardyse me taght
> To accord me with covetyse, my kynde to forsake,
> That is larges and lewté that longez to knyghtez. (2379–81)

In not giving the ultimate gift of his life, Gawain has failed to live up to his chivalric identity as one who practices "larges," a virtue significantly related in this formulation to loyalty ("lewté") in the service of courage, just as its opposite—"covetyse"—is related to "cowardyse." In refusing to make the final sacrifice, Gawain fails to offer the "gift of death" central to chivalric ideology.[8] Gawain has failed, in economic terms, to give freely enough. He fails not because he gives too much—like a spendthrift knight—but because he gives too little.

Like the anonymous friend in Jacques Derrida's account of Baudelaire's "Counterfeit Money," Gawain tries to give what Derrida calls a "counterfeit" gift: paying off his antagonist with false coin, keeping his life (by keeping the "magic" girdle) while seeming to give it away. Derrida uses Baudelaire's story to suggest that the gift itself is "the impossible," and one way to read *Gawain* is to say that it, too, suggests the extent to which the desire for a pure gift is illusory, beyond the power of a "fallen humanity" to enact. This is why, in trying to enact it, Gawain flinches—a holding back that literalizes at the level of bodily discipline the covetousness for life (if nothing else) that Gawain's retention of the girdle signifies at the level of exchange.

Yet as Derrida's analysis of the gift suggests, this might be looking at the problem in the wrong way. Maybe the problem is not simply with Gawain, or even with humanity, but with the gift itself. The gift—like Gawain's need to live—cannot exist *without* being excessive. Derrida merely follows anthropological tradition in recognizing in this "excess of the gift" something potentially violent, observable in the "instant of madness that tears time apart" and even threatens "to burn up" the very meaning of the word "gift."[9] As will become clear, this dangerous excess haunts *Gawain* as a poem that for all its seeming focus on Gawain's failure to give enough is also, paradoxically, about surplus and its management.[10] It has been recognized that surplus is one of the basic problems of this poem, most notably as that "sygne of surfet" (2433), the oft-discussed girdle, but also—as I will suggest—in other gifts of violence. While Gawain faults his body for its unruly desire—"the fayntyse of the flesche crabbed" (2435)—this unruliness attaches ultimately to the poem's own desires. We might even conclude that *Gawain*, at least as much as its hero, is working with false coin, pretending to generosity while at the same time celebrating the violence of the economy that underlies its vision of noble life. Seeing this requires us to look not just at what Gawain fails to give but at what does give and, in turn, what he is forced to receive back. This also means looking at the poem as the embodiment of a political economy, not just a salvific one.

Consequently, this chapter takes up in earnest Harwood's suggestion that we read the poem's gifts in terms of their meaning within the system of late feudalism. It argues further that this meaning is primary rather than secondary to the poem's Christian purpose, and thus reads chivalry as its real source of fascination.[11] That fascination figures most visibly in the poem's elaborate attention to aristocratic pastime and ritual: the hunt, the feast, the game of courtly love, the scenes of hospitality, and gift exchange itself. It is observable also in the poem's concern with tracing the circulation of violence through these chivalric forms of life, including gift exchange, which works throughout this poem to reveal the "feigned reciprocities" that structured relations of dominance and submission under late medieval feudalism—a connection to be explored in what follows.[12] The poem's function as a chivalric object of desire is suggested as well by its late medieval reception, both by its immediate readers—most notably the scribe who saw fit to append the motto of the Order of the Garter—and by later ones like the anonymous author of *Sir Gawain and the Carle of Carlisle*, who obviously knew the poem well enough to respond to its interest in the gift with a poem of his own.

These facts argue for reading the poem's interest in the gift as deriving at least as much from chivalric fantasy as from Christian ethics. A further implication is that the poem concerns not just sin but desire more broadly, as one reader has recently proposed.[13] In this the poem will ultimately suggest a set of correspondences, already remarked on in previous chapters, among gift giving, aristocratic identity, and violent desire. We might begin, however, by simply observing that the first gift for Lacan is always the name—a gift that Gawain receives at the moment when, the ax having fallen, he is hailed as the knight whose value is equivalent to a pearl: "as perle bi þe quite pese is of prys more / so is gawayn in god fayth bi oþer gay kny3tez" (2364–65). That Gawain can only experience this reaffirmation of his identity as an imposition significantly reveals "the 'masochistic' character of the chivalric subject" as grounded in "the chivalric ethos of violent domination."[14] Chivalric dominance depends on the chivalric subject's own willingness to submit himself to the violence on which his power to rule was based.

In engaging with such insights, however, I am less interested in tracing anew the desire for violence at the heart of medieval chivalry than in showing how *Sir Gawain* makes specific use of the gift to explore the paradox of desire's expression as sublimation. Gifts are themselves products of desire, as medieval economic thinkers knew very well. D. Vance Smith has shown how the gift is configured in medieval economic writing as a dangerous surplus in excess of what is strictly needed to sustain life.[15] The gift thus stands in an intriguing relation to the "surplus enjoyment" described by psychoanalytic thought as central to the regulation of desire. It makes sense, then, that a medieval poem in which desire plays a crucial role should also concern itself with the exchange of gifts in a circulation that not only begins with desire but has the effect of producing ever *more* desire. Chivalric identity depends on the ceaseless flow of this desire—the desire both to give and to take—in ways that the poem dramatizes. Yet the danger in *Sir Gawain* is that such desire might become unmanageable, the inherent surplus of the gift spilling over into forms of violent enjoyment that go beyond the purely symbolic. In the context of aristocratic gift exchange, this is in effect a danger that the "repressed" meaning of the gift as violence will become known too openly—that it will somehow exceed its intended symbolic function.[16]

As I have already suggested, this symbolic excess is what infuses the central gift-act of *Sir Gawain* with meaning: the "tappe" that threatens his life while also giving it. Nor is it a coincidence that the poem's most vividly realized scene takes the form of a gift that threatens to spill over quite literally into the Real—to become actual violence. This is the moment when the Green Knight's ax at last (after several teasing feints) bites into the flesh of Gawain's nape, spilling out the hero's blood:

> Þaʒ he homered heterly, hurt hym no more
> Bot snyrt hym on þat on syde, þat seuered þe hyde.
> Þe scharp schrank to þe flesche þurʒ þe schyre grece,
> Þat þe schene blod ouer his schulderes schot to þe erþe. (2311–14)

As Mark Miller suggests, the moment is "wonderful for its slow motion aestheticism: we are asked to see the ax descend, sever the skin, and cut through the fat to the flesh beneath it, sending blood shooting over Gawain's shoulders to the earth, as the next line tells us, to gleam on the snow." In Miller's psychoanalytic reading, this moment of aestheticized violence realizes a desire for Gawain: specifically, the desire "to register the coming of this unimaginable, long-awaited event,"[17] to witness in effect his own death. Yet the satisfaction of this desire (if that is what it is) also takes the form of an imposition: a gift.

More than an imposition, in fact, Bertilak's gift is an act of mastery. Mastery seems the only fit word for a blow that begins both swiftly (*lyghtly*, 2309) and fiercely (*heterly*, 2311) but ends in the nick caused by a glancing "tappe" (2357). Mastery in this sense measures out its violence precisely and—in this case—in spite of what would seem to be the laws of physics governing the swing of the blade that comes down straight onto the neck of one's victim. And this mastery in turn marks *Sir Gawain* as itself a particular kind of masterful performance, not least because it leaves a written trace: the "nirt" (2498) or nick that Gawain will carry with him and later, at Arthur's court, use to tell his story. What *Sir Gawain* also confesses is that mastery needs the flirtation with real violence that happens when the blade sinks into Gawain's flesh, spilling his blood onto the snow, just as it needs (in the same way) Gawain's own grisly decapitation of Bertilak himself at the beginning of the poem.

This last point is important because it has always been tempting to read *Sir Gawain* in conventionally exegetical terms, as a poem whose central gift is forgiveness of sin, the divine grace or *gratia* that forgoes vengeance. Yet Bertilak's gift appears in a different light if we follow Miller in attending to the excess of this moment, the slow-motion beauty of the swing that severs Gawain's flesh. If this is a symbol of forgiveness, as many have argued, it is at the same time an act of violence.[18] Insofar as it marks Gawain's (re-)submission to the symbolic order of chivalry, Bertilak's "tappe" can be read as the violence of the gift itself. Even more, it is a form of the symbolic that flirts dangerously with the Real—the "stuff" opened up by Gawain's wound—specifically, "þe schene blod"(2314) that spurts ("schot" [2314]) to the earth from Gawain's shoulders to lie in exaggerated relief against the white snow ("blenk on þe snawe" [2315]). That Bertilak forbears to pay out "þe remnaunt" (2342) of his deadly gift only confirms the extent to which it constitutes violence in itself. This is not to say that no profit has been made in the exchange of decapitation for a mere nick on the nape. Part of the economic magic of this romance is to make precisely this exchange: the transformation of real into symbolic violence, trading a tenuous mastery for a surer one. But the poem never lets us forget what lies behind this transformation. Thus, for instance, the threat latent in Bertilak's darkly ironic suggestion that Gawain hold himself "wel payed" (2341) by the little tap he has received in return for his own swing of the ax in the poem's opening scene.

Violence informs the structure of the poem at a fundamental level, however much it (or we) might fantasize about the sublime return of a gift that has been effectively purged of aggression, transformed into a sign of God's love. And this also means that however much we might want to turn our gaze from Gawain's scarred flesh and dwell instead on the penitential meaning of the girdle he wears, the scar is there, too. Moreover, it *must* be there for the events of the poem to be legible at all. That Gawain must reveal it in order to tell his story to Arthur's court tells us a great deal about where this poem truly locates its value as a cultural sign. That he can do so only after having first covered the "nirt" up tells us something more. The noble gift always both conceals and reveals in its nature as an open secret, a "misrecognized" and "socially repressed" form of violence that nonetheless also announces itself as such.[19] What is remarkable about *Sir Gawain* is the extent to which the poem makes this open secret the basis of its claim to literary value, the proof of its mastery in aesthetic as well as political terms. The scar will ultimately serve as the most visible proof of this mastery. Yet the violence of the gift begins circulating in this poem well before Gawain strikes his fatal blow, even before Arthur and his court enter on the scene. A fuller consideration of how that violence determines the plot of *Sir Gawain* will bring us back to the question of what Gawain's "nirt" means for this romance and, by extension, for the literary tradition that it inaugurates.

"ÞE HURT WATZ HOLE": DISCOVERING VIOLENCE

We have been looking at the gift's culmination in violence at the high point of *Sir Gawain*, but of course the poem is not typically so blunt. When the gift first returns to Gawain in this poem, in fact, it does so not as violence but as a promise of protection *from* violence: the green girdle. This instability in the gift's meaning—a semantic excess that always threatens to turn the gift into its opposite—is evident already in the poem's epic prelude, in lines that open onto a picture of the land as what Monika Otter, in her study of twelfth-century Anglo-Latin historiography, has called *gaainable tere*—land that is not only "profitable" (and thus exchangeable) but also "conquerable," with significant echoes of *gaaignier* in the sense of "to win, to acquire."[20] In echoing these historiographical accounts, especially Geoffrey of Monmouth's *History of the Kings of Britain*, *Sir Gawain* retells Arthurian prehistory as a drama of the gift. Following Geoffrey and his later imitators, the poem opens with an allusion to Aeneas and his descendants—Arthur's forefathers— as the conquerors of Western Europe. Remarkably, these lines *already* imagine the "gainable" land of England as a thing to be given away. The description pivots seamlessly from a depiction of violent conquest to a scene of gift giving, as the descendants of Aeneas first "depreced" or destroyed "prouinces" and then, in the same line, become the "patrounes" (6) of those lands—or, more specifically, of their "wele" (7) or wealth. As "patrounes," the Trojan conquerors are transformed into rulers and father figures, as the word's etymology suggests, but also, significantly, into gift givers, a familiar modern meaning of "patrounes" that was also available in Middle English, where it is found most often in the context of ecclesiastical benefaction.[21]

Whether the poet had in mind a connection between lordship and gift giving as he began *Sir Gawain*—as is evident with respect to *Pearl*— matters less than the simple fact that "patronage" is what proceeds naturally and immediately in *Gawain* from the application of physical force. Patronage in this context means first and foremost the right to impose one's name on conquered territory, extending the primal gift of that name to others. As "riche Romulus" (8) has already done for Rome, so, too, Brutus will do for Britain. That such giving has its basis in violent conquest is hardly surprising in a poem as committed to chivalric ideology as this one. Yet in admitting a little too quickly that patronage *is* after all a matter of violence, the poem's opening already hints at the ways in which violence will threaten to expose itself as the basis of chivalric identity.

Conflict will return throughout the poem, as the bold barons whose love of strife ("baret" [21]) is the cause of so much sorrow ("tene"

[22]) among Arthur's ancestors almost immediately return in the form of the Green Knight.[22] Yet for this return to have any power to shock us, the poem must first lead us to imagine violence as something safely enshrined in the ancestral past of Arthur's immensely civilized court. As we leave behind the epic prologue for the world of Arthurian romance, we find games in place of strife—games, more specifically, whose point is exchange. The first of these exchanges are the New Year's gifts or "yeres-giftes" (67) about which the members of the court "debated busyly" (68) in a contest that hints at the possibility of strife only to foreclose on it. Ladies, we are told, "laghed ful loude, thogh thay lost haden" (69), while lords are understandably "not wrothe" (70) when they win—an understatement whose full significance will only become clear later in the poem. Whatever the erotic undertones of the passage, they also give us the poem's first picture of gift exchange: a safe one in which the possibility of "debate" is put to rest as soon as it is raised.

Almost immediately, however, the poem presents a more disturbing image of the gift in Arthur's demand for a gratuitous exchange of lives—"lif for lyf" (98)—in the form of a "justyng" (97). A game in theory, the desired joust is also an exchange, as suggested by its resemblance to the exchange of blows that will shortly be initiated by the Green Knight. Coming on the heels of the giving of New Year's gifts, Arthur's desire for an exchange of lives raises again the unsettling aspects of the aristocratic economy that the New Year's gifts seem designed to contain. Bored by the spectacle of riskless exchange, Arthur seeks out a more violent possibility, as the narrator hints in remarking of the young king that "his lif liked hym light" (87). As it turns out, it is Gawain rather than Arthur who will pay the price for Arthur's reckless desire—an act of substitution that carries the logic of exchange a step further.

Arguably called into being by Arthur's chivalric longing, the Green Knight enters offering precisely the gift of violence that the king had demanded:

> If any so hardy in þis hous holdez hymseluen
> be so bolde in his blod brayn in hys hede
> þat dar stifly strike a strok for an oþer
> *I schal gif hym of my gyft* þys giserne ryche. (285–88, emphasis mine)

The Green Knight, too, imagines death as an exchange ("a strok for an oþer"), offering his ax or "giserne ryche" as the aestheticized profit of what amounts to a covenant in pursuit of mutual destruction. What the Green Knight calls the "richness" of his proffered ax finds an echo in the poetry itself, which describes in detail how the blade sinks into his neck. After the Green Knight's departure, Arthur attempts both to commemorate and to have done with this eruption of violence into his court by ordering Gawain to hang the ax on the wall as a trophy. But what Gawain already knows, even if Arthur does not, is that violence must be paid for with more violence, as the Green Knight has already reminded us in promising to repay ("yederly yolden" [453]) Gawain for his decapitating blow in one year's time. His magical survival of Gawain's blow, which neither Arthur nor Gawain had reckoned on, marks the inevitability with which the gift exacts repayment in this world, even as his later forgiveness of Gawain arguably evokes the next.[23] Indeed, the first "fytte" of the poem ends with a grim hint of the gift's inevitable return when the narrator reminds us that Arthur has had the gift he requested: "this hanselle hatz arthur of auenturus on first" (491).

If a certain inevitability of repayment structures the plot, however, it is deferral that marks the experience of the poem as narrative, generating the necessary interval that distinguishes the gift from mere exchange.[24] While the Green Knight demands repayment, his double, Bertilak, does precisely the opposite by continuing to give. This dissimilarity, however, conceals a deep kinship between seemingly opposed aspects of Gawain's antagonist. From the first lines describing their meeting, Bertilak-as-Green-Knight works to place Gawain ever more deeply in his debt. In welcoming Gawain to Hautdesert, Bertilak offers his guest the gift of hospitality in terms that link possession and power: "ȝe are welcum to welde as yow lykez / þat here is al is yowre awen to haue at yowre wylle / and welde" (835–37). Bertilak's invitation to "wield as he likes" anticipates the lady's notoriously more direct offer:

> "ȝe ar welcum to my cors,
> Yowre awen won to wale,
> Me behouez of fyne force
> Your seruaunt be, and schale." (1245–47)

The ultimate gift is the gift of the body itself, as Gawain already has good reason to fear.[25] But even in the unlikely event that Gawain does suspect something at this point, he knows the rules of gift exchange too well to be capable of ignoring Bertilak's gambit. Far from taking up his host's invitation to wield mastery, he immediately responds by emphatically surrendering himself to Bertilak's "wylle" (1039, 1081). Not slow to seize the opportunity, Bertilak at once takes hold of Gawain ("sesed hym þe syre" [1083]) and asks Gawain if he is serious in his pledge "to do þe dede þat I bidde" (1089). Gawain's reply that he is "bayn" to do Bertilak's "hest" (1092) while under his roof evokes the binding power of hospitality, anticipating the lady's more literal binding of Gawain some hundred or so lines thereafter ("I schal bynde yow in your bedde" [1211]).

Hospitality is a gift—as Derrida and others have recognized—and like other expressions of the gift it exerts a power that drives this poem forward.[26] Only now, after the asymmetrical character of their relationship as host and guest has been firmly established, does Bertilak move to clinch his deal with Gawain by suggesting the exchange-of-winnings game. Gawain is to rest himself in bed each day and furthermore ("ȝet firre" [1105])—Bertilak now presses his advantage home—to agree to the "forwarde" (1106) that whatever each man gains during the day is to be shared with the other at night. While it is a commonplace of criticism that the exchange of winnings takes place in the context of the beheading game, the more local context of Gawain's submission here to the laws of hospitality has for the most part eluded notice. Those laws are central both to *Gawain* itself and especially to some later romances about Gawain that we will be considering.[27] One of those laws, of course, is that the master of the house makes the rules—he is literally (in one etymological account of *hospes*) the "guest-master."[28] This power dynamic drives the whole plot of *Sir Gawain and the Carle of Carlisle*, as we shall see, yet *Sir Gawain and the Green Knight* anticipates *Carle* in its picture of a Green Knight who is a *hospes* in the strongest sense. Confronted by such a lord, Gawain is forced into a game premised from the start on inequality, even as the poem seems to make commensurate exchange its structuring principle. It is not true, then, that the poem recommends to us "the fundamental realities of mercantile life," although *Gawain* does certainly gesture toward those realities as they were coming into being in fourteenth-century England.[29] Subtending mercantile exchange in the poem is the initial gift that makes exchange possible while also ensuring that it will never be *truly* commensurate— that it will always bear the trace of the gift as a form of exchange whose very nature presumes inequality. The gift is what must inevitably both accompany and exceed any economy.

Bertilak suggests as much when he declares that the bargain to exchange will be sealed as soon as he and Gawain drink to the deal: "who bryngez vus þis beuerage þis bargayn is maked" (1112). Wine drunk in honor of a bargain (the so-called pledge drink) reflects the common practice, retained well into the early modern period, of ensuring the sanctity of an exchange by turning it into a gift: "the sacrifice of the gift of alcohol . . . symbolized the allegorical pledging of oneself." One historian argues that the wine drunk on such occasions signified "the life spirit," with obvious Eucharistic associations.[30] The description of such a practice in *Gawain* thus points to the gift logic under which late medieval commercial contracts continued to be secured while simultaneously hinting at the danger to which Gawain is subjecting himself in taking up Bertilak's game. In agreeing to the exchange, Gawain does not merely lay himself open to the charge of *untrewthe* should he fail to make a proper return. He also pledges his own blood as the forfeit in a ritual that directly recalls and memorializes the central gift-event of Christianity. Yet Gawain is no Christ. The poem's repeated enactments of Christian ritual remind us that Gawain need *not* make a full gift of himself precisely because Christ already has. In pledging himself in his deal with Bertilak, Gawain does symbolically perform the sacrifice that will later be rendered unnecessary—puts himself, if only for that moment, in the place of the ultimate victim of Christian history—but only so that his final release from his pledge will be a gift. If the moment hints at Gawain's vulnerability, it also reminds us that the proper framework for understanding his predicament is the gift economy by which he is bound and whose inequalities the exchange game merely reproduces, as it were, in the guise of fairness.

The profound inequity of Gawain's situation has earned him remarkably little sympathy.[31] Though offering the most sustained and satisfying account of the poem's gifts to date, Harwood's view that the poem makes Gawain the representative of "fallen humanity" is in keeping with a critical penchant that arguably seeks to allegorize and thus erase the poem's more unpleasant features. Without denying the obvious relevance of a specifically Christian soteriology to *Gawain*, I would suggest that the poem works to trouble any reading of its violence in terms of a wholly benign purpose. Despite Harwood's insistence that "the aggression manifest in the original challenge can be disclosed as latently love" by the story's end, I think we should resist the temptation to avert our gaze from what is unsettling about the poem's economy.[32]

This becomes more difficult, anyhow, as the poem progresses from the challenge implied by Bertilak's enactment of manorial lordship to a vivid depiction of what that lordship actually produces: dead bodies in the form of the animals that Bertilak hunts down and subsequently offers to his guest in fulfillment of his end of the bargain to exchange the profits gained by each. The profit here is death itself, and it holds a specific warning for Gawain. Just how far this oft-noted parallel goes is suggested by the verbal repetition of a phrase—"schyree grece" (1378, "schyre" at 2313)—to describe both the rib meat of the stag slain on the first day of the game and, later, the "fair flesh" of Gawain's own neck as the Green Knight's blade sinks in.[33] Thus, when Bertilak on the first occasion displays for Gawain's approval the body of the dead animal, what he literally "schewez" (1378) is his power to kill, presented to his guest in the barely sublimated form of a gift ("and al I *gif* yow Gawayn" [1383, emphasis mine]). We might even say that the violence of the gesture is precisely what marks it as a gift, despite its involvement in what both men have previously agreed is to be a purely commercial exchange. More than a mere tit for tat, the game is a "swete swap" (1108) marked from the start by gratuitousness and excess. What Gawain cannot yet know, of course, is that the sweet surplus of the exchange—its *violence douce*—is death itself, inscribed on the tender flesh of beast and man alike.[34]

The exchange game, like some of the other games that Bertilak plays, foreshadows the violence promised to Gawain at the Green Chapel, where he will receive the glancing blow.[35] While Harwood follows the long-established tradition of reading the Green Knight's gesture as an act of mercy, the poem's conclusion has made at least some critics uneasy.[36] Lurking behind much of that unease, I think, is the simple fact that the terms of the deal put Gawain at a disadvantage from the start. As Mann remarks, "the ostensible fairness of the exchange conceals an underlying imbalance: the Green Knight can replace his head if cut off, but Gawain cannot."[37] Gawain himself points out this "monstrous inequality" in his reply to the Green Knight's taunt ("'þaȝ my hede falle on þe stonez / I con not hit restore'" [2382–83]). But even Mann in the end blames Gawain for not seeing that "punctiliousness in keeping the terms of the bargain must accompany insouciance as to the inequality of their outcome."[38] I want to suggest, by contrast, that to read the poem in this way obscures the simple fact of the bargain's profoundly unequal nature.

It is worth lingering on the Green Knight's advantage here as a literal realization of what Roberto Esposito has termed "immunity": the exemption from the obligation to give that is granted to privileged members of the community. His argument proceeds by taking seriously Émile Benveniste's remark that *communitas* is etymologically the circle of mutual gift givers (*con + munus*). By extension, Esposito suggests *immunitas* as precisely the negation of that community in the figure of the one who is exempt from giving. As Esposito puts it, "if *communis* is he who is required to carry out the functions of an office—or to the donation of a grace—on the contrary, he is called immune who has to perform no office, and for that reason he remains ungrateful."[39]

For Esposito this logic of immunity is particularly tied to the notion of "the proper" and more broadly to the capitalist ideology of property. Medieval culture struggled to define what might constitute "the proper," especially in its fascination with those possessions most intimately related to the aristocratic self. We have already seen how the noble gift could ironically be a sign of such propriety, of the self's freedom from the obligation to give or accept on terms of equality. Such giving ensures, rather than undermines, the integrity of the self, refusing the very community that it seems to proffer. The total gift, as we have seen, would mean the destruction of chivalry itself as a form of possession. If *Sir Gawain* seems engrossed with the possibility of such a gift—a gift that would erase chivalry by enacting it to its limit—it is in part because such a gift is what the poem most fears. In this the poem resembles some others we have been reading, but *Sir Gawain* imagines how the total gift might also contain its opposite, how immunity might make it possible to *seem* to give without actually surrendering what really is most proper to the self.

That Bertilak is so often identified with God is hardly surprising, given the power he enjoys. In fact the *Gawain* poet offers plenty of ammunition for drawing the analogy in a number of his other works, including *Pearl*, whose "Prince" (1201) gives and takes just as he pleases, and *Patience*, which strikingly imagines the divine as a "rych Lord" (326) whose commands must be unhesitatingly obeyed.[40] Yet the poem undermines any such easy equation in its insistence that the immunity enjoyed by Bertilak as the Green Knight must *not* be enjoyed by Gawain—that the sign of that possibility be instead a reminder of Gawain's mortality. It is this sign, not coincidentally, that will become the basis for the poem's closure in a scene of fellowship. As we will see, the poem grounds its vision of chivalric community in its closing down of the possibility that any knight—or at least any knight of Arthur's— might be exempt from death.

The sign in question is of course the famous green girdle, the poem's most explicit gift—the one that Gawain supposes will protect him. It is the girdle that seems to offer the kind of immunity I have been describing: the possibility of keeping back what one gives. This is what makes it a sign of chivalry, as I now want to suggest. While he wears the girdle, Bertilak's lady avers, "þer is no haþel vnder heuen tohewe hym þat my3t" (1853)—a promise that proves to be false when Bertilak draws blood and reminds Gawain, pointedly, that he might have been "wroþeloker" (2344) in his dealings with his victim. If the gift, in Mauss's formulation, is what stands in for and wards off violence, the girdle would seem to perform its function in a singularly inadequate way. Promising safety from violence, the girdle-as-gift instead invites it, as Bertilak explains in tying his nicking of Gawain specifically to the latter's acceptance of the girdle: "here yow lakked a lyttel, sir" (2366). The seemingly magical power of the gift in Mauss's account to ward off violence becomes instead the very means by which violence erupts into the text.

It is thus not enough to say that the girdle will be the sign of the chivalric community, though it will be. It is, at the same time, a sign of the violence that constitutes this community; in fact, it is as much a covering as a sign, since what it covers is the wound or "nirt" (2498) that Gawain bears with him on his return journey to Camelot. The "nirt" will heal—be made "hole" (2484), as the narrator is quick to aver—and that wholeness in turn presages the solidarity of an Arthurian court that now, at the poem's end, organizes itself around the display of this "sygne" (2433) that covers Gawain's wound. The girdle will become synonymous with the "renoun" (2519) of Camelot, the chivalric capital that Arthur's court accrues to itself by means of the common sign that its members wear, the object that Gawain again here, in the closing scene, calls the "token" (2509) of his adventure.

If many readers have felt that there is something superficial in the court's response to that adventure—something that misses the point entirely—this is no doubt partly because Camelot refuses to acknowledge what Gawain so urgently wants to draw its attention to:

> This is the bende of this blame I bere in my nek,
> This is the lathe and the loss that I light have. (2506–7)

"This" is the "bend"—the girdle—but what it actually points to, Gawain insists, is the "blame" carved upon his flesh. It is the latter that Gawain clearly means when he refers to the "lathe and the loss" that he bears. Yet what Gawain sees as the shame of chivalry—the mark it leaves on the body, that body's subjection to death—is for Arthur the basis of chivalric prestige. Accordingly, it is not the wound but the girdle that Arthur sees and adopts as the sign of his court: "and he honoured that hit hade evermore after" (2520). The truth of chivalry must be covered up, denied and yet capitalized on, and so it is the girdle that becomes the poem's "sign" (as it has remained in much of the modern critical tradition). Still, shame will haunt the poem's vision of what chivalry finally amounts to, not just in its historical vulnerability but in its inability to give itself fully to its own professed ideals. The motto appended to the poem by one anonymous scribe suggests as much in its aggressive displacement of all shame onto those who would dare to think it: *Honi soit qui mal y pense!*[41]

This might help to explain why the "nirt" vanishes from later romances of Gawain, even in stories that persist in making Gawain the recipient of the threatened beheading. Chivalry, having once admitted to its nakedness, will not be so indiscreet again, at least in this tradition. Yet the potential for humiliation encoded by the scar continues to haunt later English stories about Gawain. One of these is a fifteenth-century romance called *Sir Gawain and the Carle of Carlisle*, aptly described by Jeffrey Jerome Cohen as the "obscene double" of more overtly "disciplinary" productions like its fourteenth-century ancestor.[42] *Carle* mirrors its original in many ways, and in so doing it performs an exchange with the older poem—in fact a series of exchanges—culminating in a scene of violence that is itself the central gift of *Carle*, its response to the wound left by the earlier poem's flirtation with a gift that might undo possession itself.

MURDEROUS HOSPITALITY

Sir Gawain and the Carle of Carlisle is a "bourgeois" romance insofar as it reckons the profits of violence even more precisely than its fourteenth-century predecessor, but this does not make *Carle* in any sense critical of chivalry and its ideals, as has sometimes been claimed. More explicitly than its predecessor, *Carle* is about transformation, and it does transform the motifs of the earlier poem in new and striking ways. But beneath those transformations lies an essential kinship of purpose with *Carle*'s more firmly elite literary cousin. For *Carle*, too, knows how to make itself into the kind of gift that in fact ensures possession.

Sir Gawain and the Carle of Carlisle survives in Porkington MS 10, composed in the northwest Midlands around 1400, as well as in the Percy Folio, dated circa 1650. The seventeenth-century redaction's value lies primarily in its inclusion of a central episode—omitted in the earlier version on which I mostly rely—in which Gawain beheads the carl at the latter's request. As its climactic beheading suggests, the story of *Carle* works to realize the violence that the fourteenth-century masterpiece mostly sublimates. *Carle* explores a nightmare world in which the gift can only appear as a violence that culminates in death, even as the poem depends for its resolution on the possibility of distinguishing a peaceful gift from a deadly one. It is among *Carle*'s surprisingly rich ironies that the crucial possibility of peaceful exchange depends on a transformation that can be realized only *through* a gift of death—a beheading that exorcizes violence by enacting its mortal limit.

Carle concerns a powerful but monstrous lord of a rich manor—the carl or "churl" of the title—who long ago took a vow to murder any knight lodged with him unless the unlucky guest should agree to the carl's every command, no matter how bizarre. As the poem opens, we already know that Gawain, equipped with his usual faultless courtesy, will succeed in this task where all others have failed, or will do so in the course of the story. Here the foils for Gawain's unflappable *suavité* are Sir Baldwin and Sir Kay, companions of Gawain who repeatedly disobey the carl's injunctions only to receive blows in return for their defiance. Gawain, by contrast, behaves submissively, kneeling before his host and removing his own magnificent destrier from the carl's stables so that the latter's foal will be kept safe from the rain. After gamely obeying each of the carl's commands—even slipping into bed with the carl's own wife, having actual intercourse with the daughter, and finally (in the Percy version) beheading the carl—Gawain through his total obedience either inspires or allows the carl (depending on the manuscript) to abandon his vow and join the Round Table. The aggression latent in what the carl repeatedly calls "courtesy" could hardly be more apparent than in this story of blows given and received. Yet *Carle* resembles its more elite ancestor in inviting us to avert our gaze from the violence that it also enjoins us to acknowledge.

One measure of this ostensibly "popular" romance's capacity for chivalric mystification is that for all its later explicitness about violence, the poem opens with the safely mediated symbolism of the stag hunt. Among the hunters is Sir Ironside—who "coude mor of venery and of wer / Then all the kyngus that wer ther" (knew more about hunting and war than all the kings there, 85–86).[43] Yet hunting as opposed to war is the possibility realized in what follows, just as Ironside himself—whose twenty-line description would lead any first-time reader of the poem to mistake him for the hero—gets displaced by a knight who knows less about war but more about how to manipulate the kinds of exchanges that his own displacement of Ironside performs. If there is something excessive about the fact that Arthur and his men manage to kill "fife hundrerd der" (112) by mid-morning, the scene nevertheless defends against the possibility of the hunt's alternative insofar as the deer stand in for a military plot that *Carle* ultimately refuses. Compared to the relative propriety of the hunting as conducted in *Sir Gawain and the Green Knight*, the later poem's interest in detailing a sylvan holocaust is bound to appear sanguinary. Yet the enthusiasm with which the poem arranges these corpses before the audience's gaze—"alonge undur a lynde" (in a row under a linden tree, 114)—is matched by a certain reticence when it comes to knightly corpses, as will become clear only later in the poem, when Gawain gets a peek at the contents of the carl's dungeon.

As in *Sir Gawain and the Green Knight*, the hunt in *Carle* enacts a violence that also lurks in what should be the relative safety of the domestic scene. In *Carle*, however, the trouble is apparent from the moment when Sir Baldwin tells of a carl in a nearby castle who offers only "evyll harbrowe" (evil lodging, 147). In its harboring of threat rather than safety, the carl's castle promises danger from its first mention, in turn activating Kay's violent determination to pry open the castle with a crowbar, or what he euphemistically refers to as the "kyngus keyis" (king's keys, 203).[44] In place of the magically appearing Hautdesert of *Sir Gawain*, the poet of *Carle* imagines a solidly real place whose door might have to be forced—a difference that emphasizes the extent to which *Carle* will revolve, even more directly than in *Gawain*, around the giving and taking of hospitality, which the poet of *Carle* identifies specifically with the value of courtesy. Hospitality thus becomes "carllus corttessy" (278), the term used by the carl himself to describe what he offers his guests. As a parody but also a critique of more conventional scenes of hospitality in romance, "carllus corttessy," like "evyll harbrowe," names the tensions inherent in the practice of hospitality as a form of aristocratic giving.

Hospitality poses the problem of the gift in an especially urgent form insofar as it asks who really owns the things of a household that has been opened to others—guests who can now lay claim to the possessions that lie closest to the self. Drawing on the work of Émile Benveniste, Derrida suggests that hospitality, insofar as it invokes the logic of gift exchange, expresses the gift's "impossibility."[45] This is because the host, if he is to exercise the giving away of his substance that hospitality entails, must at the same time remain the indisputable master of all he possesses—what Gawain in the Percy version of *Carle* calls "lord within his owne" (126). That absoluteness of possession also attaches itself to the guest who enters the host's domain in a way that threatens to reduce the guest to the status of a thing possessed. Benveniste even suggests "guest-master" as the original meaning of *hospes*.[46] Yet hospitality is at the same time maintained by a fiction of reciprocity. "The primitive notion," Benveniste declares, "is that of equality by compensation: a *hostis* is one who repays my gifts by a counter-gift" (where *hostis* originally could mean either the guest or the host in our modern sense).[47] As Benveniste's and Derrida's explorations of *hospes-hostis* suggests, the practice of hospitality hinges on a basic paradox: what is mine is yours, but only *because* it is mine. Every act of hospitality is simultaneously an assertion of mastery.

Romance has always known about the possessive spirit of hospitality, at least from the moment when Chrétien de Troyes imagines a king who emphatically insists on lodging all itinerant knights in his castle:

> No knight of high standing . . . can enter the town in search of hospitality without being welcomed by king Evrain. The king is so noble and gracious that he has made a proclamation to his burghers that, if they value their lives, no nobleman who comes from outside must find lodging in their houses. Honouring men of valour is a charge the king takes on himself. (II. 5471–84)[48]

That a "burgher" might dare to offer his own hospitality is of course the possibility that drives the plot of *Carle*. Like King Evrain, moreover—whose guests' heads routinely end up on spikes in the castle garden—the carl, very much the lord of *his* manor, threatens to reduce his guests to the status of inanimate objects, adding them to the store of household wealth locked away in his dungeon.

So the carl is naturally all too happy to welcome his guests. Far from barring their entry, as Kay had feared, an eager carl plies Arthur's knights with outsized hospitality served out in an endless flow of wine from golden goblets that hold "nine gallons" each (293). A potentially more transgressive kind of excess materializes when the carl invites Gawain to enjoy the women of the castle—an invitation that the gallicized Gawain of this romance heartily embraces. Cohen reads this fantasy of indulgence as a critique of "chivalric male embodiment," especially the mirroring of that process in the physical excessiveness of a giant carl standing in height "nine taylloris yerdus" (nine tailor's yards, (259) or about twenty-five feet, with a breadth of "two tayllors yardus" (257) to match. Yet Cohen points to another way of reading the poem's excesses when he remarks that the carl, even before his transformation into a knight of Arthur's court, "already plays the game of courtliness through steadfast adherence to a set of rules."[49] Monstrous excessiveness resides not just in the carl's gigantic bulk, in other words, but also in those practices of hospitality and gift exchange that the text asks us to see as admirable but also somehow threatening. By the time the carl asks Gawain to take his host's life by striking off his head, we have already witnessed Gawain almost go too far in offering to rape the carl's wife—an act of violent possessiveness that even the carl steps in to prevent: " 'Whoo ther! / That game I the forbede' " (467–68). Like the chivalric ritual of the hunt that enacts while diverting the threat of war, the carl's hospitality performs excess as the potential for violence. As in *Sir Gawain*, hospitality and hunting turn out to be different ways of encoding the same fantasy of domination. Yet *Carle* suggests that the enactment of this fantasy depends for its effect less on the identity of the performer than on the performance itself.

"Carllus corttessy" (278)—the text's name for its violent hospitality—in fact turns out to be no more contradictory than conventional hospitality. What the carl later calls his "wyckyd lawys" (541) are nothing more than the law of submission contained within any act of hospitality and which attaches equally, if paradoxically, to both host and guest. Gawain, who acknowledges this law when he kneels before the carl and subsequently performs his bidding, is rewarded with absolute mastery over the carl and his possessions, up to and including the taking of the carl's life. Kay and Baldwin, by contrast, fail to submit and hence— according to this paradoxical and therefore "wyckyd" law—not only fail in their own bid for mastery but are forced into an acknowledgment of their host's mastery over them. Their story acts as a foil to Gawain's and establishes the extent to which "carllus corttessy" reproduces its socially sanctioned double.[50] This reproduction of the official norm explains why the carl—who supposedly "can no corttessy" (193, see also 279)—is nonetheless quick to find fault with any lack of courtesy in others. When Sir Baldwin shoves the carl's humble foal out into the rain because he objects to having it stabled by his own elegant steed, the carl appears at the scene as if by magic to accuse the knight: "cannyst thou noght of corttessyghe" (314). Like Kay after him, Baldwin receives, in payment for his rudeness, a powerful "boffett" that knocks him "to the ground . . . / I sonynge" (to the ground unconscious, 316–17)—an assault that evokes by analogy, but also replaces, the death penalty that we have already been told is normally allotted to the carl's guests. The notion that an aristocrat need not exchange with a commoner marks a return to the question of who might be immune in this story, who is exempt from the need to exchange. Like Gawain himself in the earlier poem, Baldwin and Kay will discover the futility of their attempts to avoid exchange. Gawain's acquiescence, by contrast, accepts and affirms community and equality.

Yet in fact, as we shall see, the community that *Carle* imagines is ultimately based on violence and self-interest. *Carle*, like its more famous analogue, can in the end only imagine the gift as a form of possession. This is hinted at, already, in the strange fact that when the carl's hospitality is acknowledged, he proves not just docile but submissive to the point of extremity. The poem's economy, it seems, cannot at any point achieve stable reciprocity, and this also means that the question of who does possess takes on a radical violence. This accounts for the paradox that the more Gawain submits, the more he obliges the carl to make a similar return, until by the poem's end it is the carl rather than Gawain who adopts the ultimate posture of submission, going "downe on his kne" (601) before Arthur in a repetition of Gawain's earlier gesture to him. This fantasy of dominance via submission recalls other *Gawain*-romances, notably *The Knightly Tale of Gologras and Gawain* (circa 1500), which dramatizes how Gawain's willing and thus honorable submission to his opponent magically "produces more honor and more submission"[51] from Gologras, another outsider to the Arthurian court who gets subsumed into the Round Table in the remorseless process of cultural assimilation that *Gawain*-romances as a whole perform. While *Gologras* imagines this exchange as a mere postlude to a real battle that Gawain has already won before he submits, *Carle* makes exchange itself the means of victory. Merely by making an appropriate return to the carl in the form of his submission, Gawain wins a mastery that in other romances, including *Gologras*, must first be won by more conventional means. If the carl's deadly hospitality realizes the violence at the heart of the gift, Gawain's submission turns that violence back on the carl.

Yet submission is finally not Gawain's only weapon in this romance, which also celebrates its hero's ability to return the carl's hospitality in kind: to make the countergift. Unlike his predecessor in the fourteenth-century *Sir Gawain*, Gawain in *Carle* marks his superiority by giving actively, even to the extent of taking on the role of host himself. The key moment occurs when Gawain leads the foal—described, in the romance's only moment of sentimentality, as "all wett" (345) from the freezing rain—back into the stables to feed, covering the horse with his own mantle. Gawain explicitly codes his gesture as a repayment, telling the foal that he and his companions "spend her that thy master dothe get" (350), while his command to the foal—"eette thy mette" (349)—antici- pates the precise wording of the carl's parallel injunction to Gawain in the immediately following scene: "'Sytt styll,' quod the Carl, 'and eete thy mette'" (376). By making a return gift, Gawain symbolically takes on the role of "guest-master" that has up to this point belonged to the carl, who now defies his own self-characterization as uncourteous by magically appearing yet again, this time to thank the gallant Gawain "full curttes- lye" (353). Significantly, the scene also initiates a change in the nature of the carl's offers—the point at which he moves from the conventional if outsized gestures of hospitality encoded in excessive feasting and drink- ing to the performance of hospitality as an extreme form of self-sacrifice, beginning with the offer of his wife and daughter and culminating in the request that Gawain remove his head. By performing hospitality as reciprocal, Gawain effectively reduces the carl to submission in his own house, forcing him into an escalating war of gift giving that the carl can win only at the cost of symbolic death (a beheading that also turns out to be a disenchantment). Gawain's submission to the carl in carrying out the requested beheading should not obscure the extent to which Gawain here also performs the violence of the gift.

Considered in this context, the decapitation scene merely con- firms the extent to which Gawain has *already* taken the carl's place as a giver of gifts—the position of mastery that in *Sir Gawain* belonged to Bertilak—even as his "gift of death" purges the carl of the monstrous excess of a giant's head and height. What Gawain in the earlier poem had referred to as his "surfet" (2433) and the "fayntyse of the flesche crabbed" (2435) is represented in *Carle* as a literal excess of flesh, which when shorn away reveals the carl to be simply a man "of the height of Sir Gawaine" (399). Yet if the later poem seems in one way to imagine excess as a more literal kind of problem, it nonetheless recognizes that excess haunts not just human bodies but the practices and rituals of chivalry itself, even if that more troubling surplus can only appear in the mysterious form of a "false witchcraft" (403) imposed on chivalry from without and dispelled as soon as it is acknowledged. Gawain's blow performs this ambivalence in its double status as both a gift and an enacting of mortal violence.[52] Because *Carle* is a romance, moreover, this stunningly concrete realization of the gift's violence also allows the banishment of that violence once and for all, as the now-disenchanted carl vows to become a member of the Round Table, accept all guests in charity for Gawain's sake, and build a chantry stocked with "ten prestis syngynge til domysday" (549) for the souls of knights he has slain.

In its magical resolution of tensions, *Carle* seems to exemplify the comic and even satiric qualities of "bourgeois romance," which works to "give aristocratic identity a new lease on life . . . [through] alliance with an increasingly powerful bourgeoisie" even as it simultaneously creates "a space for satire and resistance to elite values."[53] Thus the carl, for one critic, is "a threatening embodiment of anti nobility" who shows that "the ruling class has no automatic prerogative to dictate the terms of its relationship to those below," while, for another reader, "the main theme of the poem is that unless the established classes accommodate the churls, they will be in trouble."[54] Tellingly, *Carle* can only recognize this possibility for accommodation between the classes as a fantasy of possession, nor is this fantasy, as we might suppose, strictly a mercantile one. Certainly the romance's conclusion, in which Gawain gets the carl's daughter and a packhorse "ichargid wyth golde" (567) to his dowry, would seem to support a reading of this romance as a piece of bourgeois triumphalism—one whose message is summed up in the carl's smugly rhetorical question to Gawain: "holst the well payde?" (do you consider

yourself well paid?, 481). Yet attention to the poem's aggression reveals
the limits of such a reading and points to the poem's fascination with
chivalry as a procedure for keeping back what one seems to give.

For all its avidity in reckoning up the carl's material wealth—in gold
plate, elaborate feasts, and fine robes that "cost a thousand pound and
mar" (419)—the poem also brings into focus a different kind of accu-
mulation when the carl reveals to Gawain what he has been keeping in
his dungeon all this time. There are, we learn, "ten fodir of dede menn
bonys" (ten cartloads of dead men's bones, 533–34) lurking in a "wilsome
wonys" (desolate dwelling, 532) attached to the castle, a space ironically
made even more desolate by its realization of what the carl's hospitality
has produced. The bones suggest a horrifying version of mercantile accu-
mulation even as they exemplify this romance's fascination with chivalric
identity, evident here in the significant detail that "many a blody serke,
/ And eche of heme a dyvers marke" (many a bloody shirt, / each with a
different heraldic design, 535–36) lies strewn among the remains.

Since "mark" in Middle English names both a form of symbolic
capital restricted to the armigerous as well as a unit of monetary value
known in medieval England, its use to describe what the carl has been
storing up says much about the threatening power of an arriviste churl
as a competitor for the symbolic capital of chivalry.[55] Yet the moment
also hints at the ways in which chivalry itself makes violence and sac-
rifice into the sorts of objects that can be hoarded up and valued as
though they were, somehow, *things*. The phrase "blody serke" (535) is
significant here in recalling a traditional story of knightly sacrifice often
allegorized in later Middle English writing as an emblem of Christ's gift
of himself to humanity.[56] The intriguing possibility that the carl is not
just sacrificing but also storing up complicates our understanding of
what his bone hoard signifies for the economy of this romance. If the
remains in the carl's dungeon initially seem distinct from the poem's
earlier corpses both in their (formerly) human status and in their need
to be hidden from view, their revelation at the poem's conclusion makes
plain the extent to which the carl, too, relies for his identity on the per-
formance of violence.

The scene suggests that he does so at the very moment when he
promises to stop, especially given the placement of the episode just

before his welcome of King Arthur and subsequent knighting. The carl's strangely unmotivated revelation of the contents of his dungeon contains an implicit boast—"Look! I am one of you after all"—that paradoxically ensures his assimilation into the Round Table. And it turns out that the carl has more to give than money. He also gives identity, in the form of a blood-red steed to the angry Kay and a miter, cross, ring, and cloth of gold to the bishop-knight Sir Baldwin. And in turn he receives it, as Arthur responds to the carl's hospitality by naming him Carlisle, now earl rather than churl. Yet the stubborn presence of the "carl" in this newborn Carlisle suggests that what occurs here is less a rebirth than a kind of semantic extension.

This disturbing possibility is also suggested by the poem's final image, in which the carl builds another house—a "ryche abbey" (649)—and stuffs it with the bodies not of dead knights but living "monkys gray / To rede and synge tille domysday" (655–56). The carl's largesse recalls the similar endings of more explicitly penitential romances like *Sir Gowther*, whose hero also builds an abbey in payment for his many crimes. Such endings give literary expression to the fearful piety of a medieval warrior aristocracy who, in the words of one historian, "tried to buy off the consequences of their aggression by offering a share of the loot to those whose prayers would hopefully resolve their dilemma."[57] Yet *Carle* goes one better than a more conventional "knights behaving badly" romance like *Gowther* when it announces that the monks will pray specifically for the souls of "the men that [the carl] had slayne" (658). While this added detail might seem to make *Carle* the *more* penitential romance, since it explicitly connects crime and gift payment, it also promises a reckoning of the carl's knightly potential, attested to by the names of the dead, that will last to the end of the world. A purified mirror image of the carl's "house of death," the abbey will function like a house of memory, paying down the debt on (but also immortalizing) the carl's transgressions against the law of hospitality. The building itself encodes the ambiguity of its signifying function: ostensibly an abbey, it is also a sort of castle—built "stronge and wele" (653)—that houses spiritual lordship in its (presumably later) status as a "byschoppis see" (654).

Like the carl's castle, the "ryche" abbey is destined to become a seat of wealth and power, one that expresses the carl's own power to

immure men within its walls until the end of time. The poem's con-
cluding emphasis on the abbey's construction suggests the importance
accorded to the memorializing function that this final moment enacts.
Precisely because *Carle* (unlike *Gowther*) can imagine no real use for
knightly violence, the memory of a now-forbidden enjoyment must be
forever renewed in the interests of chivalric prestige.

The ambiguous mourning of its final scene, like so much else about
Carle, complicates attempts to read the poem as a bourgeois romance
with a reformist message, a call for an expansion of the late medieval
community. While the poem clearly emerges in some sense from late
medieval mercantile culture, it does not follow that the point of *Carle*
is to show (in the words of one recent reader) "how imitation of nobil-
ity, supported by immense wealth, becomes the real thing, or perhaps
something better."[58] Rather, the carl *is* nobility revealed in all its brutal
glory. As we have seen, in fact, the central moment of transformation
that must have been part of the basic story is missing from the poem
in its earliest known medieval version. The carl of *Carle* quite precisely
does not become anything new when he shifts his allegiance to Arthur.
While scholarly consensus has tended to regard the elision of the trans-
formation scene as the result of damage to the manuscript or scribal
neglect, its effect is to confront us with the ambiguity of a nobleman
who remains in every sense the carl that he always was.[59]

Whatever the possibilities opened up by the apparent lacuna in the
Porkington *Carle*, the poem's subsequent reception suggests the discom-
fort that the story provoked among at least some late medieval and
early modern readers. Roughly one hundred years after the appearance
of the Porkington *Carle*, a broadly analogous poem, *The Turke and Sir
Gawain*, remedies the omission in the earliest *Carle* by transforming its
"Turke"—a carlish figure who is threateningly exotic to boot—into a
proper Christian knight in a scene that appears to owe much to a later
redaction of *Carle* (with which *Turke* appears in the Percy MS). In place
of the carl's cartloads of dead knights, *Turke* more innocently imagines
the liberation of "many a worthy man" (299) from the castle of the
villainous King of Man when the Turk, immediately after his transfor-
mation, leads Gawain into another part of the castle in what seems to be
a clear reminder of the dungeon scene in *Carle*. If the *Turke* composer

knew *Carle* in one of its versions—as seems likely, given their shared manuscript context—his revision suggests an awareness of the original episode's uncanny horror.

Turke in fact never even mentions the dungeon, reporting only that Gawain encounters inhabitants of the castle "that before they never see" (300), a difference that transforms the carl's compulsive and symbolically fraught revelation of his crimes into a fairy-tale-like moment of restoration that simply and easily extends the Turk's own transformation. Yet even *Turke* registers the dangerous power of hospitality, which appears here in the condensed form of enchanted food that must not be eaten.[60] When the transformed Turk invites Gawain at the poem's end to eat at his table "withouten threat" (301), the moment evokes, by way of an apotropaic gesture, violent possibilities that this story otherwise tends to render ludicrously comic.[61] Even as it suggests retrospectively the complexities of a romance like *Carle*, then, *Turke* expresses its own genealogy as a *Gawain*-romance in its lingering commitment to forms of chivalric desire that it can barely articulate.

That even a very late *Gawain*-romance like *Turke* struggles to contain the excessiveness of the gift is remarkable, given how easy it would be to read the emphasis on reciprocity in all of these poems as an index of their belatedness—the extent to which even *Sir Gawain and the Green Knight* already embodies a "civilizing process."[62] "Courtesy," imagined in these romances as mutual deference, enacts seemingly reciprocal terms of exchange between Camelot and Hautdesert, carls and aristocrats, "Turks" and Christians. Yet true reciprocity is precisely what these romances never quite manage to achieve, so that the history of *Gawain*-romance is marked—like that of English romance in general—by a stubborn residue of violence that can never be fully economized, safely accounted for, or traded away. Rather, Gawain becomes a site for exchange as inevitably *un*equal, alternately compelled and compelling, as he either cedes power on behalf of the Arthurian order or (in later stories) imposes that power on an Other almost dangerously willing to submit itself. Gawain in these stories names the power inherent in the gift, a concern of the tradition from the moment when Arthur imagines that one life might be traded, giftlike, for another.

Gawain's presence in a story almost guarantees that it will ask the question that confronts any spendthrift hero: How much is finally too much to give? This is why Gawain, who begins his history in English romance by failing to give enough, nevertheless comes to stand for the problem of the gift's excess. It is a development anticipated by Chaucer's Squire, who naturally chooses "Gawayne" as the knight to whom a bearer of exotic gifts might fitly be compared. And we have seen that what Gawain gives is, to quote the Squire again, "olde courteisye" itself, a social performance that signifies submission ("obeisance") as precisely the stuff of which mastery is made.[63] The violence of this performance, teasingly latent in *The Squire's Tale* as it is in the roughly contemporaneous *Sir Gawain*, gets realized with stunning clarity in the subsequent course of *Gawain*-romance that this chapter has endeavored to trace.

The final chapter of this study turns to a tradition of late medieval narratives that, like *Carle*, consider the possibility of affinity between the knightly and nonknightly, set in the mercantile, emergently modern world of towns, money, and royal law that the Robin Hood stories take for granted. Yet such stories, for all their seeming modernity, also imagine how chivalry will persist as the imaginative focus for the emergent forms of community that such stories record. Like the *Gawain*-romances, whose history of "downward cultural diffusion" they in some respects mirror, outlaw tales like *The Gest of Robyn Hode* perform the gift as central to the cult of chivalry as it would be played out across early modern culture and beyond.[64] As we shall see, the *Gest* in particular transcends its belatedness (and what Middle English summoning of the chivalric spirit could be anything but belated?) by daring to imagine nothing less than chivalry's primal scene.

CHAPTER 5

"What Shall These Bowes Do?"

If romance knows itself as a form of persistence, then there is perhaps an inevitability to the future of romance as a genre destined to outlive even itself. Romance, after all, is the paradigm for the survival of older genres that "do not . . . die out, but persist in the half-life of the subliterary genres of mass culture."[1] Medieval English romance always-already bears this taint of the commercial, and so the subsequent history of romance in England might seem like nothing more than the elaboration of its commodified origins, a symptom of the precocity with which England accomplished what Michael Nerlich has called the "dialectical process of making courtly literature or ideology bourgeois and making the rising bourgeoisic courtly."[2] If, on the other hand, this book has done something to suggest the limits of such a view, then might it be that the afterlives of this tradition, too, can be read differently from the way they typically have been?

This chapter will argue that this is indeed the case with respect to at least one of romance's generic descendants: the outlaw literature of the fifteenth century. Outlaw tales dramatize how the ideal of the noble gift—originally a mark of aristocratic propriety—comes to serve as the social glue binding together much broader forms of association.[3] The destructiveness of the gift in these tales comes to stand not primarily for class distinction, but rather for the possibility of community itself. In that sense, outlaw literature realizes the yearning for community that was a part of English romance from its beginnings, since these fictions—especially in comparison with other European examples of the form—typically did imagine themselves as speaking to a broad and socially diverse audience. These texts thus offer what might seem to be in many respects a utopian vision, in which the gift comes to stand as a general sign for the possibility of social wholeness and cohesion in the context of an unstable and rapidly changing world. Yet like the romances they so often resemble, these texts also participate in the fantasy of chivalry as a mode of possession—of taking back in the act of seeming to give. In that sense, as we shall see, these texts remain deeply chivalric even when they seem to gesture beyond the confines of romance.

One of the surest signs of chivalry's persistence in these tales can be found in the extent to which the history of their reception in modern scholarship has tended to follow the lines laid down by scholarship on the romances themselves. This has meant that, just like the romances, the ballads based on them have been read as impoverished in relation to their sources: "simply fragments of Romances," "debasements of earlier romances . . . the last crude residue when popular tradition had done its worst with courtly romance." And this has also meant that these fictions, again like the romances, have been interpreted as middle- or even lower-class in their associations on the basis of a supposed "degeneration" from earlier forms that reveals them to be, if not "the property of the lowest classes of society," then at best "mercantile" in their origins and audience.[4]

Like the romances also, these texts are saturated with violence. As one reader notes, if anything these tales dramatize how "violence and cruelty were intensified when occurring as part of social conflict."[5] That English outlaw stories are indeed violent will not be news to anyone who has read a few of them. Stuart M. Kane provides a useful tour of the gallery of horrors that awaits readers, including "the mutilation-murders of a monk and his young page, dogs feasting on the body of a slain assassin, [and] the decapitation and symbolic 'skinning' of a horsehide-clad bounty-hunter."[6] As Kane's list suggests, the violence of these texts is symbolic as well as literal, teasingly interrogating the line between the figurative (the metaphorical "skinning" of a man dressed in an animal hide) and the real (the man's actual murder and subsequent mutilation by Robin Hood). If there is, as Richard Firth Green suggests, a tension in these poems between "occlusive" and "spectacular" violence—between what hides and what shows itself openly—this may help to explain why such poems, like the romances to which they may be compared, perform violence as their central symbolic act.[7] The profound ambiguity of violence in these texts is crucial to recognize because it allows outlaw tales to carry forward the project of romance. What such poems give us is above all an economy of violence, a way of knowing violence as somehow both a disciplinary regime and—at the same time—a fantasy of rebellion against that regime.

The Anglo-Norman poem of complaint known as *The Outlaw's Song of Trailbaston* (circa 1305), long central to attempts to establish the historical context of the earliest outlaw literature, expresses this complexity of meaning and function in the space of a few lines. The narrator, who presents himself as a wrongly accused fugitive, imagines with sadistic relish what he will do to the corrupt judges who have outlawed him if only he can get his hands on them:

> Je lur apre[n]droy le giw de Traylebastoun,
> E lur bruseroy Feschyne e le cropoun,
> Les bras e les jaunbes, ce serreit resoun,
> La lange lur tondroy e la bouche ensoun. (stanza 10)

> [I would teach them the game of Trailbaston
> And would break their backs and their rumps,
> Their arms and their legs: it would be right;
> I would also cut out their tongues and their mouths.][8]

Such inverted violence, turned on the heads of the functionaries of the punitive regime itself, will figure prominently in the outlaw tradition of later medieval England, as when the hero of the *Tale of Gamelyn* hangs both the judge and the jury that have sentenced him to death, or when the associates of the outlaw William of Cloudesley improbably murder "three hundred men and mo" (141)—from the justice, sheriff, and mayor down to the beadles—in the process of rescuing their companion.[9] Yet the *Outlaw's Song* demonstrates that the violence of these tales is itself disciplinary. Violence is a right whose origins can be found in traditional hierarchies. So the narrator of the poem laments that "if I wish to chastise my boy [*mon garsoun*, my servant], / With a slap or two, to correct him, / He will take out a bill against me, and have me attached [i.e., arrested]" (stanza 3). In fact, it is the failure of such disciplinary violence that threatens the anarchy of total war, as the narrator predicts: "If God does not prevent it, I think that war will arise" (stanza 1).

It would be easy enough, especially in the case of the *Outlaw's Song*, to read such anxieties in relation to a narrative of chivalric decline, and the poem's speaker, though he speaks in Anglo-Norman, can sound remarkably like the displaced hero of an English metrical romance such as *Sir Cleges*:

> J'ai servi my sire le roy en pées e en guere,
> En Flaundres, Escoce, en Gascoyne sa terre;
> Mès ore ne me sai-je point chevisaance fere; —
> Tot mon temps ay mis en veyn pur tiel honme plere. (stanza 7)

> [I have served my lord the king in peace and war,
> In Flanders, Scotland and Gascony, his own land;
> But now I do not know how to make a livelihood.
> I have spent all my time in vain to please such a man.]

Yet there is also here a more general sense of confusion, indeed of radical disillusionment, that will be formative for later and less elite articulations of the outlaw theme. We might read something of that confusion in the narrator's strange confession: "Formerly I knew a little about what was good; now I am less wise" (stanza 18). The sarcasm of such lines skirts dangerously close to self-accusation. The failure of violence to be *meaningful* becomes the crisis of a poem that finally admits its ignorance about its own historical situation.

The attempt here to manage and measure violence, to render it a locus of meaning, connects a poem like the *Outlaw's Song* to the romances in intriguing ways. It is tempting, perhaps, to see in such radical dislocation the demise of chivalry as a way of understanding the world. My reading does not deny that outlawry can signify chivalric marginalization and decline, but it does suggest that we should recognize in outlawry forms of displacement and exile that have always been central to romance. As Timothy S. Jones suggests in his reading of the outlaw motif in *Tristan and Iseult*: "What is outlawry but a change in fortune and social context? Who is the outlaw but someone who has been deprived of all his property, evicted from the social order and cast into the wilderness? And what is an errant knight but one who leaves the certainty of the feudal community for the uncertainty of the forest?"[10]

Jones's questions raise the possibility that outlawry is romance's basic situation, akin to that of those "blameworthy knights" of French feudal epic whom Georges Bataille described as "driven by a spirit of excess, turning themselves into outlaws."[11] If on the one hand the knightly outlaw cannot be the hero of romance as directly as he is in some epics of political grievance, romance nonetheless marks a new focus on outlawry as the social fate of an entire class. In Chrétien's *Erec et Enide*—by some accounts the first romance ever written—the hero encounters over and over again the mirror image of his own displaced situation, the outlaw who lives by robbery (*de roberie vivoit*):

> Uns chevaliers del bois issi,
> Qui de roberie vivoit.
> Deus conpeignons o lui avoit,
> Et s'estoient arm' tuit troi.
> Mout covoitent le palefroi
> Que Enide va chevauchant. (2796–2801)

> [Out of the woods came a knight who lived by robbery. He had two companions with him, and all three were armed. They cast very covetous eyes on the palfrey Enide is riding.][12]

The outlaws are defeated, but they can never really disappear, indeed multiplying as Chrétien's poem develops:

N'orent pas une liue alee,
Quant devant an une valee
Lor vindrent cinc chevalier autre,
Chascuns sa lance sor le fautre,
Les escuz as cos anbraciez,
Et les hiaumes bruniz laciez;
Roberie querant aloient. (2925–31)

[They had not gone a league when before them in a valley there came five other knights, with lances in rest, shields held close at their necks, and polished helmets laced; they were on the lookout for plunder.]

Erec's encounters follow a conventional pattern of ever-increasing displays of prowess on the part of the hero, who vanquishes first three outlaws, then five, and so on. Simultaneously, however, the episodes map out a logic of dispossession that seems inescapable: the more impoverished and desperate knights Erec vanquishes, the more outlaws are thereby created, so that (we might conclude) only the hero's arrival at the pinnacle of sovereign power, in the romance's final scene, can stave off once and for all the threatening resemblance between him and them.

In England, the traumatic dispossession brought about by the Norman Conquest took imaginative form in outlaw stories as early as the twelfth-century *Gesta Herewardi*, a Latin text that nevertheless has some claim to being thought of as a romance, and the thirteenth-century Anglo-Norman *Fouke li Fitz Warin* and *Romans de Wistasse li Moine*, texts that parallel broader developments in Anglo-Norman romance while preserving and elaborating the outlaw theme. The outlaw makes his appearance most explicitly in Middle English in *The Tale of Gamelyn* (circa 1350)—to be examined below—with more distant echoes in romances such as *Sir Orfeo* and more broadly in the numerous English romances whose plots revolve around disenfranchisement and so are "in this loose sense 'outlaw tales.'"[13] Such precursors help to establish a romance context for later outlaw heroes in the ballads, such as Adam Bell, Clim of the Clough, William of Cloudesley, and Robin Hood. Indeed, the very earliest reference in English to such tales, in *Piers*

Plowman, fails to distinguish between what one character calls "rymes of Robyn Hood and Randolf Erl of Chestre," the latter of which, though an obscure figure, is described in at least one of the manuscripts of *Piers* as the subject of "Romaunces."[14] Such moments remind us that "in the late Middle Ages there is often not a very clear distinction between popular romances and what are now called 'ballads.'"[15]

Certainly the lack of any clear distinction is evident by the sixteenth century, as Douglas Gray demonstrates in his account of the generic confusion evident in some early modern accounts of medieval secular literature, one of which refers to "stories of the old time, as the *Tale of Sir Thopas*, the reportes of *Bevis of Southamptoun*, *Guy of Warwicke*, *Adam Bell*, and *Clymme of the Clough* and other such old Romances or historicall rimes." Likewise, some sixteenth-century manuscripts of Chaucer's *Tale of Sir Thopas* substitute "Robynhoode" for "Sir Bevis" in a list of "romances of prys," and "wyld Robein under bewch" appears together with the romance heroes "Gy off Gysburne" and "Bevis" of Hampton in William Dunbar's "Schir Thamas Norny."[16] Such confusion testifies to outlaw tales' participation in a late medieval and early modern "confluence of form," Thomas J. Garbaty's term for the process by which the ballad emerged out of metrical romance beginning in the fifteenth century.[17] Work on the medieval ballads by Garbaty and others, notably Richard Firth Green, has effectively served to refute an older view of the genre as an inherently post-medieval form, especially in the case of the outlaw tales whose emergence as a written literature can be traced back to at least the mid-fifteenth century.[18]

Yet what does such confluence mean? If criticism has moved away from a purely evaluative view of these tales as "debasements" or "fragments of Romances," how do we account for the "change in taste" that resulted in a shift away from romance and toward balladry? Supposing that these texts do represent a kind of "downward diffusion," are we to read their resemblances to earlier romances as mere "ideology lag" (in the words of one scholar) or, somewhat more complexly, as fulfilling "the need for a mercantile hero to replace the knightly hero of the aristocratic romances"?[19] While such possibilities are not totally antithetical to my own reading, both views, I think, underestimate the extent to which these tales imagine themselves as expressions of chivalric culture.

Romance is not just an outworn husk in these texts but a vital component of their cultural work as vehicles for ensuring chivalry's future.

The confluence of romance and outlaw ballad is perhaps nowhere more vividly imagined than in a short lament from the seventeenth-century Percy Folio, "In Olde Times Paste," which begins by invoking "Lancelott of Dulake" in the same breath as later outlaw protagonists like Robin Hood, William of Cloudesley, Adam Bell, and Clim of the Clough. The anonymous poet's ready conflation of knights with outlaws mirrors the oft-noted formal indeterminacy of Percy's contents, which can themselves be hard to place firmly as either romance or ballad.[20] If the poet's willingness to take outlaws as synonymous with knights imagines one way in which chivalric culture might persist, however, the poem concludes with a striking account of economic crisis that signifies a more general failure of chivalric continuity:

> More sparinge for a pennye nowe
> then then was for a pound;
> rich men, alas, they know not how
> to keepe ne hawke nor hound.
> All merriments are quite fforgot,
> & bowes are laid aside;
> all is to litle now, god wott,
> to maintaine worldlye pryde.
> Where I began, there will I end,
> the olde time sure was best;
> vnless that misers quickly mend,
> old mirth may take his rest,
> pray wee then good bowmen may rise,
> as hath beene here to-ffore,
> to-ffore, to-ffore,
> to mamtaine, to Maintaine,
> & make our mirth the more,
> the more, the more. (53–70)[21]

The poet's desire for good bowmen to rise in order "to maintaine . . . mirth" identifies an economic imperative of feudal life ("maintenance" in the sense of an economic payment to retainers) with the symbolic persistence or "maintenance" of chivalric culture more generally, whose decline is marked by the simultaneous failure of both the gifts rich men will no longer give and the forms of violent masculine performance that are endangered when "bowes are laid aside." One of the more remarkable features of the poem is the extent to which it imagines the "rise" of good bowmen as at once a revolt against the established order—recalling perhaps even the Rising of 1381 itself—and an ongoing attempt to ensure the persistence of chivalric culture ("as hath been here to-ffore"). Expressions of social protest become ironically a form of "maintenance," a defense against modernity that must be periodically renewed.

To what extent can a poem like this tell us something about the cultural place and function of the earlier, medieval literature of outlawry in England? Like the Percy lament, the earlier outlaw tales it cites are haunted by anxiety about the failure of noble giving, the central symbolic act of the texts we have been exploring. And this means that however different "In Olde Times Paste" might be in its historical situation and audience from the outlaw tales that inspire its vision—so that the "dangerous, chaotic, imminent outlaw of the medieval tradition" is here rendered mostly "unthreatening, orderly, and remote"—the poem is nonetheless entirely faithful to that tradition in imagining gift giving as a pleasurable excess, a form of "maintenance" that signifies violent resistance to the encroachments of modernity.[22] In that sense, the nostalgia performed by a seventeenth-century poem of complaint is remarkably similar to that of outlaw tales, whose heroes stand, for the Percy composer, as lost exemplars of chivalric integrity. In order to see how this might be so, we should turn now to the outlaw tradition itself.

"WE WIL SPENDE LARGELY"

If the outlaw is in some sense the mirror image of the chivalric knight from the very beginnings of romance, it is not until the mid-fourteenth century that a romance in Middle English takes this parallel seriously enough to make an outlaw its hero. Though one might indeed call it a "romance"—its traditional label—*The Tale of Gamelyn* (circa

1350) already illustrates the tendency toward formal confluence that will become more marked in the fifteenth century, and thus the poem exhibits characteristics of both metrical romance and of the later ballads for which it evidently served as a source of inspiration.[23] One scene in particular—Gamelyn's wrestling match with a murderous "champioun"—plays a crucial if underappreciated role in the "ballad epic" of *The Gest of Robyn Hode*, as we shall see. Yet *Gamelyn*'s importance for romance's future arguably depends less on the way in which it will serve as the raw material for later outlaw tales than on the sheer vehemence with which this poem insists on the durability of the chivalric. That insistence is how *Gamelyn* knows itself to be a romance, even if it is also (among other things) a ballad of the sort that might have been told by Chaucer's Cook.[24]

Like the romances we have been exploring throughout this book, the poem's figure for chivalric persistence is the noble gift, most conspicuously in the moment when a crowd led by the poem's dispossessed hero, the eponymous Gamelyn, breaks into the house of his older brother, a stingy villain who has wrongfully deprived Gamelyn of his land. Gamelyn proceeds to throw a wild party for his new friends that lasts for an entire week, a festivity he inaugurates by explicitly contrasting his own generosity with his brother's parsimony and offering a warning to anyone who might think to hinder the potlatch-like festivities:

> My brother is a nigon, I swere be Cristes oore,
> And we wil spende largely that he hath spared yore;
> And who that make grucchinge that we here dwelle,
> He shal to the porter into the drowe-welle. (321–24)[25]

Gamelyn's largesse here evokes the gift as a way of performing community—a word that conjoins *con* ("shared") and *munus*, which originally meant "gift"—as "the semantic and social field . . . circumscribed by the exclusive circle of mutual gift-givers."[26] As in many later outlaw stories, gifts in *Gamelyn* serve as a basis for an ad hoc and broadly defined late medieval social nexus—typically glossed in the ballads as "felaushyp"—here, the community embraced by the socially indeterminate "faire company" (308) that assembles with the hero to feast for an entire week. Such a community might mirror what has been assumed to be the "composite focal audience" of the poem as a whole, which "brings together the interests of dispossessed landholders in Gamelyn himself, the falsely accused, like the king of the outlaws, upper servitors like Adam who have to decide whom to serve, and the bondsmen who resist the pressures imposed by Gamelyn's vicious eldest brother."[27] Seen in this light, Gamelyn's undiscriminating hospitality offers a vision of social and political wholeness even more inclusive than that of earlier romances characterized by a "movement toward social amelioration."[28] Far from being a sign of aristocratic propriety, Gamelyn's giving seems to undo that propriety by enacting it without limit.

But as in an earlier Latin romance called *Hereward the Wake* (from which this scene probably derives), Gamelyn's giving can be read in another light, as an assertion of violent possessiveness.[29] As one reader notes, "it is typical of the violence which is part not only of [Gamelyn's] character, but of the poem as a whole, that his idea of hospitality should be to entertain half the county for seven days nonstop drinking."[30] We might go further and say that the power to give gets expressed here as the *right* to violence, which dissenters ignore at the risk of being thrown down a well ("into the drow-welle"). A violent assertion of ownership is in fact the whole point of Gamelyn's generosity, as the hero's brother recognizes. His angry question to Gamelyn—"Who made the so bold / For to stroien the stoor of myn household?" (351–52)—equates possession with the power to destroy wealth by giving it away in noble fashion. By dispensing the wealth of the household "largely," that is, Gamelyn establishes his claim to the goods so distributed—in this case, to that very portion of the inheritance that he has been denied at the poem's outset. His behavior in this scene might thus be explained by the counterintuitive logic at the heart of the noble gift described by Pierre Bourdieu, in which the giver "possesses in order to give," but, equally, "possesses by giving."[31] Gamelyn embraces this logic when he asserts his right to the inheritance by giving away a substantial portion of it.

Such an act only makes sense to the extent that noble giving is conceived of in this poem as a recognizable way of establishing possession, a strategy whose aim is always partly domination. In *Gamelyn* especially, the violence inscribed in such moments speaks to a world in which "only force can accomplish" the hero's restoration and a (tentative and fragile) reform of a corrupt social order.[32] This is after all also a poem in which "a mannys brayn" can be made "to lyen on his hode" (594) and a suborned royal jury "honged hie, / To weyven with the ropes and the winde drye" (879–80)—images that have understandably provoked the charge of "barbarism."[33]

The gift, as symbolic instead of overt violence, works to hold together a poem defined by the paradox that it is both gleefully transgressive throughout, as it revels in theft, destruction, and murder, and yet somehow "finally a quite conservative story" that ends with Gamelyn's reinstatement into his rightful inheritance and a return to normalcy.[34] It is telling in this respect that the poem's initial failure to ensure chivalry's future is marked by a failure of giving, when the dying Sir John declares that he will give Gamelyn his fine horses as well as most of his land. Yet Gamelyn—whose name has been glossed as "old man's son"—is the poem's figure for the belatedness that imperils the secure transmission of aristocratic privilege. Gamelyn has come too late into the world and has to contend as a result with a greedy elder brother who, with the connivance of the dead knight's landed neighbors, conspires to rob Gamelyn of his allotted portion.

Significantly, the poem's other figure for this belatedness is Gamelyn's portion itself, which is specifically said to include the "fiftene ploughs of londe" (356) that Gamelyn's father amassed by "purchas" (14) rather than inheritance or military service. On the one hand, the power of this "mercantile surplus" to ensure an aristocratic future for the hero is what enables the poem's first gift, when the hero's father—in defiance of the principle of primogeniture and his neighbors' advice—decides to alienate the land in favor of Gamelyn. On the other hand, the uncertain legal status of this surplus is the whole problem of the romance. This seems to be the point of Sir John's distinction between the portion destined for the eldest son—the patrilineal "heritage" (58) presumably secured by entail—and the portions destined for the two younger brothers, both the "fyve plowes" (59) that Sir John won "with my right honed" (60)—to be apportioned to the middle brother—and the remaining fifteen ploughs' worth that he bought outright, which fall to the hero. Gamelyn's portion is indeed surplus in every sense—both literally *more* than the other portions and tied implicitly to the ways in which novel forms of surplus were being generated by the late medieval economy.[35] We might thus understand Gamelyn's land as the poem's basic problem: both the means by which aristocratic culture might reproduce itself and—in the portability that characterizes its life as a surplus—a threat to that very culture.

Read in these terms, Sir John's gift to his youngest son marks the dying knight's attempt to recruit a mercantile surplus for the uses of chivalry, an act that Sir John associates with charity when he invokes "Seint Martyne" (53), best known to medieval audiences for dividing his cloak with a beggar, and thus a figure whose invocation emphasizes the impulse toward the gift that structures the poem from its opening.[36] Sir John, as he reminds his reluctant advisors, is still alive and thus able to alienate land as he pleases in the form of a bequest, in this way circumventing the implicit constraints of primogeniture: "for al that ye han done / yit is the londe myne" (54). While there has been some debate about the poem's accuracy in terms of fourteenth-century law, Sir John obviously believes his action to be legally valid, as is suggested by his reference to the "lawe" (64).[37] At the same time, the problematic nature of the father's decision, as it plays out in the poem, also suggests the extent to which his gift is surplus to the usual economy of aristocratic transmission. Proposed in the peaceful contexts of law and Christian charity, Sir John's gift is nonetheless noble in its attempt to express the will of the giver over against the norms of his society. It is just such giving that will later be asserted by the outsized hero as violence, the reckless destruction of "stoor" that characterizes aristocratic expenditure.

Not just an inheritance romance, then, *Gamelyn* is more precisely a romance of the gift.[38] The question of who *gets* to give—and thus who possesses—is central to the poem's meaning. This in turn ought to complicate our view of a relatively late romance that has traditionally been read as either "emphatically non-chivalric" or simply uninterested in matters of chivalry altogether, probably written for an audience that "had no personal stake in chivalry."[39] The gift in *Gamelyn* points to the more nuanced possibility that chivalry persists even in what seems to oppose it. This is because *Gamelyn* represents a world in which only what is outside chivalry can save it. It is therefore vital to the future of chivalry that Gamelyn be outlawed, even bound by physical constraints in one of the poem's significant recurring images, and thus marked as separate from the "attenuated" chivalric order represented by the hero's "distinctly chivalric" but "strangely ineffectual" middle brother, Sir Ote.[40] Absent for most of the poem, Ote's reappearance at its end as a conventionally chivalric hero—"als good an knyght and hende" (724)—suggests the poem's need for a mediating term that can redirect the social energies embodied by Gamelyn. The poem's work in accomplishing this is summed up in its carefully modulated resolution: Gamelyn, the future of chivalry, will be Sir Ote's heir. If the poem closes with a vision of potentially mercantile reciprocity, in which Gamelyn pays his enemies back—"Thus wane Gamelyn his land and his lede, / And wreke him on his enemyes and quytte hem her med" (891–92)— Sir Ote's gift in the next line works to ensure the continuity of aristocratic life to which this poem is so deeply committed: "And Sir Ote his brother made him his heire" (893). Attending to the poem's other gifts suggests that we should not read this as mere chivalric window dressing but as a measure of the extent to which chivalry will survive in outlaw literature as a way of imagining broader forms of affinity. It is paradoxically by breaking the rules of aristocratic transmission that the stability of this transmission will be assured.

The power of transgression to ensure chivalry's future is also the subject of later outlaw tales, which find their most canonical expression in an interlaced collection of ballads known as *A Gest of Robyn Hode*. Written roughly a century after *Gamelyn*, the *Gest* seems on its face to dramatize chivalry's failure to sustain itself in an emergently modern world of towns, money, and trade—a failure given generic form, we might conclude, in the *Gest*'s (partial) refusal of a romance structure for that of the outlaw ballad.[41] Yet while few readers would go so far as to call the *Gest* a romance, I do want to suggest that this poem dramatizes an important moment in the history of chivalric culture: the moment at which romance, in order to persist more fully as an ideological form, ends up staging its own death as a literary one. Ultimately, this means that the question of what exactly the *Gest* is—and of related questions to do with audience, class ideology, and so on—will turn out to be surprisingly irrelevant to this poem's work. In other words, romance will persist in the *Gest* in spite of what the poem itself says about the impossibility of this persistence. The poem's figure for this impossible persistence will be, naturally, a gift.

ROBIN HOOD'S GIFTS AND THE FUTURE OF CHIVALRY

The *Gest* illustrates the critical commonplace that the "real" Robin Hood was not the figure of charity he would later become, as the only evidence for philanthropy it offers comes in the poem's concluding lines: "he was a good outlaw, / And did pore men moch god" (1823–24).[42] Instead, the first real evidence for a socially conscious Robin dates to Martin Parker's *The True Tale of Robin Hood* (1632), which shows Robin for the first time actively helping the poor:

> Poore men might safely passe by him,
> And some that way would chuse,
> For well they knew that to help them
> He evermore did use.
>
> But where he knew a miser rich,
> That did the poore oppresse,
> To feele his coyne his hand did itch;
> Hee'de have it, more or lesse. (201–8)[43]

Yet the noble gift is very much a part of early Robin Hood ballads, even if charity is not. For the gift of these tales is not eleemosynary but rather noble in the sense that we have been tracing: a symbolic act whose ultimate end is domination. In fact, it is a significant aspect of this literature's subsequent development that the violence of its economy will be evacuated in the name of a post-feudal order. Thus, for example, in the Restoration propaganda play *Robin Hood and His Crew of Souldiers* (1661), a royalist interlocutor claims victory over Robin and his crew of outlaws in part by arguing that "laws were not made as you formerly imagine, to enslave the Generous, but Curb the Proud and Violent" (100–101).[44] Early modern attempts to defeudalize Robin (even as they ironically make him an earl) suggest the extent to which the economy of the original tales is one of violent self-interest.

The world of the *Gest*, like that of *Gamelyn*, is a belated and insecure one. The *Gest* in many ways dramatizes belatedness even more urgently, but still the *Gest* has much in common with the earlier text. Both exemplify the confluence of form central to the history of romance's development in England. The *Gest*, like *Gamelyn*, seems to have enjoyed an audience best described as "composite," one that "commentators seem now to agree . . . was probably mixed."[45] This is perhaps only to be expected of a tale in which a yeoman outlaw helps a knight, a situation that echoes the déclassé Gamelyn's rescue of his more explicitly chivalric brother Ote. Nor should the resemblance surprise us, since both poems offer a measure of the extent to which the transition from feudal to mercantile culture entailed a "complex dialectical process," as Thomas H. Ohlgren has argued with respect to the *Gest*. It is actually crucial that we could describe the work of *Gamelyn* in much the same way, for this suggests that romance, far from being reducible to anti-mercantile satire, knows the complexity that will characterize its afterlife in a poem like the *Gest*. By the same token, the *Gest* will turn out to be less a fable of an emergent modernity's victory over a declining chivalry—"mercantile culture appropriating and dominating courtly culture"—than a working out of the complex ways in which chivalry will persist in a world that already knows itself to be modern.[46]

As in the earlier poem, persistence takes the form of a gift. Perhaps the surest sign that this poem belongs to the gift is the extent to which scholarship has devoted itself to the question of whether there *is* a gift here. I do not mean by this simply that it is impossible to know whether, as Jacques Derrida has wondered, there is such a thing as a pure gift, innocent of calculation.[47] Rather, it is my contention that the *Gest* itself does not know whether its exchanges are gifts or not, and that this is exactly their point as practices that mean ambiguously both gift and not-gift—and, by extension, both chivalric and mercantile, as well as, ultimately, both violence and its displacement. It is telling from this point of view that the poem's many exchanges can be, for J. C. Holt, instances of "extravagant generosity" legible as expressions of "the knightly code," while for Ohlgren those same exchanges show how "the virtue of generosity has been reconfigured [in the poem] as a loan to be repaid," or again, that where Gray sees "demonstrations of largesse worthy of any knight of romance," Richard Tardif argues instead for "the freedom of the town rather than . . . chivalric largesse" as the focus of the poem.[48] Such statements measure the extent to which in scholarship on this poem the gift has become a figure for more general disagreements about the audience and social function of outlaw literature.[49] Yet if it is now generally recognized that this audience was probably mixed and its function accordingly complex, these facts might themselves tell us something about why the gift is the poem's figure to begin with.

It should not be surprising, then, that the *Gest* begins with a gift— or, more precisely, with the question of whether there is one. When we first meet Robin, he is in the greenwood awaiting the arrival of some wayfarer on whom to force his coercive hospitality. In a conventional trope of the outlaw ballads, Robin offers a sumptuous dinner to passersby under the guise of generosity, only to make them pay with whatever money they are carrying. "Pay or ye wende" (145), Robin will demand of his first victim, and the immediacy of Robin's demand denies the time that makes the gift in favor of the commodity exchange that (as Bourdieu says) "telescopes gift and counter-gift into the same instant."[50] For Ohlgren, the point of this scene of impatience is mercantile, the episode for him recalling the ceremonial dinners of fifteenth-century guilds in which new inductees were required to pay a fee upon the conclusion of the banquet.[51] While the commodity is what interrupts the gift in this opening scene, it is telling that what the outlaws have on their mind is violence: "where we shall robbe / where we shal reve, / Where we shall bete and bynde?" (46–48), as Little John asks his master. Little John's question already suggests that violence, not the commodity, is what will lie closest to the heart of this poem's gifts.

Yet where can the gift be found in a world defined by its ironic distance from romance? If this opening seems to measure Robin's exile from the space of romance as he lies in the greenwood waiting, as though he were Arthur, for a marvel in the form of an "unkouth gest" (24), he soon (like Arthur) gets exactly what he wanted: a source of "moche wonder" (175). But where Arthur got a green knight to marvel over, Robin gets a poor one: the "wonder" is simply that this knight's "clothynge is so thin" (176). We would be forgiven for suspecting that Sir Richard at the Lee—the knight in question—is a spendthrift on the order of a Sir Launfal, and Sir Richard indeed confesses to Robin that he has lost all his wealth "for my greate foly . . . and for my kyndnesse" (203–4), preparing us for a story of economic imprudence. And as in the spendthrift romances explored in chapter 2, the failure of aristocratic expenditure in the *Gest* signals not just an economic but a more broadly cultural crisis, in which the future of chivalry as a whole will be cast into doubt.

But it turns out that Sir Richard has not been giving gifts at all. His predicament is entirely more modern, arising from exorbitant legal fees in connection with the defense of his son, who has murdered two other combatants during a "just" (96) or tournament. As a result, Sir Richard laments, he has been driven to mortgage his lands to a local abbot eager to repossess them from the now-bankrupt knight. If Robin is displaced from romance, so too, it transpires, is Sir Richard. The breadth and depth of that displacement is evident not just in the outlawing of tournaments—which were periodically banned by royal authorities in England as early as the reign of Henry II—but in the fragility of what might be called this poem's "play violence," the ease with which the symbolic play of a tournament might turn deadly, so that Sir Richard can later identify the danger of such violence as the reason his creditors should take pity on him:

> "In joustes and in tournement
> Full ferre than have I be,
> And put my selfe as ferre in press
> As ony that ever I se." (461–64)

The knight's defense echoes, even as it tellingly revises, the traditional complaint of declining knighthood from *Sir Cleges* to *The Outlaw's Song of Trailbaston*. Instead of military service, the knight's worth is to be measured in the extent to which his activities recode violence as play. Robin, too, has just been playing with violence, and the stakes involved in that play become retrospectively apparent when the knight gives his account of symbolic play gone wrong. Chivalric ritual, including gift exchange, ideally works to manage and limit violence even as it allows for its expression in a controlled form. Yet the knight's story, like Robin's comic hospitality, points to the fragility of ritual. In the knight's story ritual not only fails to conceal but actually becomes violence plain and simple, erasing the distinction between ritual and reality on which chivalric culture depends. If the noble gift is a kind of symbolic playing at violence—as I have suggested—than we might see the precariousness of that play as central to this poem's questions about whether there *will* be a gift.

In fact, at least the possibility of a gift appears immediately after the knight tells his story. It is true that the four hundred pounds that Robin now gives the distressed knight come "in the form of a *loan*, not an outright gift," but the loan later becomes a gift when Robin forgives the debt.[52] Moreover, Robin's gift-loan is accompanied even here by a number of "pure" gifts—or what Little John explicitly calls "almus to helpe a gentyll knyght" (275)—including a new suit of clothes, boots, gilt spurs, two horses with accoutrements, and Little John himself as Sir Richard's attending squire. Little John's comically generous provision of cloth for the knight's new suit in this scene encodes largesse, marking "a fundamental *difference* as well as comic comparison to mercantile practice."[53] Yet Little John's identification of these gifts as "almus" should not keep us from recognizing their noble meaning: the ways in which the gift means violence in this scene of aristocratic exchange.

We might begin by noting that Little John's unit of measure is his "bowe-tree" (288)—a favored weapon of the outlaws—already a reminder that violence is at stake here, even in what seems to be primarily a scene of charity. This scene alludes to violence in broader ways as well, in its refusal to distinguish between persons and things (so that Little John is here given away as freely as the objects that accompany him) as well as in its focus on the material means of knightly violence. The outlaws' gift of a warhorse is especially significant since it not only gives us the knight's proper name (*chevalier*) but allows that displaced warrior "to mayntene hym in his right" (306), a euphemistic formula that connects the practice of violence with the feudal right to the legitimate exercise of force. This same right is what Sir Richard has already said he tried to defend in the person of his son—"to save hym in his ryght" (211)—after the son's murder of his fellow combatants, and the echo of this formula in the ceremony that accompanies the outlaws' rehabilitation of the knight again codes violence as crucial to aristocratic identity.

Robin's gift will also paradoxically make violence unnecessary. One symptom of this displacement is that Sir Richard, even though he threatens the greedy abbot with violence should he not receive his land back—"But I have my londe agayne, / Full dere it shall be bought" (441–44)—in fact does more than fling a sack of gold at his erstwhile creditor. Robin's gift thus begins a recuperation of the symbolic (of violence as "ryght") that will also work to elide the grounding of aristocratic distinction *in* violence. The gift here enacts the careful ambiguity that ensures the persistence of its symbolic work.

The gift is what keeps coming back in this poem, a fact that itself suggests we should read such gifts as something more dangerous than charity. We might even say that the remainder of the poem is concerned with the ways in which the knight repays Robin's initial generosity, and does so with the aggressivity inherent in noble giving. In offering a series of countergifts, Sir Richard lives up to "the obligation to reciprocate presents received" that drives the aristocratic economy.[54] More than simply leveling the score between Robin and the knight, the latter's countergifts reproduce the violence at the heart of Robin's initial gesture. Sir Richard's reciprocating gesture marks this violence in a variety of ways, most palpably in the knight's dangerously lavish countergift of a hundred bows and arrows "inocked all with whyte silver" (527) that he offers, with mock humility, as a "pore present" (1100) to the outlaws. Specifically described as a present rather than a repayment, the gift of arrows significantly comes on top of the principal sum of four hundred pounds that Sir Richard owes to Robin as well as the "twenty marke" (1079) that the knight offers as a euphemized form of interest and which he calls—employing the term used in medieval English records—"curteysy" (1080).[55] Surplus to such monetized "courteysy," the arrows mean not just violence but the specifically chivalric possibility that violence might be a thing of lavish beauty.

Like the marvelous weapons that mystify violence in chivalric romances, Sir Richard's gift bears an imagined surplus value that is equivalent to the value of chivalry itself. The euphemizing power of Sir Richard's gesture here has a specific resonance in the broader context in which the poem situates his gift-act. Like the knight's initial story, the story of how his return gift came to be is one of violence. Unlike that initial story, however, the knight's second story is about violence averted and rendered safely symbolic—transformed, in fact, into a gift—but only barely. I refer here to Sir Richard's description of how he helped "a pore yeman, / With wronge was put behynde" (1071–72) at a peasant wrestling match.

In one sense, Maruice Keen is surely right that in terms of plot logic "there is no reason at all . . . why Sir Richard atte Lee and his men should stumble on a country wrestling match on their way to visit Robin Hood."[56] Still, it matters that we can trace a romance pedigree for this episode, in particular a connection to Gamelyn's helping of a franklin whose sons are endangered in a wrestling match (191–282).[57] For the *Gest*, too, is about the future of chivalry, of sons who might die or be dispossessed, of the uses of knightly violence in a world that seems to preclude it, and of the gift as what ensures chivalry's returns. It is no coincidence that Sir Richard's stumbling on the match involves his entrance into the space of romance *aventure*—of the chance encounter signaled by a narratorial "but":

> But at Wentbrydge ther was a wrastlyng,
> And there taryed was he,
> And there was all the best yemen
> Of all the west countree. (537–40)

Even though we have been told earlier that Sir Richard has been on crusade (388)—an episode that this poem otherwise elides—it is here, in the agrarian life of a small village, that Sir Richard will rediscover his knightly function. He will do so, moreover, in a way that rewrites the history of his own decline.

Sir Richard, seeing the violent play of the wrestling match about to turn deadly, steps in to ensure the proper functioning of the ritualized violence whose failure earlier in the story was also the end of aristocratic continuity, the trauma that precipitated the crisis of his son's exile from the space of romance. Here again, the violent play that makes this poem's world cohere threatens to overflow its proper boundaries, the "full fayre game" (541) veering into attempted murder at the moment when a clear winner emerges:

> There was a yoman in that place,
> And best worthy was he,
> And for he was ferre and frembde bested,
> Slayne he shulde have be. (549–52)[58]

Though the lines are hard to parse, it seems that the yeoman who has won the play is far from home ("ferre") and thus placed in the position of a stranger ("frembe bested"), which in turn provokes the jealousy of villagers angry to see the victory go to someone outside the county. Like the crypto-Norman "champioun" who wins the play in *Gamelyn*, there is something troublingly alien about this yeoman who comes from afar to upset the village economy.[59]

Yet *Gamelyn* also provides the model for what is more profoundly at issue here: economic as opposed to cultural difference. That difference is measured not just in the distance between a franklin and a déclassé knight (in *Gamelyn*) or between such a knight and a yeoman like the ones encountered by Sir Richard in the *Gest*, but rather—and more urgently—in the distance that competition generates among the yeomen themselves. For what is remarkable here is the breakdown of precisely the kind of "felaushyp" that outlaw literature typically celebrates, described by Robin at the start of the poem as the community of people among whom violence is forbidden:

> No more ye shall no gode yeman
> That walketh by grene wode shawe,
> Ne no knyght ne no squyer
> That wol be a gode felawe. (53–56)

Yet if Robin's notion of fellowship promises an end to class warfare, at least for those who will be good fellows, the cutthroat nature of the wrestling match raises the possibility that such conflict is inevitable not just between but within classes—that such violence may in fact be fundamental to the workings of *any* economy, realized here as a scene of competitive struggle among late medieval small landholders. Noteworthy in this respect is the remarkable value of what is at stake in this wrestling match. The exotic yeoman's strength wins him not the modest ram and ring offered as prizes at such matches, but rather a bridled horse, pair of gloves, gold ring, and cask of wine (548)—prizes of unusual value that the poem's most recent editors gloss as possible evidence of "an 'art' or literary context for the *Gest*."[60]

In fact, what the prizes also suggest is the possibility of romance, the notion that one might wrestle one's way into possession of the signifiers of gentle status. If there is some historical truth to this short fable of capitalist origins—locatable in agrarian economic competition as much as in the economies of trade represented by the medieval town—it is noteworthy that the poem knows this possibility as romance rather than history.[61] For romance is exactly what now ensues. The most troubling sort of Other for the villagers, the yeoman becomes for Sir Richard a figure worthy of knightly defense, just as Gamelyn demonstrates his essentially chivalric nature by helping a franklin against the murderous "champioun" in the earlier poem's analogous scene. The reversal by which the monstrous Other of *Gamelyn* becomes the beset-upon yeoman of the *Gest* should not keep us from noting the similarities of poems that imagine a future for chivalry in the person of the knightly protagonist. The *Gest*, too, will become a romance precisely in the moment it registers the possibility of conflict most explicitly.

The conflict that begins with the villagers' attempt to murder the victorious yeoman ends, significantly, only when Sir Richard threatens to defend the victor with force if necessary—a threat he backs up by summoning to his aid no less than one hundred armed retainers, whom he has somewhat inexplicably managed to hire in the time intervening between his initial meeting of Robin Hood and his return from the Holy Land. Though later seemingly absent from the text at the time of the knight's second meeting with Robin, the "hundredth men" (529) here are clearly present as the "hundredth" who "folowed hym in fere, / With bowes bent and arowes sharpe" (558–59) when Sir Richard intervenes to stop the attempted murder. Backed by this veritable army, the knight threatens "for to shende that companye" (560) of resentful losers, takes the winner by the hand, and awards him the prizes. If chivalry names in part the possibility that violence can be a kind of game, its survival depends on the fair play that Sir Richard's policing of this scene of conflict ensures.

Yet the extent to which this chivalric anecdote is rigged, staged precisely by means of the violence that ritual works to mystify, can help to explain what happens next. Having threatened the onlookers with death, Sir Richard now—remarkably, given what has just transpired—plays the hospitable lord in a scene of largesse that marks yet another of this poem's points of similarity with *Gamelyn*. Just as Gamelyn celebrates his triumph over the champion wrestler by broaching "fyve tonne of wine" (316) from his brother's cellar (as discussed above), so Sir Richard now buys the pipe of wine that the yeoman has won as a prize and shares it out among the very onlookers who have just tried to murder the victor and were in turn threatened by Sir Richard himself:

> He gave hym fyve marke for his wyne,
> There it lay on the molde,
> And bad it shulde be set a broche,
> Drynke who so wolde. (565–68)

For Nancy Mason Bradbury, "the instantaneous switch from near-murder to raising glasses together is characteristic" of both poems in a way that proves their kinship, so that the *Gest* "retells" an episode from *Gamelyn*, which in its turn bears traces of a previous life as an independent story.[62] Yet it is significant that the form taken by this toggling between violence and convivial fellowship, in both poems, is the gift that means both these things at once: an ambiguity instantiated here in wine that might have been blood, a moment of Eucharistic communion that might have gone very differently. So it is understandable that Sir Richard, in a hurry to get to Robin Hood, still finds time to observe the end—"long tarried . . . tyll that play was done" (569–70)—even as the leisurely enjoyment of play sits uneasily with possibilities whose dangerous immanence is the poem's open secret.

The luxury of time is crucial to the broader function of this episode in the poem's overall structure. The wrestling match and its aftermath, a drama of the gift in miniature, are connected to the poem's central transactions in a variety of ways, most obviously in the fact that the knight's gifts to Robin will include the same bows and arrows that the knight and his men have just wielded to restore order, in the previous scene, to a late medieval agrarian community that only force can render coherent. After the match, the knight returns to repay the outlaws, and his late arrival affords the "gift of time"—the "time-lag" in between the gift and its return—that helps to differentiate gift giving from mere exchange.[63] Sir Richard's apology to Robin for his lateness thus becomes an opportunity to tell the story of the wrestling match, which is also, of course, the story of how a delay was created:

> But take not a grefe, that I have be so longe;
> I came by a wrastelynge,
> And there I holpe a pore yeman,
> With wronge was put behynde. (1069–72)

The righting of the yeoman's wrong took time, and Robin's return gift is the limitless quantity of time that alone can turn the loan of the four hundred pounds into a gift, as Robin does now in inviting the knight to "broke it well for ay" (1082) or enjoy it forever.

That timing is indeed everything when it comes to the gift is the moral of this scene, for it is only now, after the time of the gift has made us safe again, that Robin notices the silver-gilt bows and arrows that Sir Richard has brought as his own gift, the surplus that exceeds, as I note above, even the interest that the knight has brought along in the form of money. "'But what shall these bowes do?'" (1097), Robin asks, and it is perhaps worth dwelling for a time ourselves on the semantic possibilities of his disarming question. In a literal sense, the answer to the outlaw's query is obvious. What the bows do—what they have already done, in a striking reversal of the kind of work we might have expected of an outlaw tale—is to get people to behave themselves. But Robin's polite question also configures the "bowes" as an unnecessary present, whose gratuitousness he acknowledges in the expected way (i.e., "you shouldn't have"). The claim to be unable to imagine a use for the gift is the tribute that the recipient pays to the excessive generosity of the giver, even when accompanied, in our own society, by a concession to capitalist efficiency in the form of the assertion that the gift is exactly "what I needed."

If Robin's question works to the first purpose, imagining the bows as pure surplus, we know by now that they are exactly what this poem cannot do without, even if their sumptuary extravagance begs us to read them anew as objects whose meaning is primarily aesthetic—a surplus recognizable in what Robin will now give in return for them: four hundred *more* pounds from his "treasuré" (1102) and a promise that the knight can return "yf thou fayle ony spendynge" (1109). The possibility that the gift might indeed "fayle"—that the future of chivalry is in doubt—will seem before the end of this poem to be very real.

The specter of failure is evident in the story of how Robin, having secured a royal pardon at the intercession of the knight, goes to court and attempts to live like a feudal lord. In an ironic twist, Robin promptly bankrupts himself, with the result that he is placed in the knight's initial position:

> Had Robyn dwelled in the kynges courte
> But twelve monethes and thre,
> That he had spent an hondred pounde,
> And all his mennes fe.
>
> In every place where Robyn came
> Ever more he layde downe,
> Both for knyghtes and for squyres,
> To gete hym grete renowne. (1729–36)

Robin's largesse evokes the excessiveness of the potlatch while his desire for "renowne" recalls Mauss's account of noble giving as above all a struggle for rank. But the unsustainable nature of such generosity soon becomes clear, as Robin, left with "no man but twayne" (1738), laments that his "welthe is went away" (1744).[64] This loss of wealth mirrors a waning of potency that Robin mourns in the lines that immediately follow:

> Somtyme I was an archere good,
> A styffe and eke a stronge;
> I was comted the best archere
> That was in mery Englonde. (1745–46)

Robin's economic and military impotence threatens his own chivalric future, as his men drift one by one out into the forest and leave him behind. Their abandonment of Robin inverts the trajectory of the "spendthrift knight" romances explored in chapter 2, in which an initial wasting of funds and disintegration of the hero's household is followed by the restoration of wealth and chivalric status. Here, by contrast, recovery (in the story of the knight) is followed once again by loss in the story of Robin himself. More explicitly than in the romances, the failure of Robin's largesse also marks a failure of his capacity for violence and thus of any possible means of recuperation within chivalric society.

But if this suggests the limits of our attempt to read the future of romance in a poem like the *Gest*, it is significant that the poem's ending is equally legible as a reenactment of chivalry's primal scene—one that in fact reinverts Robin's career of decline. For the poem will not give up on chivalry so easily. Even as the scene of romance located in the court proves a dead end, the greenwood offers a fantastic realm where Robin can be restored to potency. When he returns there at the end of the *Gest*, his first act performs a violence that the outlaws recognize and obey instinctively:

> Robyn slewe a full grete harte,
> His horne than gan he blow,
> That all the outlawes of that forest
> That horne coud they knowe,
>
> And gadred them togyder,
> In a lytell throwe;
> Seven score of wyght yonge men
> Came redy on a rowe. (1785–92)

Such ready submission echoes, even as it transposes, the story of abandonment that ensued upon Sir Richard's impoverishment as described near the poem's opening:

"And nowe they renne away fro me,
    As bestis on a rowe." (237–40)

The humiliating bestiality that remains when chivalry is gone will prove a kind of fragile reassurance, when Robin slays the "full grete harte" that is this poem's final gift. As the outlaws doff their "hodes" (1793) and "set them on theyr kne" (1794), their submission acknowledges the power of Robin's deadly gesture to reconstitute the outlaws as a community, remaking itself now as easily as it had melted away. Robin's slaying of the great hart is a summons to a feast—a lordly gift indeed—that encodes violence as the originary moment of the social order. While this return to a primal scene may be a regression, it does not come empty-handed. The ultimate figure of romance's persistence, the gift is what the *Gest* cannot afford to lose.

— • —

If a fifteenth-century poem like the *Gest* offers us an index of romance's persistence as what Fredric Jameson would call an "ideologeme," can it also tell us something about the death of romance as a historically specific form?[65] One obvious question raised by the approach I have taken throughout this book is why, if romance is what persists, its demise as a form should ever have taken place. How might we account for the undeniable fact that romance in the specific, generic sense that we refer to as "the metrical tradition" of medieval England does fade from view, albeit perhaps less quickly than was once thought? If I am right in insisting on romance as a ghost that continues to haunt us, where did it go to begin with? If, on the other hand, romance never went anywhere, why should this book end here?

At its root this is a question about the durability of the kind of violence that romance performs. It is the highly ritualized violence that

Bourdieu sees as withering away in the face of social and economic rationalization:

> If it be true that symbolic violence is the gentle, hidden form violence takes when overt violence is impossible, it is understandable why symbolic forms of domination should have progressively withered away as objective mechanisms came to be constituted which, in rendering superfluous the work of euphemization, tended to produce the "disenchanted" dispositions their development demanded.[66]

The violence that romance does, we might conclude, has no place in a world where coercion no longer needs to be ambiguous in order to be effective. Disenchantment in the literary sphere expresses itself as a preference for prose and ultimately for the novel, a form that binds romance more tightly to the truth claims of historiography. Meanwhile, the chivalric idealism of the original romances finds expression only in the disintegrated and fragmentary form of the ballad, whose stuttering repetitiveness marks at the lexical level the desire to retain a form of life that can no longer actually be narrated.

Such an account, familiar enough in its basic outlines, would seem to offer us a very different reading of the *Gest* from the one I have proposed above. It would be significant, on such a reading, that Robin's unhappy death clearly frustrates the expectations of romance: that having fled once more into the greenwood, he will be done in by an evil prioress who is somehow also the hero's cousin. The murder of Robin by means of a deliberately botched bloodletting—a moment rife with family intrigue of the sort that also characterizes the prose romances of the late Middle Ages—provides an index of the extent to which the fifteenth century was an age of counterromance, increasingly dominated by narratives whose "more realistic and bleaker view of the world" demands "a rethinking of our conception of the genre."[67] It might be no coincidence, on this reading, that the *Gest* can be compared in structure to Malory's *Le Morte Darthur*, whose tragic outcome it echoes.[68] The *Gest*'s interlaced structure might further remind us of its likely textual history as a gathering together of ballads, so that the poem's very existence testifies less to the direct persistence of a metrical form than to the ways in which the disintegration of that form has already led to an effort at reconstitution.

Might the failure of aristocratic expenditure that the *Gest* dramatizes have something to do with the sorts of changes that this poem also exemplifies at the level of form, in its ambiguous status as what I am calling a reconstituted object? Do we know how such an object got made to begin with? It seems beyond dispute that the compiler of the *Gest* was working from written sources, which he sutured together with considerable care. Less clear is whether this means that the poem was primarily meant to be read rather than recited, and whether that in turn implies the absence of a "minstrel." Whatever the truth, the scene of oral composition imagined by the *Gest* (if not actually implied by it) was rapidly vanishing from the world of post-Chaucerian England. As a sixteenth-century minstrel named Richard Sheale laments,

> For wher the haue no mony in store
> Ytes tyme for the mynstrell to gete owt ath dore. (7–8)

Sheale's complaint reminds us that the turn away from romance in the late Middle Ages can be located partly in the eclipse of an oral culture whose economic basis was a specific form of patronage.[69] *Sir Cleges* is perhaps the most explicitly anxious of the English romances on this score, as I suggested in chapter 2, and in that respect *Cleges* was prescient about changes that the *Gest*, composed about two generations later, dramatizes in its very structure as a suturing together of earlier tales. The failure of the aristocratic economy imagined by the *Gest* is, among other things, also the failure of the conditions that drive the production of long-form metrical narrative. Such narrative does not disappear, of course, but it will be increasingly challenged by newer forms in post-Chaucerian England. The *Gest* might thus tentatively be read as one early attempt to recuperate a form that was already on its way out.

If the *Gest* does in some sense mark an end—the point at which romance shades into something else—we have seen that the poem simultaneously imagines itself as a return.[70] Robin's return to the forest evokes what Roberto Esposito calls "the scene of originary violence"—the coerciveness out of which all community emerges. This original act of violence, Esposito argues, "inevitably refers to every future founding of community." Such violence "returns again, and indeed never disappears," so that it at once "precedes and also embraces the project of its modern 'domestication.'"[71] This is what the *Gest* knows when it reimagines the trauma of modernity as a scene of primitive violence. In this it resembles the more firmly romance texts that this book has been exploring, since I have tried to show that English romance is always reconstituting itself, imagining the future as a repetition of the past. One effect of this compulsion is that even as such texts describe a world in which violence is increasingly caught up in abstract procedures of exchange, they nevertheless imagine the return of the violence that all such texts desire—the founding gesture that ensures the coherence of the community. The returns of such violence are arguably the central fascination of the English romances.

This book has focused specifically on the noble gift as the primary way in which romance fantasizes about such returns, yet the need for imagining those returns is dictated in large measure by the modernity of the texts. As we have seen, the romances most explicitly interested in the gift are also those that are the most anxious about the commodity. The ghosts of these texts—in their realization of the abstract power of the commodity—evoke what Christopher Cannon has aptly called the "spirit" of romance, even as such ghosts also intimate the return of something more archaic. Such ghosts are indeed properly specters rather than mere spirits, since they contain—as Derrida suggests of the commodity—a kind of trace materiality, a "bodiless body which we have recognized as making the difference between the specter and the spirit."[72] One way of thinking of that body is to call it, as Marx did, "congealed labor-time." Keston Sutherland draws our attention to Marx's specific term for this substance—*Gallerte*—as a site of horror and disgust in its naming of the gelatinous animal product derived from boiled skin, bone, and connective tissue.[73] More than a rhetorical flourish, the term is intended by Marx to emphasize what the commodity really is, the soup that results when "the individual himself is divided up."[74]

The symbolic violence of such a procedure is undeniably more abstract, less directly performative than the kind of violence that Cleges offers to the greedy courtiers (see chapter 2) or that the Green Knight performs on Gawain's body (see chapter 4). Yet if late romances suggest that such violence constitutes a "withering away"—a becoming ghostly—the same texts demonstrate that the disappearance of violence into the spectral forms of the commodity will never be complete, that the ghost is a return as well as a denial of violence. We have seen indeed that romance desires such returns precisely because its vision is so often emergently modern.

Of course, we still fantasize about such returns. If English romances were the "pulp fictions" of the Middle Ages, *Pulp Fiction* itself enjoined us, back in the 1990s, to delight in violence for the sake of nostalgia— to enjoy freely what was after all not really ours but someone else's. Over twenty years later, getting medieval remains not just a matter of violence, but of the ways in which violence can be enjoyed as what is *always* someone else's. Indeed, the continued need for such enjoyment is really an admission that we like romance, too. Not just Westerns and superhero movies, either, but horror films, grindhouse flicks, Manga, the hyper-violence of a visual culture that no longer sees its representations of pain and suffering as real but as referring always to other representations—violence that manages to be at once fully present and thoroughly mediated, ours and somebody else's.

Indeed, wherever our violence does not vanish seamlessly into the interstices of discourse and institution, we, too, are enjoying a romance. By the same token, medieval romances are thoroughly aware of the power of their own complexly mediated representations. To encounter them is to recognize that our own ambivalent desires have a long prehistory.

Notes

Preface

    1. Bloomfield, "Episodic Juxtaposition," was perhaps the first to note the ways in which romance lends itself to retrospective reading.

    2. See Knight, "Social Function," 101. His discussion is the most direct argument for a Marxist reading of the Middle English romances in particular.

    3. Fradenburg, "Simply Marvelous," 8.

    4. Ganim, *Style and Consciousness*, 18. The chapter in which this remark is found—"Community and Consciousness in Early English Romance" (16–54)—offers one early formulation of this idea and some of its stylistic consequences for the English romances.

    5. The injunction to "think the gift" is Derrida's (*Given Time*, 28–29). Bataille is quoted in Esposito, *Communitas*, 124, in the context of the latter's argument for a notion of community as a site of the gift—one that constitutes "a lack, a limit that is configured as an onus" (6). See especially the last two chapters in *Communitas* on Heidegger and Bataille, 86–134. For more on the concept of the noble gift, see chapter 1, note 24.

    6. On the idea that some Middle English romances can be understood as "critical texts" that are skeptical of chivalric ideals, see Knight, "Social Function," 114–15.

Chapter 1

    1. See Mehl, *The Middle English Romances*, 19.

2. See, respectively, Davenport, *Medieval Narrative*, 26; Hibbard, *Mediaeval Romance in England*, 144; and Cannon, *The Grounds of English Literature*, 175.

3. For *King Horn*, see Herzman, Drake, and Salisbury, eds., *Four Romances of England*, 17.

4. I refer both to the last chapter of Cannon's *Grounds*—titled "The Spirit of Romance: *King Horn, Havelok the Dane*, and *Floris and Blanche-flour*"—and to Putter and Gilbert, eds., *The Spirit of Medieval English Popular Romance*. For Mauss's discussion of the *hau* of the gift, see *The Gift*, 11.

5. Crane, *Insular Romance*, 23.

6. See Mauss, *The Gift*, 45. In *Given Time* Jacques Derrida refers to the "time of the gift" in the course of his extension and revision of Mauss's logic. For more on the concept of the noble gift, see note 24, below.

7. A classic statement of this argument, with particular respect to the manuscript containing the largest number of Middle English romances, is Hibbard, "The Auchinleck Manuscript." Though subsequently revised and sometimes challenged, her theory has been largely accepted. A refinement is suggested by Pearsall and Cunningham, eds., *The Auchinleck Manuscript*, viii–ix.

8. These evaluations can be found, respectively, in Hibbard, *Mediaeval Romance in England*, 144; McDonald, "A Polemical Introduction," 1; Ramsey, *Chivalric Romances*, 125; Kline, *Medieval Literature for Children*, 299; Tigges, "Romance and Parody," 143; and Furrow, "Chanson de Geste as Romance," 67.

9. See, respectively, Riddy, "Middle English Romance," 235; Meale, "'God Men / Wiues Maydnes and Alle Men,'" 219–20; Pearsall, "The Development of Middle English Romance," 18–19; Halverson, "*Havelok the Dane* and Society," 150; and Foster, ed., *Amis and Amiloun, Robert of Cisyle, and Sir Amadace*, 111. Riddy in particular was among the first to see how chivalric concerns could appeal to mercantile readers, asserting that the romance hero could be "a focus for the fantasies of people who are not themselves members of the knightly class, just as cowboys are part of the imaginative lives of people who have never ridden a horse" (238).

10. See Duggan, *The Cantar de Mio Cid*; Kay, *Chansons de Geste*; Kellogg, *Medieval Artistry and Exchange*; Miller, *Bloodtaking and Peacemaking*, 77–109; Baker, *Honour, Exchange, and Violence*; and especially Cowell, *Medieval Warrior Aristocracy*.

11. Smith, *Arts of Possession*, xv. Smith's consecutive chapters on *Sir Launfal* and the *Alliterative Morte* can be found on 154–222. For Jameson, see "Magical Narratives," 141–42.

12. Lacan, *Écrits*, 106.

13. Holsinger, *The Premodern Condition*, 81. Holsinger makes the case for Lacan's debt to Bataille most strongly earlier in the same chapter, when he

asserts that "Lacan sought to instill at the very core of psychoanalytic practice" an "ethics of sovereignty and expenditure" (60).

14. On gift exchange among the North Kabyle as "symbolic violence," see Bourdieu, *Outline of a Theory of Practice*, 192.

15. Harper, "*Pearl* in the Context of Fourteenth-Century Gift Economies," 424–25.

16. Ibid.

17. While not a signet ring, Richard's ring arguably functions as a symbol of the king's authority in this exchange. The measure of the duke's success would in that case be indicated by his ability to counter Richard's ultimate gift—the ring as a symbol of royal authority—with a yet more valuable example of the same object. What Richard seemingly wants to represent as absolute and most proximate to his royal identity—his authority as symbolized by the ring—turns out to be vexingly relative and open to negotiation.

18. Walsingham, *Chronica Maiora*, 297.

19. Bourdieu, *Outline of a Theory of Practice*, 173.

20. I refer to MacFarlane's classic account in *The Culture of Capitalism*.

21. Cowell, *Medieval Warrior Aristocracy*, 10–11.

22. The quotation is from Howell, *Commerce Before Capitalism*, 149. For other recent work in this area, see Davis, *The Gift in Sixteenth-Century France*; Groebner, *Liquid Assets, Dangerous Gifts*; and Ben-Amos, *Culture of Giving*.

23. Cowell, *Medieval Warrior Aristocracy*, 39.

24. See Harwood, who remarks that in the *Historia Walciodorensis Monasterii*, for instance, "the relation between nobility and the gift becomes a sort of refrain: the gift itself is noble (*nobile donum*), made by people behaving noble (*ut nobilis faciens donationem*), displaying their nobility by adding to others' wealth in noble fashion (*ut nobilis, nobiliter, ampliaverunt*)" ("*Gawain* and the Gift," 484).

25. Mauss, *The Gift*, 8.

26. Gasché, "Heliocentric Exchange," 101.

27. Mauss, *The Gift*, 104.

28. Ibid., 8, 20.

29. Ibid., 77.

30. Ibid., 4.

31. Bataille, "Notion of Expenditure," 121; and Sahlins, "Spirit of the Gift," 88, 84.

32. Bataille, *Accursed Share*, 45–62; and Sahlins, "Sprit of the Gift," 86.

33. This vivid summation of Bataille's enthusiasm for medieval *dépense* is offered by Holsinger, *Premodern Condition*, 45.

34. Duby, *Early Growth of the European Economy*, 50.

35. Bourdieu, *Practical Reason*, 94, and *Logic of Practice*, 110.

36. Bourdieu, *Logic of Practice*, 126.

37. Ibid., 133.

38. We might even say that symbolic violence is rendered, strictly speaking, impossible by the terms of Bourdieu's own analysis. I suggest in the ensuing chapters that this is something more than a post-structuralist cliché, though it obviously echoes pronouncements by (most recently) Slavoj Žižek about the impossibility of the symbolic and—closer to the concerns of gift theory—Jacques Derrida's notion of the gift as "the impossible" itself. What is "impossible" here is a kind of signifying work that—as we shall see—must repeat itself endlessly because it can never be fully realized, so that the very impossibility of such work becomes, paradoxically, the grounds of its persistence. For Žižek's most explicit statement of this Lacanian insight about "the impossibility of the Symbolic fully to 'become itself,' " see "Class Struggle or Postmodernism?," 120. For Derrida's insistence on the gift as "not impossible, but *the* impossible," see *Given Time*, 7.

39. Bourdieu, *Logic of Practice*, 126.

40. Cooper, *English Romance in Time*, 409–29.

41. Pearsall, "Development of Middle English Romance," 26.

42. Hibbard, *Mediaeval Romance in England*, 144.

43. Jost, "Why Is Middle English Romance So Violent?"

44. Duggan and Turville-Petre, eds., *Wars of Alexander*.

45. For *Havelok*, see Herzman, Drake, and Salisbury, eds., *Four Romances of England*, 146.

46. *Sir Gowther* can be found in Laskaya and Salisbury, eds., *Middle English Breton Lays*, 263–307, and *Libeaus* in Shuffelton, ed., *Codex Ashmole 61*, 111–63. For a comparison of these two romances in terms of their treatment of violence, see Mitchell-Smith, "Defining Violence in Middle English Romance," 148–61.

47. Simpson, "Violence, Narrative and Proper Name," 128.

48. Ganim, *Style and Consciousness*, 30.

49. Cohen, *Of Giants*; Heng, *Empire of Magic*; Ingham, *Sovereign Fantasies*.

50. For Crane's argument that English romances "primarily address the aristocracy's deteriorating situation," see her *Insular Romance*, 219. Riddy somewhat more capaciously defines the audience and ideology of the romances as "bourgeois-gentry" ("Middle English Romance," 132), yet she, too, notes the tendency of the romances to uphold traditional chivalric values.

51. Cannon, *Grounds of English Literature*, 14.

52. Whetter, *Understanding Genre*, 73.

53. *Floris*, lines 591–99, from Kooper, *Sentimental and Humorous Romances*. Subsequent citations are taken from this edition and cited by line number. Translations are mine unless otherwise noted.

54. Pelan, *Floire et Blancheflor*, lines 1638–40. Subsequent citations are given by line number.

55. This is implied by Murray's questioning of the "Sarazins kene" at lines 43–44: "He axede what hi soghte / Other to londe broghte." See Herzman, Drake, and Salisbury, eds., *Four Romances of England*, 18.

56. Kelly, "The Bartering of Blauncheflur."

57. Bahr, *Fragments and Assemblages*, 130. Bahr is concerned specifically with the version in the Auchinleck MS, likely produced for a mercantile audience in London.

58. Cannon, *Grounds of English Literature*, 188.

59. Galloway, "Layamon's Gift," 725.

60. Kooper, *Sentimental and Humorous Romances*, 19.

61. Ibid., 16.

62. Ibid., 19.

63. Kelly, "The Bartering of Blauncheflur," 103.

64. This precise rhyme (or, in one case, a slight variation) occurs in *Floris* at lines 523–24, 575–76, 758–59, and 772–73.

65. For the description of Tristrem as a "chess hustler," see Lupack, *Lancelot of the Laik and Sir Tristrem*, 151.

66. Adams, *Power Play*, 108. For "los" as loss of money or goods sustained through rash gambling, see *Middle English Dictionary*, s.v. "los," note 2(a).

67. See Pelan, *Floire et Blancheflor*, which has Floire refer explicitly in the scene to repayment: "*por çou qu'il m'ert gerredonés / se mon besoing ja mais veés*" (for my [gift] will be repaid / if ever you see my need) (lines 2235–36).

68. Kelly, "The Bartering of Blauncheflur," 106.

69. Here the French source instead describes the Judgment of Paris (*Floire et Blancheflor*, lines 465–90).

70. *Floire*, for instance, makes no mention of the means by which Aeneas attains possession of the cup. See *Floire et Blancheflor*, lines 490–91.

71. For a detailed comparison of the extant English manuscripts in this respect, see Geck, "'For Goddes Love, Sir, Mercy!'"

72. Bahr, *Fragments and Assemblages*, 130.

73. Ibid.

74. Ibid.

Chapter 2

1. All citations of *The Awntyrs off Arthure* are from Hahn, ed., *Sir Gawain*.

2. Hahn, ed., *Sir Gawain*, 171.

3. All citations for *Sir Launfal* are from Laskaya and Salisbury, eds., *The Middle English Breton Lays*, while those for *Sir Amadace* are taken from Foster, ed., *Amis and Amiloun*.

4. For the older view of the poem as an amalgam of the work of two distinct authors, perhaps with the mediation of a third hand, see Lübke, "*The Aunters of Arthur*," and Hanna, "*The Awntyrs off Arthure*." The most significant challenge to this view is from Spearing, who argues for a reading of the poem as a diptych (*Medieval to Renaissance*, 129). Phillips suggests a tripartite structure ("*The Awntyrs off Arthure*," 71).

5. For more on the concept of the noble gift, see chapter 1, note 24.

6. Spearing, *Medieval to Renaissance*, 138.

7. Ibid., 139.

8. Martin, "*The Awntyrs off Arthure*," 194.

9. Chism, *Alliterative Revivals*, 255.

10. Ibid.

11. Citations for *Sir Cleges* are taken from Laskaya and Salisbury, eds., *The Middle English Breton Lays*.

12. Foster, ed., *Amis and Amiloun*, 120.

13. Ibid.

14. Cannon, *The Grounds of English Literature*, 172–209.

15. Mehl, *The Middle English Romances*, 85.

16. Putter, "Arthurian Romance," 241, 244.

17. For Crane's argument that English romances "primarily address the aristocracy's deteriorating situation" (219), see her *Insular Romance*.

18. See, respectively, Mehl, *The Middle English Romances*, 85; Foster, "Simplicity, Complexity, and Morality," 400; Shuffelton, ed., *Codex Ashmole 61*, 491; and Hazell, who finds the violence of the romance's payback scene "disquieting" and argues that the scene's excessiveness "darkens the elevated themes that open and close the poem" (*Poverty in Late Middle English Literature*, 43–44). Yet where she sees a disjuncture between the violence of the scene and the overall tone of the poem, I want to suggest that in fact this violence is central to the poem's meaning.

19. Muscatine, *The Old French Fabliaux*, 73.

20. Schelp sees the reference to Cleges's fallen "pryde" as evidence that the poem is an exemplary romance and Cleges himself an overly prideful hero (*Exemplarische Romanzen im Mittelenglischen*, 93–97). Knight argues convincingly, however, that Isumbras is the "the opposite of Cleges" in being "deprived of his lordly and familial joys because of 'pryde of gold and fee'" ("Celticity and Christianity," 35). Like Knight, I see no evidence that Cleges's pride is an issue in the poem, especially as his giving is directed toward explicitly devotional ends.

21. Putter, "Arthurian Romance," 242.

22. Dame Clarys does overhear her husband's "mournyng" (121), but nothing in her subsequent advice to him suggests that she is aware of the miracle that has just occurred. See lines 125–44.

23. See, for instance, Loomis, "*Sir Cleges* and Unseasonable Growth in Hagiology."

24. Though the first to demonstrate a likely source for the poet's knowledge of the Miraculous Cherries in the N-Town mystery cycle, Carr himself rejects the notion that the cherries have a purely figural meaning as reminders of Christ's nativity ("The Middle English Nativity Cherry Tree," 135, 147). His caution is a valuable corrective to readings discussed above that have stressed the poem's miraculous and devotional elements.

25. Laskaya and Salisbury, eds., *Middle English Breton Lays*, 402, note to line 194.

26. Carr remarks similarly that "Uther would scarcely value seasonable cherries as highly as he does this miraculous fruit" ("The Middle English Nativity Cherry Tree," 146).

27. Shuffelton, ed., *Codex Ashmole 61*, 492.

28. John Gower uses the phrase "al is bot a chirie faire" (*Confessio* 1.454). Shuffelton discusses the proverbial nature of the motif ("Romance, Popular Style, and the *Confessio Amantis*," 80–81).

29. Derrida, *Given Time*.

30. See *Sir Amadace*, lines 253–64, and *Sir Launfal*, lines 409–15.

31. The general point that the romance Other reflects contradictions internal to aristocratic society is made in an influential form by Jameson, "Magical Narratives," 161.

32. Shuffelton, ed., *Codex Ashmole 61*, 492. A discussion of this motif can be found in Reinhard, "Strokes Shared."

33. Laskaya and Salisbury, eds., *Middle English Breton Lays*, 372.

34. See also Hazell: "It is always tempting to rewrite text as we would like to see it, and it is easy to imagine Cleges appealing to Uther for justice" (*Poverty in Late Middle English Literature*, 43).

35. See, for instance, McKnight's claim that Cleges is "particularly a minstrel hero" (*Middle English Humorous Tales*, lxii).

36. Putter, "Arthurian Romance," 242.

37. Noted also by Laskaya and Salisbury, eds., *Middle English Breton Lays*, in their critical introduction: "as if Cleges were a minstrel himself, he tells the story of retribution so compellingly that the 'lordes lewghe [laugh], both old and yenge' (line 517), and, like many a talented minstrel, he is amply rewarded for his services" (374).

38. The variation is noted by Laskaya and Salisbury, eds., *Middle English Breton Lays*, 406, note to line 484, although they do not remark on its significance.

39. See, for instance, George Kane's dismissal of the poem as "undistinguished," full of "bourgeois primness and affected gentility" (*Middle English Literature*, 19).

40. Shuffelton, for one, understandably splits the difference, speaking of the poem's "Arthurian (or pre-Arthurian) setting" (*Codex Ashmole 61*, 492).

41. Putter, "Arthurian Romance," 244.

42. See *Middle English Dictionary*, s. v. "gost," n2a, "The soul of a dead person." The earliest use listed is attributed to Chaucer's *Knight's Tale*, line 2768. A related sense with earlier attested dates is (2b) "a damned soul, whether in hell or returned to earth," which gives 1225 as an early date. Yet that use, in the *Trinity Homilies*, refers to ghosts that are hellbound or already there, as does the reference listed for the *Speculum Guy of Warwick* (circa 1330). The evidence would thus seem to suggest the late fourteenth century as the moment in which the dominant modern sense of the term begins to take shape.

43. See, respectively, Heng, *Empire of Magic*, 56, and Knight, "The Social Function," 107.

44. Foster, ed., *Amis and Amiloun*, 142.

45. Spearing, *Medieval Poet as Voyeur*, 107.

46. Bliss, ed., *Sir Launfal*, 94.

47. Knight, "The Social Function," 106–7, discusses the Lombard associations of a terrifying giant named "Lamberte" in *Lybeaus Desconus*, a Middle English romance that—like *Launfal*—draws on Lombardy as a site of anxiety. See also Shuffelton, ed., *Codex Ashmole 61*, note to line 1574 of *Lybeaus Desconus*.

48. Smith, *Arts of Possession*, 183.

49. See also the Middle English *Octavian*, in which the hero must borrow armor described as "full rysty" (939) in order to do battle with a giant. The most recent edition is by Hudson, ed., *Four Middle English Romances*, 45–114.

50. Spearing, *Medieval Poet as Voyeur*, 107.

51. An early account of the episode is provided by Cross, who notes its parallels with the *Gesta Romanorum*, among other analogues ("The Celtic Elements," 635).

52. Smith, *Arts of Possession*, 186–87.

53. See also Putter, "Gifts and Commodities," 380.

54. Simpson, *Reform and Cultural Revolution*, 268–69. See also Foster's remark that "*Sir Amadace* seems to be a 'commercial romance'" (*Amis and Amiloun*, 114). Yet see lines 391–92, 497, 608–9, 722–25, and 845 for the poem's insistence on the feudal nature of the wealth it imagines, with almost haunting repetitiveness, as consisting in the perquisites of lordship: "fild and frithe, toune and towre."

55. The phrase occurs at act 2, scene 9, line 90, and can be found in Greenblatt, ed., *The Norton Shakespeare*.

56. See lines 387–401 of *Sir Orfeo* in Laskaya and Salisbury, eds., *Middle English Breton Lays*.

57. Steel, comment (dated April 13, 2007, 4:20 pm) on "Quote of the Day."

58. Brewer, "The Popular English Metrical Romances," 59.

59. Johnston, "Knights and Merchants Unite," 738–39.

60. Simpson, *Reform and Cultural Revolution*, reads this as a scene in which "the knight must commodify his own wife and son" so that he is in effect forced to "act like a merchant, and pay back exactly what he promised, *without the possibility of paying more*" (268). But see Putter's remark that "goods" here "include people as well as things, and so the line cannot be drawn at commodities" ("Gifts and Commodities," 389). Whether there is a commodity here or not is arguably the anxiety of this scene.

61. See, respectively, Johnston, *Romance and the Gentry*, 238; Hardman, "The Unity of the Ireland Manuscript," 60; Foster, "Simplicity, Complexity, and Morality," 406. But see also Putter, "Gifts and Commodities," whose reading seems to imply, as does Johnston's, a gentry context.

62. See Simpson's claim that "reassertion of the enclosed system of noble generosity in *Amadace* can only be made by a preparedness to accept all that threatens enclosure" (*Reform and Cultural Revolution*, 268).

63. The poem's most recent editor remarks on this comparison, noting how the test put by the ghost "parallels that of God's testing of Abraham (*Genesis* 22), where the father will slay his son rather than break his vow to God. Like Isaac, the child is spared when the angel bids 'cease' and provides the redemptive substitution of a ram stuck in thorns, which medieval commentaries interpreted as a figuration of Him who died on the Cross. Perhaps this is why the poet sets Amadace's test on the Eve of Christ's nativity" (Foster, ed., *Amis and Amiloun*, note to line 801 of *Sir Amadace*).

Chapter 3

A previous version of this argument focuses on Chaucer's relationship to the idea of chivalric adventure. See Walter Wadiak, "Chaucer's *Knight's Tale* and the Politics of Distinction," *Philological Quarterly* 89, nos. 2/3 (2010): 159–84.

1. For "burgesses," Chesterton, *Chaucer*, 39; "delusions," Cannon, *The Grounds of English Literature*, 201; "ethos," Koff, *Chaucer and the Art of Storytelling*, 35; "ostentatiously nonaristocratic," Patterson, *Chaucer and the Subject of History*, 40.

2. This and all subsequent references to Chaucer's poetry are from Benson, *The Riverside Chaucer*.

3. The point that accounting is vital to Chaucer's sense of himself as a poet is made by Galloway, "The Account Book and the Treasure," 92–103. Galloway, too, recognizes the potential for Chaucer's poetry to fuse noble and mercantile values, remarking that in "Envoy to Bukton," Chaucer's deployment of the "technologies of mercantile accounting . . . constitutes a gift in the covertly reciprocal spirit of noble culture" (103).

4. Cannon, *The Grounds of English Literature*, 207.

5. For a detailed account of Chaucer's precise social location as a squire "en service," see Strohm, *Social Chaucer*, 13.

6. Crow and Olson, eds., *Chaucer Life-Records*, 17, 275, 113, 133, 272.

7. Carlson, *Chaucer's Jobs*, 5.

8. On Chaucer as "synonymous with surplus value in literature," see Cannon, *The Grounds of English Literature*, 207.

9. Meyer-Lee, *Poets and Power*, 1–12.

10. Benson, *The Riverside Chaucer*, 987, note to line 1315.

11. I refer, of course, to Dryden's famous line about Chaucer: "Here is God's plenty." It was also Dryden who first imagined Chaucer to be the "father of English poetry" ("Preface to Fables Ancient and Modern," 2.280). On the ways in which early modern writers in particular imagined Chaucer's legacy as a gift, see Krier, "Receiving Chaucer," 1–9.

12. For more on the concept of the noble gift, see chapter 1, note 24.

13. Cannon, *The Grounds of English Literature*, 198–200.

14. Mauss, *The Gift*, 47–48, and Harwood, "Chaucer and the Gift," 38.

15. Harwood, "Chaucer and the Gift," 33.

16. See, for instance, David, "Sentimental Comedy," and Crane, *Gender and Romance*, 93–131.

17. This reading of *The Shipman's Tale* (though not in the context of its possible comparison to *The Franklin's Tale*) is explored most fully by Patterson, *Chaucer and the Subject of History*, 349.

18. Harwood, "Chaucer and the Gift," 31, reads the feast of *The Squire's Tale* with which the Franklin's textual fragment begins in this way. See Harwood's related assertion that the gift in both *The Squire's Tale* and *The Franklin's Tale* "solicits a return" and thus "economizes itself" (33).

19. For the argument that the Knight has a personal investment in the scenes that he narrates, see Patterson, *Chaucer and the Subject of History*, 227–28.

20. Muscatine, "Form, Texture, and Meaning," 920.

21. This phrase appears in the title of Patterson's chapter on *The Knight's Tale* in *Chaucer and the Subject of History*, 165–230.

22. Jones in *Chaucer's Knight* advances what has become a famously iconoclastic reading of the Knight as a mercenary, perhaps on the model of Sir John

Hawkwood, a fourteenth-century *condottiere* who died in 1394 and whom Chaucer is known to have met more than once.

23. Crane, *Gender and Romance*, 10; Pearsall, "The Development of Middle English Romance," 12.

24. Kahrl, "Chaucer's 'Squire's Tale' and the Decline of Chivalry."

25. See Shoaf's assertion that the Miller "pays the Knight back, 'quites' him, by almost retelling the *Knight's Tale*" (*Chaucer, Dante, and the Currency of the Word*, 168).

26. Fradenburg, *Sacrifice Your Love*, 167.

27. Epstein, "'With Many a Floryn,'" 63.

28. Ibid.

29. Ibid., 65.

30. Levi-Strauss's well-known analysis of the role of women as gift objects in precapitalist societies, especially in relation to the incest taboo, is found in his *Elementary Structures of Kinship*. For a detailed analysis of Emilye's pivotal role in the tale, see Crane, *Gender and Romance*, 169–203.

31. Muscatine, "Form, Texture, and Meaning," is the founding text of this tradition. A sampling of those inspired by Muscatine's reading would include Halverson, "Aspects of Order in the *Knight's Tale*"; Olson, "Chaucer's Epic Statement"; and Van, "Theseus and the 'Right Way.'"

32. An early example of suspicion about Theseus is offered by Webb, "A Reinterpretation of Chaucer's Theseus." See also Aers, *Chaucer, Langland, and the Creative Imagination*, 174–95; Patterson, *Chaucer and the Subject of History*, 165–230; and Blake, "Order and the Noble Life," who offers a critique of Theseus on theological grounds.

33. See, for instance, Brown and Butcher, *The Age of Saturn*, 235–36.

34. Fradenburg, *Sacrifice Your Love*, 167; emphasis in the original.

35. Such love service could itself be a form of the gift, as Massey suggests in relation to *Troilus and Ciseyde*. Indeed, for Massey, the *Troilus* involves "an ideal act of unidirectional gift-giving originating in a feminized male lover" ("'The Double Bind,'" 21). If so, it is perhaps not a coincidence that *The Knight's Tale*, Chaucer's other ambitious romance, also concerns an attempt to "think the gift," as I propose later in this chapter.

36. Green, "Arcite at Court."

37. Blodgett, "Chaucerian Pryvetee," 486.

38. One way of resolving this dilemma would be to read "honestly" here to mean "fittingly, properly," as the *Middle English Dictionary* chooses to do. This leaves unresolved, however, the question of what might be fitting about Arcite's slyness, especially since another meaning of "honestly" is "in an upright way, virtuously." See *Middle English Dictionary*, s. v. "honestliche."

39. These objects disappear, respectively, in the romances narrated by the Wife, Squire, and Franklin.

40. Boccaccio states with contrasting brevity that Arcite "went to the house of Theseus." See Boccaccio, *Theseid*, 143. The phrase "cynical Latin gallantries" is from Lewis, "What Chaucer Really Did," 75.

41. Wallace, *Chaucerian Polity*, 205. This is again the sense in which Chaucer refers to "aventure" in *The Canon's Yeoman's Tale*, when a character declares that those who would turn a profit "moste putte oure good in aventure" (VIII. 964) like "a marchant" (965).

42. The identification of "romances of prys" as literally romances with a certain "price" is made by Cannon, *The Grounds of English Literature*, 204–5.

43. On the ways in which *The Franklin's Tale* plays with the idea of adventure, see Crane, *Gender and Romance*, 166.

44. Though see Jones, *Chaucer's Knight*, 92.

45. See Patterson's observation that "the shape of the narrative argues that what appears to be 'aventure' or 'cas' is in fact 'destynee'" (*Chaucer and the Subject of History*, 208).

46. On the idea of Arcite as a remnant, see Fradenburg, *Sacrifice Your Love*, 167.

47. See, for instance, Hallissy's assertion that "Chaucer's godlike creativity surpasses Theseus's in Athens" ("Writing a Building," 256). The highly influential reading of the tale as a representation of "noble life" is by Muscatine ("Form, Texture, and Meaning," 929), who cites the architecture of Theseus's "lystes" as an example of the tale's "symmetry" (915–16).

48. Carlson, *Chaucer's Jobs*, 27.

49. Brewer, *Chaucer and His World*, 190.

50. McTaggart, *Shame and Guilt in Chaucer*, 58.

51. Ibid., 59.

52. Esposito, *Communitas*, 33.

53. Fradenburg, "Sacrificial Desire," 65; emphasis added.

Chapter 4

I am grateful to Patrick Blong, my former classmate and a fellow medievalist, for a chance conversation in which he suggested that the green girdle is first and foremost a covering for Gawain's wound. Our conversation enriched my understanding of how the girdle works, not just as a gift, but as a screen intended to disguise the hero's vulnerability. It will be clear what my reading of the girdle owes to this insight.

1. See, for instance, Johnson, *The Voice of the Gawain-Poet*, 40–46. But see also Chism, who argues that the poem ultimately "situates Gawain in a different narrative, not cyclical, festive, and unchanging, but linear and irrevocable" (*Alliterative Revivals*, 105).

2. All citations of *Sir Gawain and the Green Knight* are from the edition of Tolkien and Gordon.

3. For more on the concept of the noble gift, see chapter 1, note 24.

4. See Muscatine, *Poetry and Crisis*, 37–69, esp. 56ff.; Taylor, "Commerce and Comedy"; Mann, "Price and Value"; and Shoaf, *The Poem as Green Girdle*, 68. For other discussions of the poem's ambiguously commercial logic, see Burrow, *Reading of Sir Gawain*, 76–77 and 88–89, and Trigg, "Romance of Exchange."

5. Like Mann's "Price and Value," Riddy, "Giving and Receiving," stresses the function of exchange in this poem as bringing together court and urban circles: "the gifts—the chessboard and the Sword with the Two Rings in *Walewein* and the green girdle in *Sir Gawain and the Green Knight*—which seem to be emblems of the aristocratic value system, are a point at which the city and the court come together" (112).

6. Aers, *Faith, Ethics, and Church*, 79–80.

7. Harwood, "*Gawain* and the Gift," 490.

8. For Fradenburg, the chivalric subject is "already lost to life" in his cultivation of "an intentional relationship to violence" (*Sacrifice Your Love*, 206).

9. Derrida, *Given Time*, 10, 147.

10. For an interesting account of Gawain's traditional associations with plenitude and surplus, see Walters, "More Bread from Stone."

11. As will be clear, I side with interpretations that—without neglecting the poem's close engagement with the theological—nonetheless recognize chivalry as the value system that is ultimately most central to the poem and serves as its principal fascination. Harwood, "*Gawain* and the Gift," 492–93n1, offers a concise summary of this debate. Obviously, though, it is impossible to fully separate the poem's chivalric from its theological concerns, as I argue below in attending to the Eucharistic associations of Gawain's pledge drink with Bertilak and (later in the poem) the identification of the Green Knight's "tappe" with divine *gratia*—an identification that gives ironic point to the violence of the poem's climactic scene.

12. Algazi, "Feigned Reciprocities," 122.

13. Miller, "The Ends of Excitement," 221.

14. Ibid., 245.

15. Smith, *Arts of Possession*, xvi.

16. On the uses and limits of the gift as "repression" in the psychoanalytic sense, see Derrida, *Given Time*, 16. Derrida's argument that this intended

repressive function of the gift is in some sense "impossible" is borne out spectacularly by the events of *Sir Gawain*, as I argue below.

17. Miller, "The Ends of Excitement," 218, 215.

18. Harwood, "*Gawain* and the Gift," offers the most sophisticated explication of this view. See also Champion, "Grace versus Merit." Shoaf, *The Poem as Green Girdle*, offers an intriguing reading of the nick or "nirt" as a symbolic act of circumcision.

19. Bourdieu, *Outline of a Theory of Practice*, 172.

20. See Otter, *Inventiones*, 59–61. Otter does not discuss *Sir Gawain*, but the poem's opening is obviously indebted to the historiographical tradition that she explores.

21. See *Middle English Dictionary*, s.v. "patroun" (n.), 1a ("the lord of a person or place; owner of riches") but also 1b ("the founder of a religious order or faith; also, a benefactor of a religious institution, patron") and 2b ("one who has the right of patronage").

22. Also remarked by Shoaf, *The Poem as Green Girdle*, 56. Unlike him, however, I see the initial point of the passage as contrastive in relation to the plenary-court scene that follows. Only later will it become clear that Arthur, too, loves strife, and even then it is a desire that gets expressed in a strictly mediated form, as I show below.

23. As Harwood remarks, "it is perhaps a bad sign that [Gawain] ends fit 1 by hanging up the ax, as if it were a profit" ("*Gawain* and the Gift," 488).

24. Bourdieu, *The Logic of Practice*, 105–7.

25. The lady's notorious reference to her "cors" is hard to pin down, as "my cors" may simply mean "me." As Burrow remarks, "there is a saving ambiguity in the lady's offer" (*A Reading of Sir Gawain and the Green Knight*, 81).

26. See Derrida, *Of Hospitality*.

27. Scala notes that the contract only "appears to be a lively manifestation of hospitality" (*Absent Narratives*, 52). As an offer that Gawain cannot politely refuse, Bertilak's request arguably constitutes his first act of aggression.

28. Benveniste, *Indo-European Language and Society*, 72.

29. Mann, "Price and Value," 313.

30. Tlusty, *Bacchus and Civic Order*, 106.

31. Of course, many critics do read Gawain sympathetically, but the history of scholarship on the poem has been marked at the same time by a strong tendency to qualify and even to moralize away that sympathy, to insist on the ways in which "sympathy" should be "accompanied by a certain detachment" (Spearing, *The Gawain-Poet*, 187). See also Barron's almost identical notion of "detached sympathy" (*Sir Gawain and the Green Knight*, 15), as well as Davenport, *The Art of the Gawain-Poet*, 183. The legacy of such readings can be observed in the unusual degree to which interpretation continues to be framed

in terms of the characterological, even as allowances are generously made for Gawain's situation. I want to suggest that his situation—his enmeshment in an economy of violent giving and taking—drives the poem's course and determines its meaning in ways that have not been fully recognized.

32. Harwood, "*Gawain* and the Gift," 491.

33. On this point, see Borroff, "'Sir Gawain and the Green Knight,'" 110, as well as Miller, "The Ends of Excitement," 225.

34. I refer to Bourdieu's distinction between *violence douce* and *violence ouverte*, literally "sweet" and "overt" violence, roughly tracking the distinction made in English between "real" and "symbolic" violence.

35. Among them is the so-called hood game initiated by Bertilak at lines 983–85, when he hangs his hood on a spear in what Cook calls "a grim reminder [for Gawain] of the head-game he was involved in" ("The Play-Element in *Sir Gawain and the Green Knight*," 22).

36. Chism, for instance, speaks of "a fated contest against an opponent who held dice that this time were weighted cunningly against him" (*Alliterative Revivals*, 103).

37. Mann, "Price and Value," 312.

38. Ibid., 313.

39. Esposito, *Communitas*, 6.

40. All citations of both *Pearl* and *Patience* are taken from Andrew and Waldron, *The Poems of the Pearl Manuscript*.

41. This motto famously belongs to the Most Noble Order of the Garter, created by Edward III in 1348, and was appended to the poem's concluding stanza by the scribe of Cotton Nero A.x. On the ambiguous role of shame in the formation of the order, see Trigg, *Shame and Honor*.

42. Cohen, *Of Giants*, 165.

43. All citations for both versions of *Carle*, as well as for *The Turke and Sir Gawain*, are taken from Hahn, *Sir Gawain*.

44. Hahn, *Sir Gawain*, argues for this identification of the "kyngus keyis," the idea being that entry can be forced in execution of a royal writ (note to line 203).

45. Indeed, the question of hospitality, for Derrida, takes us "from impossibility to impossibility" (*Of Hospitality*, 75).

46. Benveniste, *Indo-European Language and Society*, 72.

47. Ibid., 71.

48. Translation of lines from *Erec et Enide* by James Simpson. It is precisely "Evrain's *franchise* [his "freedom" or generosity] that instructs him to kill any bourgeois who takes in a knight of renown," as Simpson remarks (*Troubling Arthurian Histories*, 402).

49. Cohen, *Of Giants*, 165.

50. See Cohen's placement of the poem as a whole "in the arena of the law's obscene double" (163).

51. Hahn, *Sir Gawain*, 229.

52. References to lines 399 and 403 are to *The Carle of Carlisle*. Subsequent references are to the older *Sir Gawain and the Carle of Carlisle*. Both versions are from Hahn, *Sir Gawain*.

53. See, respectively, Fradenburg, "The Wife of Bath's Passing Fancy," 34–35, and Hahn, *Sir Gawain*, 8.

54. Wright, "Churl's Courtesy," 658; and Brandsen, "*Sir Gawain and the Carl of Carlisle*," 306.

55. As Smith notes in his discussion of the roughly contemporaneous *Wynnere and Wastoure* (circa 1353), merchants could have "marks" in both senses, since they often created identifying signs in imitation of the nobility (*Arts of Possession*, 87–101).

56. Hahn, *Sir Gawain*, 111, considers this possibility in light of surviving versions from devotional literature—stories whose details, however, remain obscure.

57. Mason, "Timeo Barones et Dona Ferentes," 67. The trope of penitential abbey building is of course a mainstay of romance from Marie de France onward, and medieval magnates often founded abbeys in their wills.

58. Pollack, "Border States," 22, 19.

59. Barber argues for a "missing leaf" from the Porkington MS, but the poem's most recent editor is less sure, stating only that the beheading scene is "inexplicably missing" from the Porkington version and thus leaving open the possibility of some form of scribal intention. See Barber, *Arthur of Albion*, 107, and Hahn, *Sir Gawain*, 391.

60. Hahn, *Sir Gawain*, 353, cites the Grail story as the source of the motif here, and there is evidence for the influence of that story on other Gawain-romances such as *Gologras*, but the notion of enchanted food that must not be eaten goes back at least to the myth of Persephone.

61. *Turke* renders its scenes of violence comic in a number of ways, notably in its description of a game of tennis played with a giant "ball of brasse" (line 187). Such moments work to domesticate what in *Carle* are very real possibilities of harm, culminating in death.

62. Thus, for instance, Scaglione, referring to Elias, argues that "*Sir Gawain* clearly marks a high point in the history of the civilizing process" (*Knights at Court*, 137).

63. "Gawayn" in Chaucer's *The Squire's Tale* names the possessor of a giftlike cultural capital, an "olde courteisye" grounded in the capacity to enact submission in the form of "heigh reverence and obeisaunce" (V. 93, 94–95).

64. On the role of "downward cultural diffusion" in the transition from romance to ballad, see Coss, "Aspects of Cultural Diffusion," 73.

Chapter 5

This chapter expands and revises a reading of the *Gest* that initially appeared, in a less developed form, in Walter Wadiak, " 'What Shall These Bowes Do?': Violence and the Gift in *A Gest of Robyn Hode*," *Exemplaria* 24, no. 3 (2012): 238–59.

1. Jameson, *The Political Unconscious*, 107.

2. The quotation is from Nerlich, *Ideology of Adventure*, 62. Nerlich himself asserts (in the full passage on the same page) that this process "began relatively early in England." See also Cannon, *The Grounds of English Literature*, 172–209.

3. For more on the concept of the noble gift, see chapter 1, note 24.

4. Pearsall, "The Development of Middle English Romance," 12.

5. Hilton, "The Origins of Robin Hood," 36.

6. Kane, "Horseplay," 101.

7. Green, "Violence in the Early Robin Hood Poems," 276.

8. The translation cited for *The Outlaw's Song of Trailbaston* is that of Dobson and Taylor, *Rymes of Robin Hood*, 250–54. The original poem can be found in Aspin, *Anglo-Norman Political Songs*, 67–78.

9. The tale *Adam Bell, Clim of the Clough, and William of Cloudesley* can be found in Knight and Ohlgren, *Robin Hood and Other Outlaw Tales*, 235–67.

10. Jones, " 'Oublïé ai Chevalerie,' " 90.

11. Bataille, "Medieval French Literature," 208. For the view that the ballads owe much to epic and saga, see Holt, *Robin Hood*, 63.

12. This and subsequent citations of the poem are from Chrétien de Troyes, *Erec et Enide*. Translations are from Chrétien de Troyes, *Arthurian Romances*.

13. Cannon, *Middle English Literature*, 56. On the subtext of outlawry in *Sir Orfeo*, see Evans, "*Sir Orfeo* and Bare Life," 208.

14. Spence, "A Lost Manuscript," 1.

15. Gray, "The Robin Hood Poems," 12.

16. Ibid.

17. Garbaty, "Rhyme, Romance, Ballad, Burlesque, and the Confluence of Form."

18. Fowler, *A Literary History of the Popular Ballad*, argues that the ballad is an essentially post-medieval form, whatever its obscure roots in medieval oral tradition. For a refutation, see Green, "The Ballad and the Middle Ages."

19. Tardif, "The 'Mystery' of Robin Hood," 133; Ohlgren, *Robin Hood*, 136.

20. For a compelling argument that this indeterminacy provides evidence of cross-fertilization, see Radulescu, "Ballad and Popular Romance in the Percy Folio."

21. Hales and Furnivall, eds., *Bishop Percy's Folio Manuscript*, 122.

22. Singman, *Robin Hood*, 132.

23. Ramsey, for instance, defines the tale as a "rebel romance" (*Chivalric Romances*, 93), while Skeat classes it as a ballad (*The Tale of Gamelyn*, vii). For Pollard, the tale "links the Robin Hood tales . . . with an older tradition of exiled aristocratic outlaws" (*Imagining Robin Hood*, 14). The poem's most recent editors favor Francis James Child's term "popular epic," while comparing the poem to "long battle ballads of the sixteenth century such as *Chevy Chase* or *The Battle of Otterburn*" (Knight and Ohlgren, eds., *Robin Hood and Other Outlaw Tales*, 185).

24. Returning to an old theory that links *Gamelyn* to *The Cook's Tale*, Edwards has recently mounted a strong case that *Gamelyn* was "probably intended to be included in the *Canterbury Tales* from an early stage in the textual history of the work" ("*The Canterbury Tales* and *Gamelyn*," 90).

25. All citations to *The Tale of Gamelyn* are from Knight and Ohlgren, eds., *Robin Hood and Other Outlaw Tales*, 80–168.

26. Putter, "Gifts and Commodities," 378. For an analysis of the etymological connections between gift exchange and community, see Benveniste, *Indo-European Language and Society*, 79.

27. Knight and Ohlgren, eds., *Robin Hood and Other Outlaw Tales*, 186.

28. This description is applied by Herzman, Drake, and Salisbury to *Havelok the Dane* (*Four Romances of England*, 77).

29. The *Gesta Herewardi* is a Latin romance of outlawry written in England in the early twelfth century. Like Gamelyn, Hereward, the poem's hero, is a figure of dangerous excess—"readily provoking fights among those of his own age and often stirring up strife among his elders in town and village"— yet also "particularly liberal" (Ohlgren, ed., *Medieval Outlaws*, 41). It is in fact Hereward's liberality that marks the romance's initial crisis:

> When his father went visiting his estates, Hereward and his gang often got there first, distributing his father's goods amongst his own friends and supporters. And on some of his father's properties he even appointed stewards and servants of his own to see to provisions for his men. And so his father ensured that he was banished from his homeland by Edward the Confessor, disclosing everything that he had perpetrated against his parents and against the inhabitants of the locality. And this being done, he at once acquired the name of Outlaw, being driven away from his father and

his native land when he was eighteen years old. (Ohlgren, ed., *Medieval Outlaws*, 41)

A dispute over household management (albeit with a father rather than a brother) is central to this scene as it is to the analogous moment in *Gamelyn*. More profoundly, both scenes imagine chivalric community as arising out of gifts given and received—a restoration of feudal relations otherwise under threat in the various ways these poems chronicle.

30. Keen, *Outlaws of Medieval Legend*, 90.

31. Bourdieu, *The Logic of Practice*, 126.

32. Crane, *Insular Romance*, 74.

33. Scattergood, "*The Tale of Gamelyn*," 160.

34. Knight and Ohlgren, eds., *Robin Hood and Other Outlaw Tales*, 190.

35. For a reading that takes seriously the problems raised by Sir John's award of more land to Gamelyn, see Iersel, "The Twenty-Five Ploughs of Sir John."

36. Knight and Ohlgren point out that this saint is "an appropriate person for a knight to swear by, perhaps especially as Sir John divides his possessions" (*Robin Hood and Other Outlaw Tales*, 220–21). Saint Martin is often invoked during scenes of charity in Middle English romances. See, for instance, the reference to "Seyn Martin" at line 2014 in *Amis and Amiloun*, at the point when Amis offers drink to Amiloun while the latter is disguised as a beggar (Foster, *Amis and Amiloun, Robert of Cisyle, and Sir Amadace*, 66).

37. Shannon argues that Sir John's decision "was not so unusual as might be supposed" and would have been permitted by contemporary law under the specific conditions established by the story ("Medieval Law in *The Tale of Gamelyn*," 459).

38. See Menuge, *Medieval English Wardship*, 41–61, for a sophisticated reading of the tale's inheritance themes.

39. Bradbury, "*Gamelyn*," 133, 130.

40. Ibid., 144, 142, 141.

41. The genre of the poem continues to be a matter of debate. Child's placement of the tale with the ballads (*English and Scottish Ballads*, 5.42–123) has been challenged or qualified by more recent criticism suggesting affinities to romance, among other genres. See, for instance, Bessinger's definition of the poem as a "heroic ballad-romance" ("*The Gest of Robin Hood* Revisited," 364). It seems clear, at the very least, that the *Gest* is "not strictly a ballad" (Dobson and Taylor, eds., *Rymes of Robyn Hood*, 8). My reading similarly locates the poem's genre somewhere between ballad and romance.

42. See, for instance, Holt, "The Origins and Audience," 215.

43. *The True Tale of Robin Hood* can be found in Knight and Ohlgren, eds., *Robin Hood and Other Outlaw Tales*, 602–25.

44. This amusingly reactionary play, in which the outlaws surrender their weapons and caper gladsomely upon learning of the accession of Charles II, can be found in Knight and Ohlgren, eds., *Robin Hood and Other Outlaw Tales*, 441–52.

45. Ibid., 82.

46. Ohlgren, *Robin Hood*, 82.

47. Even if the *Gest* serves to illustrate the truth of Derrida's contention that "the gift, *if there is any*, would no doubt be related to economy" (*Given Time*, 7, emphasis in original).

48. Holt, "The Origins and Audience," 221; Ohlgren, *Robin Hood*, 177; Gray, "The Robin Hood Poems," 26; Tardif, "The 'Mystery' of Robin Hood," 357.

49. A useful summary of the debate over audience is offered by Knight and Ohlgren, eds., *Robin Hood and Other Outlaw Tales*, 81–82.

50. Bourdieu, *The Logic of Practice*, 105.

51. Ohlgren, *Robin Hood*, 184.

52. Ibid., 186.

53. Gray, "Everybody's Robin Hood," 32.

54. Mauss, *The Gift*, 13.

55. As Kitell remarks, "*courtoisie* is a term with many meanings, from gift to bribery," and can also signify "interest for loans" (*From "Ad Hoc" to Routine*, 163). The ambiguity of the term reflects what I read as the broader ambiguity inhering in Sir Richard's dealings with Robin, which are characterized by a movement from loan to gift.

56. Keen, *Outlaws of Medieval Legend*, 131–32.

57. See, for instance, Coss's claim that the episode is "very reminiscent of the midland tale [i.e., *Gamelyn*], which may have been among the compiler's sources" ("Aspects of Cultural Diffusion," 336). Andrew James Johnston stresses the violence of both episodes in ways that are more directly relevant to my argument when he remarks that, in both poems, "wrestling establishes what one might anachronistically call an episode of relative sportsmanlike fairness that contrasts with, but also foreshadows, the violence and conflict that mark the tale proper" ("Wrestling in the Moonlight," 58).

58. Knight and Ohlgren provide the gloss "set far (from home) and as a stranger" (*Robin Hood and Other Outlaw Tales*, 157). This description of the yeoman evokes Bourdieu's portrait of the "virtual strangers (people from other villages)" with whom the Kabyle engage in "interested calculation" as opposed to gift exchange. For Bourdieu, such encounters reveal a form of exchange "closer to its economic truth" (*The Logic of Practice*, 115). Based on mutual suspicion, the exchanges are fraught with anxiety in part because they call into

question the fiction of disinterested giving. It is this fiction of disinterest that I argue is reestablished at the conclusion of the wrestling scene in the *Gest*.

59. The analogous scene in *Gamelyn* occurs at lines 169–286. Knight and Ohlgren note that "there is some resemblance hereabouts to the action in the *Gest* when the knight helps a yeoman at a rural sport festival" (*Robin Hood and Other Outlaw Tales*, 222), though the differences are admittedly significant. Unlike the yeoman champion of the *Gest*, the "champion" (203) in *Gamelyn* is a malevolent figure whom the hero must best. This becomes clear when the anonymous franklin of *Gamelyn* begs the hero for help against the champion, who has threatened to kill the franklin's two sons. In the *Gest*, by contrast, the champion is wrongly set upon by the losers and has, moreover, committed no crime. The scene in the *Gest* is thus in some ways an inversion of that found in *Gamelyn*. One scene is about sympathy for the downtrodden; the other privileges competition and justifies the rewards that flow from it. Yet the similarities are ultimately more telling, as I argue here.

60. Knight and Ohlgren, eds., *Robin Hood and Other Outlaw Tales*, 157.

61. This fable is the well-known "Brenner thesis," which holds that changes in the structure of agrarian class relations, rather than demographic factors or the development of international trade, account for the precocious development of capitalism in England. Brenner's claim sparked a debate conducted largely in the same historical studies journal—*Past and Present*—that served as a platform for early debate about the audience of the Robin Hood ballads, inaugurated by Hilton's 1958 "The Origins of Robin Hood." For Brenner's original article as well as the most significant responses, see Ashton and Philpin, eds., *The Brenner Debate*.

62. Bradbury, *Writing Aloud*, 62.

63. Derrida, *Given Time*, 41; Bourdieu, *The Logic of Practice*, 106.

64. For the sixteenth-century chronicler William Grafton, Robin's prodigality in such giving is in fact the initial reason for his outlawry. Having been advanced to an earldom by virtue of "manhoode and chivalry," Robin, according to Grafton, "so prodigally exceeded on charges and expences, that he fell into great debt, by reason whereof, so many actions and sutes were commenced against him, wherunto he aunswered not, that by order of lawe he was outlawed." For Grafton's account, see Knight and Ohlgren, eds., *Robin Hood and Other Outlaw Tales*, 27–29.

65. Jameson, *The Political Unconscious*, 76.

66. Bourdieu, *The Logic of Practice*, 133.

67. Cooper, *The English Romance in Time*, 142.

68. On the structural similarities, see Bessinger, "*The Gest of Robin Hood* Revisited," 46–50.

69. The poem "O God What a World" can be found in Taylor, *The Songs and Travels of a Tudor Minstrel*, 170–75.

70. Cooper, "Counter-Romance."

71. Esposito reminds us that awareness of the formative role of such violence stretches back to the "community of guilt" named by Augustine: that first city founded by Cain after the murder of his brother. Cain's murder of Abel, says Esposito, is an act whose violence "inevitably refers to every future founding of community" (*Communitas*, 11).

72. Cannon, *The Grounds of English Literature*, 172–209; and Derrida, *Spectres of Marx*, 189.

73. Sutherland, *Stupefaction*, 26–90.

74. Marx, *Capital*, 481.

Works Cited

Adams, Jenny. *Power Play: The Literature and Politics of Chess in the Late Middle Ages*. Philadelphia: University of Pennsylvania Press, 2006.

Aers, David. *Chaucer, Langland, and the Creative Imagination*. London: Routledge and Kegan Paul, 1980.

———. *Faith, Ethics, and Church: 1360–1409*. Cambridge: Brewer, 2000.

Algazi, Gadi. "Feigned Reciprocities: Lords, Peasants, and the Afterlife of Late Medieval Social Strategies." In *Negotiating the Gift: Premodern Figurations of Exchange*, edited by Gadi Algazi et al. Göttingen: Veröffent-lichungen des Max-Planck-Instituts für Geschichte, 2003.

Amtower, Laurel. "Mimetic Desire and the Misappropriation of the Ideal." *Exemplaria* 8, no. 1 (1996): 125–44.

Andrew, Malcolm, and Ronald Waldron, eds. *The Poems of the Pearl Manuscript: "Pearl," "Cleanness," "Patience," "Sir Gawain and the Green Knight."* 5th ed. Exeter, UK: Exeter University Press, 2007.

Ashton, T. H., and C. H. E. Philpin, eds. *The Brenner Debate: Agrarian Class Structure and Economic Development in Pre-Industrial Europe*. Cambridge: Cambridge University Press, 1987.

Aspin, I. S. T. *Anglo-Norman Political Songs*. Oxford: Anglo-Norman Text Society, 1953.

Bahr, Arthur. *Fragments and Assemblages: Forming Compilations of Medieval London*. Chicago: University of Chicago Press, 2013.

Baker, Peter S. *Honour, Exchange, and Violence in Beowulf.* Cambridge: Brewer, 2013.

Barber, Richard W. *Arthur of Albion: An Introduction to the Arthurian Literature and Legends of England*. London: Barrie and Rockliff, 1961.

Barron, W. R. J. *Sir Gawain and the Green Knight*. Manchester, UK: Manchester University Press, 1974.

Bataille, Georges. *The Accursed Share: An Essay on General Economy, Volume 1: Consumption*. Translated by Robert Hurley. New York: Zone Books, 1988.

———. "Medieval French Literature, Chivalric Morals, and Passion." Translated by Laurence Pratt. In *The Premodern Condition: Medievalism and the Making of Theory*, edited by Bruce Holsinger, 204–20. Chicago: University of Chicago Press, 2005.

———. "The Notion of Expenditure." In *Visions of Excess: Selected Writings, 1927–1939*, translated by Alan Stoekl, 116–29. Minneapolis: University of Minnesota Press, 1985.

Ben-Amos, Ilana K. *The Culture of Giving: Informal Support and Gift-Exchange in Early Modern England*. Cambridge: Cambridge University Press, 2008.

Benson, Larry D., ed. *The Riverside Chaucer*. 3rd ed. Oxford: Oxford University Press, 1987.

Benveniste, Émile. *Indo-European Language and Society*. Translated by Elizabeth Palmer. London: Faber, 1973.

Bessinger, J. B., Jr. "*The Gest of Robin Hood* Revisited." In *Robin Hood: An Anthology of Scholarship and Criticism*, edited by Stephen Knight, 39–50. Cambridge: Brewer, 1999.

Blake, Kathleen A. "Order and the Noble Life in Chaucer's *Knight's Tale*." *Modern Language Quarterly* 34 (1973): 3–19.

Bliss, A. J., ed. *Sir Launfal*. London: Nelson, 1960.

Blodgett, E. D. "Chaucerian Pryvetee and the Opposition to Time." *Speculum* 51 (1976): 477–93.

Bloomfield, Morton. "Episodic Juxtaposition or the Syntax of Episodes in Narration." In *Studies in English Linguistics for Randolph Quirk*, 210–20. London: Longman, 1980.

———. "Episodic Motivation and Marvels in Epic and Romance." In *Essays and Explorations: Studies in Ideas, Language, and Literature*, 97–128. Cambridge, MA: Harvard University Press, 1970.

Boccaccio, Giovanni. *Theseid of the Nuptials of Emilia / Teseida delle nozze di Emilia*. Edited and translated by Vincenzo Traversa. New York: Peter Lang, 2002.

Bollier, David. "The Stubborn Vitality of the Gift Economy." In *Silent Theft: The Private Plunder of Our Common Wealth*, 27–41. New York: Routledge, 2002.

Borroff, Marie. "'Sir Gawain and the Green Knight': The Passing of Judgment." In *The Passing of Arthur: New Essays in the Arthurian Tradition*, edited by Christopher Braswell and William Sharpe, 105–28. New York: Garland, 1988.

Bourdieu, Pierre. *The Logic of Practice.* Translated by Richard Nice. Cambridge: Polity, 1990.

———. *Outline of a Theory of Practice.* Translated by Richard Nice. Cambridge: Cambridge University Press, 1977.

———. *Practical Reason: On the Theory of Action.* Translated by Randal Johnson. Stanford, CA: Stanford University Press, 1998.

Bradbury, Nancy Mason. "Gamelyn." In *Heroes and Anti-Heroes in Medieval Romance,* edited by Neil Cartlidge, 129–44. Cambridge: Brewer, 2012.

———. *Writing Aloud: Storytelling in Late Medieval England.* Chicago: University of Illinois Press, 1998.

Brandsen, T. "*Sir Gawain and the Carl of Carlisle.*" *Neophilologus* 81 (1997): 299–307.

Brewer, Derek. *Chaucer and His World.* 2nd ed. Woodbridge, UK: Brewer, 1992.

———. "The Popular English Metrical Romances." In *A Companion to Romance: From Classical to Contemporary,* edited by Corinne Saunders, 45–64. Oxford: Blackwell, 2004.

Brown, Peter, and Andrew Butcher. *The Age of Saturn: Literature and History in the Canterbury Tales.* Oxford: Blackwell, 1991.

Burrow, J. A. *A Reading of Sir Gawain and the Green Knight.* New York: Barnes & Noble, 1966.

Cannon, Christopher. *The Grounds of English Literature.* Oxford: Oxford University Press, 2005.

———. *Middle English Literature.* Cambridge: Polity, 2013.

Carlson, David. *Chaucer's Jobs.* New York: Palgrave, 2004.

Carr, Sherwyn T. "The Middle English Nativity Cherry Tree: The Dissemination of a Popular Motif." *Modern Language Quarterly* 36 (1975): 133–47.

Cartlidge, Neil. *Heroes and Anti Heroes in Medieval Romance.* Cambridge: Brewer, 2012.

Champion, L. S. "Grace versus Merit in *Sir Gawain and the Green Knight.*" *Modern Language Quarterly* 28 (1967): 413–25.

Chesterton, G. K. *Chaucer.* London: Faber, 1959.

Child, Francis James, ed. *English and Scottish Popular Ballads.* 5 vols. Boston: Houghton Mifflin, 1882–98. Reprint, New York: Dover, 1965.

Chism, Christine. *Alliterative Revivals.* Philadelphia: University of Pennsylvania Press, 2002.

Chrétien de Troyes. *Arthurian Romances.* Translated and edited by D. D. R. Owen. London: Dent, 1993.

———. *Erec et Enide.* Edited by Jean-Marie Fritz. Paris: Lettres Gothiques, 1992.

Cohen, Jeffrey Jerome. *Of Giants: Sex, Monsters, and the Middle Ages.* Minneapolis: University of Minnesota Press, 1999.

Cook, Robert G. "The Play-Element in *Sir Gawain and the Green Knight.*" *Tulane Studies in English* 13 (1963): 5–31.

Cooper, Helen. "Counter-Romance: Civil Strife and Father-Killing in the Prose Romances." In *The Long Fifteenth Century: Essays for Douglas Gray*, edited by Helen Cooper and Sally Mapstone, 141–62. Oxford: Clarendon, 1997.

———. *The English Romance in Time: Transforming Motifs from Geoffrey of Monmouth to the Death of Shakespeare.* Oxford: Oxford University Press, 2004.

Coss, P. R. "Aspects of Cultural Diffusion in Medieval England: The Early Romances, Local Society and Robin Hood." *Past and Present* 108 (1985): 35–79.

Cowell, Andrew. *The Medieval Warrior Aristocracy: Gifts, Violence, Performance, and the Sacred.* Cambridge: Brewer, 2007.

Crane, Susan. *Gender and Romance in Chaucer's Canterbury Tales.* Princeton, NJ: Princeton University Press, 1994.

———. *Insular Romance: Politics, Faith, and Culture in Anglo-Norman and Middle English Literature.* Berkeley: University of California Press, 1986.

Cross, Tom Peete. "The Celtic Elements in the Lays of *Lanval* and *Graelent.*" *Modern Philology* 12 (1915): 585–644.

Crotch, W. J. B., ed. *The Prologues and Epilogues of William Caxton.* Early English Text Society, Ordinary Series, no. 176. London: Oxford University Press, 1928.

Crow, Martin M., and Clair C. Olson, eds. *Chaucer Life-Records.* Oxford: Clarendon; Austin: University of Texas Press, 1966.

Davenport, W. A. *The Art of the Gawain-Poet.* London: Athlone, 1978.

———. *Medieval Narrative: An Introduction.* Oxford: Oxford University Press, 2004.

David, Alfred. "Sentimental Comedy in the Franklin's Tale." *Annuale Mediaevale* 6 (1965): 19–27.

Davis, Natalie Zemon. *The Gift in Sixteenth-Century France.* Oxford: Oxford University Press, 2000.

Derrida, Jacques. *Given Time: I. Counterfeit Money.* Translated by Peggy Kamuf. Chicago: University of Chicago Press, 1992.

———. *Of Hospitality: Anne Dufourmantelle Invites Jacques Derrida to Respond.* Translated by Rachel Bowlby. Stanford, CA: Stanford University Press, 2000.

———. *Specters of Marx: The State of the Debt, the Work of Mourning and the New International.* Translated by Peggy Kamuf. New York: Routledge, 2000.

Dobson, R. B., and J. Taylor, eds. *Rymes of Robyn Hood: An Introduction to the English Outlaw.* 2nd ed. Gloucester: Alan Sutton, 1989.

Dryden, John. "Preface to Fables Ancient and Modern." In *Of Dramatic Poesy and Other Critical Essays*, edited by George Watson. London: Dent, 1962.

Duby, Georges. *The Early Growth of the European Economy*. Ithaca, NY: Cornell University Press, 1974.

Duggan, H. N., and T. Turville-Petre, eds. *The Wars of Alexander*. Early English Text Society, Special Series, no. 10. London: Oxford University Press, 1989.

Duggan, Joseph J. *The Cantar de Mio Cid: Poetic Creation in Its Economic and Social Contexts*. Cambridge: Cambridge University Press, 1989.

Edwards, A. S. G. "*The Canterbury Tales* and *Gamelyn*." In *Medieval Latin and Middle English: Essays in Honour of Jill Mann*, edited by Christopher Cannon and Maura Nolan, 76–90. Cambridge: Boydell & Brewer, 2011.

Epstein, Robert. "'With Many a Floryn He the Hewes Boghte': Ekphrasis and Symbolic Violence in the *Knight's Tale*." *Philological Quarterly* 85 (2006): 49–68.

Esposito, Roberto. *Communitas: The Origin and Destiny of Community*. Translated by Timothy Campbell. Stanford, CA: Stanford University Press, 2010.

Evans, Ruth. "*Sir Orfeo* and Bare Life." In *Medieval Cultural Studies: Essays in Honour of Stephen Knight*, edited by Ruth Evans, Helen Fulton, and David Matthews, 198–212. Cardiff: University of Wales Press, 2006.

Foster, Edward E., ed. *Amis and Amiloun, Robert of Cisyle, and Sir Amadace*. Kalamazoo, MI: Medieval Institute Publications, 2007.

———. "Simplicity, Complexity, and Morality in Four Medieval Romances." *Chaucer Review* 31 (1997): 401–19.

Fowler, David C. *A Literary History of the Popular Ballad*. Durham, NC: Duke University Press, 1968.

Fradenburg, L. O. Aranye. *Sacrifice Your Love: Psychoanalysis, Historicism, Chaucer*. Minneapolis: University of Minnesota Press, 2002.

———. "Sacrificial Desire in Chaucer's *Knight's Tale*." *Journal of Medieval and Early Modern Studies* 27 (1997): 47–75.

———. "Simply Marvelous." *Studies in the Age of Chaucer* 26 (2004): 1–26.

———. "The Wife of Bath's Passing Fancy." *Studies in the Age of Chaucer* 8 (1986): 31–58.

Freud, Sigmund. *Jokes and Their Relation to the Unconscious*. In *The Standard Edition of the Complete Psychological Works of Sigmund Freud, vol. 8*, edited and translated by J. Strachey, 1–236. London: Hogarth and Institute of Psychoanalysis, 1955.

———. *Totem and Taboo*. In *The Standard Edition of the Complete Psychological Works of Sigmund Freud, vol. 13*, edited and translated by J. Strachey, 1–161. London: Hogarth and Institute of Psychoanalysis, 1955.

Furrow, Melissa. "Chanson de Geste as Romance in England." In *The Exploitations of Medieval Romance*, edited by Laura Ashe, Ivana Djordjević, and Judith Weiss. Rochester, NY: Brewer, 2010.

Galloway, Andrew. "The Account Book and the Treasure: Gilbert Maghfeld's Textual Economy and the Poetics of Mercantile Accounting in Ricardian Literature." *Studies in the Age of Chaucer* 33 (2011): 65–124.

———. "Layamon's Gift." *Proceedings of the Modern Language Association* 121 (2006): 717–34.

Ganim, John M. *Style and Consciousness in Middle English Literature*. Princeton, NJ: Princeton University Press, 1983.

Garbaty, Thomas. "Rhyme, Romance, Ballad, Burlesque, and the Confluence of Form." In *Fifteenth-Century Studies: Recent Essays*, edited by R. F. Yeager, 283–301. Hamden, CT: Archon Books, 1984.

Gasché, Rodolphe. "Heliocentric Exchange." In *The Logic of the Gift: Toward an Ethic of Generosity*, edited by Alan D. Schrift, 100–117. London: Routledge, 1997.

Gaylord, Alan T. "The Promises in the Franklin's Tale." *English Literary History* 31 (1961): 348–50.

Geck, John A. " 'For Goddes Love, Sir, Mercy!': Recontextualising the Modern Critical Text of *Floris and Blancheflor*." In *Medieval Romance, Medieval Contexts*, edited by Rhiannon Purdie and Michael Cichon, 77–89. Cambridge: Brewer, 2011.

Girard, René. *Violence and the Sacred*. Translated by Patrick Gregory. Baltimore: Johns Hopkins University Press, 1979.

Gower, John. *Confessio Amantis*. Edited by Russell A. Peck. Kalamazoo, MI: Medieval Institute Publications, 2000.

Gray, Douglas. "Everybody's Robin Hood." In *Robin Hood: Medieval and Post-Medieval*, edited by Helen Phillips, 21–41. Dublin: Four Courts, 2005.

———. "The Robin Hood Poems." In *Robin Hood: An Anthology of Scholarship and Criticism*, edited by Stephen Knight, 3–38. Cambridge: Brewer, 1999.

Green, Richard Firth. "Arcite at Court." *English Language Notes* 18 (1981): 251–57.

———. "The Ballad and the Middle Ages." In *The Long Fifteenth Century: Essays for Douglas Gray*, edited by Helen Cooper and Sally Mapstone, 163–84. Oxford: Clarendon, 1997.

———. "Violence in the Early Robin Hood Poems." In *"A Great Effusion of Blood?" Interpreting Medieval Violence*, edited by Mark D. Meyerson, Daniel Thiery, and Oren Falk, 268–86. Toronto: University of Toronto Press, 2004.

Greenblatt, Stephen, ed. *The Norton Shakespeare*. New York: Norton, 2008.

Groebner, Valentin. *Liquid Assets, Dangerous Gifts: Presents and Politics at the End of the Middle Ages.* Translated by Pamela E. Selwyn. Philadelphia: University of Pennsylvania Press, 2002.

Hahn, Thomas, ed. *Sir Gawain: Eleven Romances and Tales.* Kalamazoo, MI: Medieval Institute Publications, 1995.

Hales, John W., and Frederick J. Furnivall, eds. *Bishop Percy's Folio Manuscript.* London: Trubner, 1868.

Hallissy, Margaret. "Writing a Building: Chaucer's Knowledge of the Construction Industry and the Language of the *Knight's Tale.*" *Chaucer Review* 32 (1998): 239–59.

Halverson, John. "Aspects of Order in the *Knight's Tale.*" *Studies in Philology* 57 (1960): 606–21.

———. "*Havelok the Dane* and Society." *Chaucer Review* 6 (1971): 142–51.

Hanna, Ralph. "*The Awntyrs off Arthure at the Terne Wathelyne*: An Edition Based on Bodleian Library MS. Douce 324." PhD diss., Yale University, 1967.

Hardman, Philippa. "The Unity of the Ireland Manuscript." *Reading Medieval Studies* 2 (1976): 45–62.

Harper, Elizabeth. "*Pearl* in the Context of Fourteenth-Century Gift Economies." *Chaucer Review* 44 (2010): 421–39.

Harwood, Britton J. "Chaucer and the Gift (If There Is Any)." *Studies in Philology* 103 (2006): 26–46.

———. "*Gawain* and the Gift." *Proceedings of the Modern Language Association* 106 (1991): 483–99.

Hazell, Dinah. *Poverty in Late Middle English Literature: The Meene and the Riche.* Dublin: Four Courts, 2009.

Heng, Geraldine. *Empire of Magic: Medieval Romance and the Politics of Cultural Fantasy.* New York: Columbia University Press, 2003.

Herzman, R. B., G. Drake, and E. Salisbury, eds. *Four Romances of England.* Kalamazoo, MI: Medieval Institute Publications, 1999.

Hibbard, Laura A. "The Auchinleck Manuscript and a Possible London Bookshop of 1330–1340." *Proceedings of the Modern Language Association* 57 (1942): 595–627.

———. *Mediaeval Romance in England: A Study of the Sources and Analogues of the Non-Cyclic Metrical Romances.* New ed. New York: Franklin, 1969.

Hilton, Rodney H. "The Origins of Robin Hood." *Past and Present* 14 (1958): 30–44.

Holsinger, Bruce. *The Premodern Condition: Medievalism and the Making of Theory.* Chicago: University of Chicago Press, 2005.

Holt, J. C. "The Origins and Audience of the Ballads of Robin Hood." In *Robin Hood: An Anthology of Scholarship and Criticism*, edited by Stephen Knight, 211–32. Cambridge: Brewer, 1999.

————. *Robin Hood*. London: Thames & Hudson, 1982.

Howell, Martha C. *Commerce Before Capitalism in Europe, 1300–1600*. Cambridge: Cambridge University Press, 2010.

Hudson, Harriet, ed. *Four Middle English Romances: Sir Isumbras, Octavian, Sir Eglamour of Artois, Sir Tryamour*. Kalamazoo, MI: Medieval Institute Publications, 1996.

Iersel, Geert van. "The Twenty-Five Ploughs of Sir John: *The Tale of Gamelyn* and the Implications of Acreage." In *People and Texts: Relationships in Medieval Literature—Studies Presented to Erik Kooper*, edited by Thea Summerfield and Keith Busby, 111–22. Amsterdam: Rodopi, 2007.

Ingham, Patricia Clare. *Sovereign Fantasies: Arthurian Romance and the Making of Britain*. Philadelphia: University of Pennsylvania Press, 2001.

Jameson, Fredric. "Magical Narratives: Romance as Genre." *New Literary History* 7 (1975): 135–63.

————. *The Political Unconscious: Narrative as a Socially Symbolic Act*. Ithaca, NY: Cornell University Press, 1981.

Johnson, Lynn Staley. *The Voice of the Gawain-Poet*. Madison: University of Wisconsin Press, 1984.

Johnston, Andrew James. "Wrestling in the Moonlight: The Politics of Masculinity in the Middle English Popular Romance *Gamelyn*." In *Constructions of Masculinity in British Literature from the Middle Ages to the Present*, edited by Stefan Horlacher, 51–67. New York: Palgrave, 2012.

Johnston, Michael. "Knights and Merchants Unite: *Sir Amadace*, the Grateful Dead, and the Moral Exemplum Tradition." *Neophilologus* 92 (2008): 735–44.

————. *Romance and the Gentry in Late Medieval England*. Oxford: Oxford University Press, 2014.

Jones, Terry. *Chaucer's Knight: Portrait of a Medieval Mercenary*. Baton Rouge: Louisiana State University Press, 1980.

Jones, Timothy S. "'Oublïé ai Chevalerie': Tristan, Malory, and the Outlaw-Knight." In *Robin Hood: Medieval and Post-Medieval*, edited by Helen Philips, 79–90. Dublin: Four Courts, 2005.

Jost, Jean. "Why Is Middle English Romance So Violent? The Literary and Aesthetic Purposes of Violence." In *Violence in Medieval Courtly Literature: A Casebook*, edited by Albrecht Classen, 241–67. New York: Routledge, 2004.

Kahrl, Stanley J. "Chaucer's 'Squire's Tale' and the Decline of Chivalry." *Chaucer Review* 7 (1973): 194–209.

Kane, George. *Middle English Literature: A Critical Study of the Romances, the Religious Lyrics, Piers Plowman*. London: Methuen, 1951.

Kane, Stuart. "Horseplay: Robin Hood, Guy of Gisborne, and the Neg(oti)ation of the Bestial." In *Robin Hood in Popular Culture: Violence, Transgression, and Justice*, edited by Thomas Hahn, 101–10. Cambridge: Brewer, 2000.

Kay, Sarah. *The Chansons de Geste in the Age of Romance: Political Fictions.* Oxford: Clarendon, 1995.

Keen, Maurice. *Outlaws of Medieval Legend.* 3rd ed. London: Routledge, 2000.

Kellogg, Judith. *Medieval Artistry and Exchange: Economic Institutions, Society, and Literary Form in Old French Narrative.* New York: Peter Lang, 1989.

Kelly, Kathleen Coyne. "The Bartering of Blauncheflur in the Middle English *Floris and Blauncheflur.*" *Studies in Philology* 91, no. 2 (1994): 101–10.

Kittell, Ellen. *From "Ad Hoc" to Routine: A Case Study in Medieval Bureaucracy.* Philadelphia: University of Pennsylvania Press, 1991.

Kline, Daniel T. *Medieval Literature for Children.* London: Routledge, 2003.

Knight, Stephen. "Celticity and Christianity." In *Christianity and Romance in Medieval England*, edited by Rosalind Field, Phillipa Hardman, and Michelle Sweeney, 26–44. Cambridge: Brewer, 2010.

———. "The Social Function of the Middle English Romance." In *Medieval Literature: Criticism, Ideology, and History*, edited by David Aers, 99–122. New York: St. Martin's, 1986.

Knight, Stephen, and Thomas Ohlgren, eds. *Robin Hood and Other Outlaw Tales.* 2nd ed. Kalamazoo, MI: Published for TEAMS in association with the University of Rochester, Medieval Institute Publications, Western Michigan University, 2000.

Koff, Leonard Michael. *Chaucer and the Art of Storytelling.* Berkeley: University of California Press, 1988.

Kooper, Erik, ed. *Sentimental and Humorous Romances: Floris and Blancheflour, Sir Degrevant, the Squire of Low Degree, the Tournament of Tottenham, and the Feast of Tottenham.* Kalamazoo, MI: Medieval Institute Publications, 2006.

Krier, Theresa. "Receiving Chaucer in Renaissance England." In *Refiguring Chaucer in the Renaissance*, edited by Theresa M. Krier, 1–18. Gainesville: University Press of Florida, 1998.

Lacan, Jacques. *Écrits: A Selection.* Translated by Alan Sheridan. London: Routledge, 2001.

Laskaya, Anne, and Eve Salisbury, eds. *The Middle English Breton Lays.* Kalamazoo, MI: Medieval Institute Publications, 1995.

Lerer, Seth. *Chaucer and His Readers.* Princeton, NJ: Princeton University Press, 1993.

Levi-Strauss, Claude. *The Elementary Structures of Kinship.* Translated by James Hade Bell, John Richard von Sturmer, and Rodney Needham. Boston: Beacon, 1969.

Lewis, C. S. "What Chaucer Really Did to *Il Filostrato*." *Essays and Studies* 17 (1932): 56–75.

Loomis, C. Grant. "*Sir Cleges* and Unseasonable Growth in Hagiology." *Modern Language Notes* 53 (1938): 591–94.

Lübke, Hermann. "*The Aunters of Arthur at the Tern-Wathelan*." PhD diss., Berlin, 1883.

Lupack, Alan, ed. *Lancelot of the Laik and Sir Tristrem*. Kalamazoo, MI: Medieval Institute Publications, 1994.

MacFarlane, Alan. *The Culture of Capitalism*. Oxford: Blackwell, 1987.

Mahowald, Kyle. "'It May Nat Be': Chaucer, Derrida, and the Impossibility of the Gift." *Studies in the Age of Chaucer* 32 (2010): 129–150.

Malarkey, Stoddard, and J. B. Toelken. "Gawain and the Green Girdle." *Journal of English and Germanic Philology* 63 (1964): 14–20.

Mann, Jill. "Price and Value in *Sir Gawain and the Green Knight*." *Essays in Criticism* 36 (1986): 294–318.

Martin, Carl Grey. "*The Awntyrs off Arthure*: An Economy of Pain." *Modern Philology* 108 (2010): 177–98.

Marx, Karl. *Capital: Volume 1: A Critique of Political Economy*. Translated by Ben Fowkes. London: Penguin, 1992.

Mason, Emma. "Timeo Barones et Dona Ferentes." In *Religious Motivation: Biographical and Sociological Problems for the Church Historian*, Studies in Church History 15, edited by Derek Baker, 61–75. Oxford: Blackwell, 1978.

Massey, Jeff. "'The Double Bind of Troilus to Tellen': The Time of the Gift in Chaucer's *Troilus and Criseyde*." *Chaucer Review* 38 (2003): 16–35.

Mauss, Marcel. *The Gift: The Form and Reason of Exchange in Archaic Societies*. Translated by W. D. Halls. London: Routledge, 1990.

McDonald, Nicola. "A Polemical Introduction." In *Pulp Fictions of Medieval England: Essays in Popular Romance*, edited by Nicola McDonald. Manchester, UK: Manchester University Press, 2004.

McKnight, George. *Middle English Humorous Tales in Verse*. New York: Gordian, 1913.

McTaggart, Anne. *Shame and Guilt in Chaucer*. New York: Palgrave, 2012.

Meale, Carol M. "'God Men / Wiues Maydnes and Alle Men': Romance and Its Audiences." In *Readings in Medieval English Romance*, edited by Carol M. Meale, 209–25. Cambridge: Brewer, 1994.

Mehl, Dieter. *The Middle English Romances of the Thirteenth and Fourteenth Centuries*. London: Routledge & Kegan Paul, 1968.

Menuge, Noël James. *Medieval English Wardship in Romance and Law*. Cambridge: Brewer, 2001.

Meyer-Lee, Robert J. *Poets and Power from Chaucer to Wyatt*. Cambridge: Cambridge University Press, 2007.

Middle English Dictionary. Edited by H. Kurath, S.M. Kuhn, and R. Lewis. Ann Arbor: University of Michigan Press, 1957–2001. Online edition: *Middle English Dictionary Online,* quod.lib.umich.edu/m/med.

Miller, Mark. "The Ends of Excitement in *Sir Gawain and the Green Knight*: Teleology, Ethics, and the Death Drive." *Studies in the Age of Chaucer* 32 (2010): 215–56.

Miller, William Ian. *Bloodtaking and Peacemaking: Feud, Law, and Society in Saga Iceland.* Chicago: University of Chicago Press, 1990.

Mitchell-Smith, Ilan. "Defining Violence in Middle English Romances: *Sir Gowther* and *Libeaus Desconus.*" *Fifteenth-Century Studies* 34 (2009): 148–61.

Muscatine, Charles. "Form, Texture, and Meaning in Chaucer's Knight's Tale." *Proceedings of the Modern Language Association* 65 (1950): 911–29.

———. *The Old French Fabliaux.* New Haven, CT: Yale University Press, 1986.

———. *Poetry and Crisis in the Age of Chaucer.* Notre Dame, IN: University of Notre Dame Press, 1972.

Nerlich, Michael. *Ideology of Adventure: Studies in Modern Consciousness, 1100–1750.* Translated by Ruth Crowley. Minneapolis: University of Minnesota Press, 1987.

Ohlgren, Thomas H., ed. *Medieval Outlaws: Twelve Tales in Modern English Translation.* Revised and expanded ed. West Lafayette, IN: Parlor, 2005.

———. *Robin Hood: The Early Poems, 1465–1560; Texts, Contexts, and Ideology.* Newark: University of Delaware Press, 2007.

Olson, Paul A. "Chaucer's Epic Statement and the Political Milieu of the Late Fourteenth Century." *Mediaevalia* 5 (1979): 61–87.

Otter, Monika. *Inventiones: Fiction and Referentiality in Twelfth-Century English Historical Writing.* Chapel Hill: University of North Carolina Press, 1996.

Patterson, Lee. *Chaucer and the Subject of History.* Madison: University of Wisconsin Press, 1991.

Pearsall, Derek. "The Development of Middle English Romance." In *Studies in Medieval English Romance: Some New Approaches,* edited by Derek Brewer. Cambridge: Brewer, 1998.

Pearsall, Derek, and I.C. Cunningham, eds. *The Auchinleck Manuscript: National Library of Scotland Advocates' MS. 19.2.1.* London: Scolar, 1977.

Pelan, Margaret, ed. *Floire et Blancheflor, seconde version éditée du ms 19152 du fonds français.* Paris: Les Belles Lettres, 1956.

Phillips, Helen. "*The Awntyrs off Arthure*: Structure and Meaning. A Reassessment." *Arthurian Literature* 12 (1993): 63–89.

Pollack, Sean. "Border States: Parody, Sovereignty and Hybrid Identity in *The Carl of Carlisle*." *Arthuriana* 19 (2009): 10–26.

Pollard, A. J. *Imagining Robin Hood: The Late-Medieval Stories in Historical Context*. London: Routledge, 2004.

Putter, Ad. "Arthurian Romance in English Popular Tradition: *Sir Percyvell of Gales*, *Sir Cleges*, and *Sir Launfal*." In *A Companion to Arthurian Literature*, edited by H. Fulton, 235–51. Oxford: Blackwell, 2009.

———. "Gifts and Commodities in *Sir Amadace*." *Review of English Studies* 51 (2000): 371–94.

Putter, Ad, and Jane Gilbert, eds. *The Spirit of Medieval English Popular Romance*. London: Longman, 2000.

Radulescu, Raluca L. "Ballad and Popular Romance in the Percy Folio." *Arthurian Literature* 23 (2006): 68–80.

Ramsey, Lee. *Chivalric Romances: Popular Literature in Medieval England*. Bloomington: Indiana University Press, 1983.

Reinhard, John R. "Strokes Shared." *Journal of American Folklore* 36 (1928): 380–400.

Richards, Jeffrey. "Robin Hood on the Screen." In *Robin Hood: Die vielen Gesichter des edlen Raubers / The Many Faces of that Celebrated English Outlaw*, edited by Kevin Carpenter, 135–44. Oldenberg, Germany: BIS, 1995.

Riddy, Felicity. "Giving and Receiving: Exchange in the *Roman van Walewein* and *Sir Gawain and the Green Knight*." In *Arthurian Literature XVII, Originality and Tradition in the Middle Dutch Roman van Walewein*, edited by Bart Bescamusca and Erik Kooper, 101–14. Cambridge: Brewer, 1999.

———. "Middle English Romance: Marriage, Family, Intimacy." In *The Cambridge Companion to Medieval Romance*, edited by Roberta L. Krueger, 235–53. Cambridge: Cambridge University Press, 2000.

Root, R. K. *The Poetry of Chaucer*. Boston: Houghton Mifflin, 1906.

Sahlins, Marshall. "The Spirit of the Gift." In *The Logic of the Gift*, edited by Alan D. Schrift, 70–99. New York: Routledge, 1997.

Scaglione, Aldo. *Knights at Court: Courtliness, Chivalry, and Courtesy from Ottonian Germany to the Italian Renaissance*. Berkeley: University of California Press, 1991.

Scala, Elizabeth. *Absent Narratives, Manuscript Textuality, and Literary Structure in Late Medieval England*. New York: Palgrave, 2002.

Scattergood, John. "*The Tale of Gamelyn*: The Noble Robber as Provincial Hero." In *Readings in Medieval English Romance*, edited by Carol M. Meale, 159–94. Cambridge: Brewer, 1994.

Schelp, Hanspeter. *Exemplarische Romanzen im Mittelenglischen.* Göttengen: Vandenhaeck & Ruprecht, 1967.

Shannon, Edgar F. "Medieval Law in *The Tale of Gamelyn.*" *Speculum* 26 (1951): 458–64.

Shoaf, R. A. *Dante, Chaucer, and the Currency of the Word: Money, Images, and Reference in Late Medieval Poetry.* Norman, OK: Pilgrim Books, 1983.

———. *The Poem as Green Girdle: Commercium in Sir Gawain and the Green Knight.* Gainesville: University Presses of Florida, 1984.

Shuffelton, George, ed. *Codex Ashmole 61: A Compilation of Popular Middle English Verse.* Kalamazoo, MI: Medieval Institute Publications, 2008.

———. "Romance, Popular Style and the *Confessio Amantis*: Conflict or Evasion?" In *John Gower, Trilingual Poet: Language, Translation, and Tradition,* edited by Elisabeth Dutton, John Hines, and R. F. Yeager, 74–84. Cambridge: Brewer, 2010.

Simpson, James. *Reform and Cultural Revolution, 1350–1547.* Oxford: Oxford University Press, 2002.

———. *Troubling Arthurian Histories: Court Culture, Performance and Scandal in Chretien de Troyes's "Erec et Enide."* Oxford: Peter Lang, 2007.

———. "Violence, Narrative and Proper Name: *Sir Degaré,* 'The Tale of Sir Gareth of Orkney,' and the Anglo-Norman *Folie Tristan d'Oxford.*" In *The Spirit of Medieval English Popular Romance,* Longman Medieval and Renaissance Library, edited by Ad Putter and Jane Gilbert. London: Longman, 2000.

Singman, Jeffrey L. *Robin Hood: The Shaping of the Legend.* Westport, CT: Greenwood, 1998.

Skeat, Walter W., ed. *The Tale of Gamelyn.* Oxford: Clarendon, 1884.

Smith, D. Vance. *Arts of Possession: The Middle English Household Imaginary.* Minneapolis: University of Minnesota Press, 2003.

Spearing, A. C. *The Gawain-Poet: A Critical Study.* Cambridge: Cambridge University Press, 1970.

———. *The Medieval Poet as Voyeur: Looking and Listening in Medieval Love-Narratives.* Cambridge: Cambridge University Press, 1993.

———. *Medieval to Renaissance in English Poetry.* Cambridge: Cambridge University Press, 1985.

Spence, John. "A Lost Manuscript of the 'Rymes of [. . .] Randolf Erl of Chestre.'" *Electronic British Library Journal* (2010).

Steel, Karl. "Quote of the Day: *Sir Amadace.*" *In the Middle,* April 13, 2007. www.inthemedievalmiddle.com/2007/04/quote-of-day-sir-amadace_13.html.

Stein, Mark. *Psychotherapy and the Remorseful Patient.* Binghamton, NY: Haworth, 1988.

Strohm, Paul. *Social Chaucer*. Cambridge, MA: Harvard University Press, 1989.

Sutherland, Keston. *Stupefaction: A Radical Anatomy of Phantoms*. London: Seagull Books, 2011.

Tardif, Richard. "The 'Mystery' of Robin Hood: A New Social Context for the Texts." In *Robin Hood: An Anthology of Scholarship and Criticism*, edited by Stephen Knight, 345–62. Cambridge: Brewer, 1999.

Taylor, Andrew. *The Songs and Travels of a Tudor Minstrel: Richard Sheale of Tamworth*. Woodbridge, UK: York Medieval, 2012.

Taylor, P. B. "Commerce and Comedy in *Sir Gawain and the Green Knight*." *Philological Quarterly* 50 (1971): 1–15.

Tigges, Wim. "Romance and Parody." In *Companion to Middle English Romance*, edited by Henk Aertsen and Alasdair A. McDonald. Amsterdam: VU University Press, 1993.

Tlusty, B. Ann. *Bacchus and Civic Order: The Culture of Drink in Early Modern Germany*. Charlottesville: University of Virginia Press, 2001.

Tolkien, J. R. R., and E. V. Gordon, eds. *Sir Gawain and the Green Knight*. 2nd ed. Revised by Norman Davis. Oxford: Clarendon, 1967.

Trigg, Stephanie. "The Romance of Exchange: *Sir Gawain and the Green Knight*." *Viator* 22 (1991): 251–66.

———. *Shame and Honor: A Vulgar History of the Order of the Garter*. Philadelphia: University of Pennsylvania Press, 2012.

Van, Thomas A. "Theseus and the 'Right Way' of the *Knight's Tale*." *Studies in the Literary Imagination* 4 (1971): 83–100.

Wadiak, Walter. "Chaucer's *Knight's Tale* and the Politics of Distinction." *Philological Quarterly* 89, nos. 2/3 (2010): 159–84.

———. " 'What Shall These Bowes Do?': Violence and the Gift in *A Gest of Robyn Hode*." *Exemplaria* 24, no. 3 (2012): 238–59.

Wallace, David. *Chaucerian Polity: Absolutist Lineages and Associational Forms in England and Italy*. Stanford, CA: Stanford University Press, 1997.

Walsingham, Thomas. *The Chronica Maiora of Thomas Walsingham*. Translated by David Preest. Suffolk: Boydell, 2005.

Walters, Lori J. "More Bread from Stone: Gauvain as a Figure of Plenitude in the French, Dutch and English Traditions." *Arthurian Literature* 24 (2007): 15–32.

Webb, Henry J. "A Reinterpretation of Chaucer's Theseus." *Review of English Studies* 23 (1947): 289–96.

Weber, Henry. *Metrical Romances of the Thirteenth, Fourteenth, and Fifteenth Centuries*. London: George Ramsay, 1810.

Whetter, K. S. *Understanding Genre and Medieval Romance*. Aldershot: Ashgate, 2008.

Wright, Glenn. "Churl's Courtesy: *Rauf Coilyear* and Its English Analogues."
   Neophilologus 85 (2001): 647–62.
Žižek, Slavoj. "Class Struggle or Postmodernism? Yes, Please!" In *Contingency,
   Hegemony, Universality: Contemporary Dialogues and the Left*, edited by
   J. Butler, E. Laclau, and S. Žižek, 90–135. London: Verso, 2000.

Index

Adams, Jenny, 25
Aers, David, 91
Amadace (poem). See *Sir Amadace*
    (poem)
aristocracy
    connections with non-nobility,
      63–64, 113–14, 163n5
    decline portrayed in *Awntyrs*, 31, 36
    decline portrayed in *Gest*, 148
    decline portrayed in *Sir Cleges*,
      39–40
    and immunity, 103–4, 111
    obligation for reciprocity, 138–39
    patronage system of, 64–67, 97
    and power of desire, 29
    problem of surplus to, 33–36,
      130–32
    role of gift exchange in, viii, 6–9,
      64–67, 138–39, 153n17,
      153n24, 163n5
    role of violence in, viii, 33–36,
      97–99, 137–38
    See also chivalry; noble giving
Arts of Possession (Smith), 4–5
Augustine, 172n71
Awntyrs off Arthur, The (poem),
    30–36, 156n4

Bahr, Arthur, 22, 28, 155n57
ballads. *See* outlaw ballads
Barber, Richard W., 166n59
Bataille, Georges, ix–x, 5–6, 12, 123,
    151n5, 152n13
Benveniste, Émile, 103, 108–9
Bliss, A. J., 52
Blong, Patrick, 162
Bourdieu, Pierre, 6, 7, 8, 13–15, 129,
    135, 147, 154n38, 165n34,
    170n58
Bradbury, Nancy Mason, 142
Brenner thesis, 171n61
Brewer, Derek, 58
Burrow, J. A., 164n25

Cannon, Christopher, 22, 67, 70, 80,
    149
Canon's Yeoman's Tale, The (Chaucer),
    162n41
Canterbury Tales, The (Chaucer)
    The Canon's Yeoman's Tale, 162n41
    commodification of literature in,
      63–64
    community mourning of, 86
    The Franklin's Tale, 67–70, 82
    The Miller's Tale, 73

romance's persistence in, 67
The Shipman's Tale, 69
The Squire's Tale, 72–73, 118,
    166n63
Tale of Sir Thopas, 82, 125
The Wife of Bath's Tale, 72
See also *Knight's Tale, The*
    (Chaucer)
capitalism
    and aristocracy's future, 130–31
    Brenner thesis of, 171n61
    impact on chivalry, 90–91
    logic of commodification, 63–64,
        67–68, 70–71
    and profits of adventure, 82–83
    role of gift exchange in, 14–15,
        22–23, 43–45, 100–101
    role of violence in, xi, 8–10,
        13–15, 28–29, 149–50
    and romance, ix, 141
    as source of antagonism, 20–22,
        51–52, 60–61, 159n60
    transition from feudalism to, 134
Carle (poem). See *Sir Gawain and the
    Carle of Carlisle* (poem)
Carlson, David, 65
Carr, Sherwyn T., 157n24, 157n26
Chaucer, Geoffrey
    House of Fame, 64, 65–66, 84
    mercantile background of, 63–64,
        83–84, 160n3
    reliance on gift economy, 64–67
    romance's impact on, 67–72,
        80–82, 84
    See also *Canterbury Tales, The*
        (Chaucer); *Knight's Tale, The*
        (Chaucer)
Chestre, Thomas, 51–52, 53
Child, Francis James, 168n23
chivalry
    and adventure, 82–83
    appeal to non-nobility, 28–29,
        152n9

cyclical nature of, 88–89
decline portrayed in *Awntyrs*,
    30–32, 36
decline portrayed in outlaw ballads,
    123, 126–27, 132, 136–37,
    144–45
decline portrayed in *Sir Cleges*,
    39–41, 48–49
decline portrayed in *Squire's Tale*,
    72–73
desire for, 5–6, 93–95
ghosts signifying return of, 49–50,
    53–54
green girdle as sign of, 88, 90, 92,
    96, 104–6, 162
impact of capitalism on, 90–91
persistence in *Awntyrs*, 35–36
persistence in *Canterbury Tales*,
    69–73
persistence in outlaw ballads, 120,
    128–29, 131–32, 134–35,
    145–46
persistence in *Sir Gawain*, 86–87
persistence of, viii–x, 3–4, 126–27
role in community formation, viii,
    87, 168n29
role of gifts in, 18–19, 36–37,
    91–92, 128–29, 134–35,
    168n29
role of violence in, viii, 17–19,
    46–49, 76–77, 85–86, 97–99,
    136–37, 145–46
surplus value of, 32–33, 52–54,
    56–59, 84–86, 113–14
and the total gift, 32–33, 91–92,
    103–4
violence memorialized, 89–90,
    114–16
violent excesses of, 36–37, 113–14,
    138–39, 168n29
See also aristocracy
Chrétien de Troyes, 109, 123–24
Chronica Moiora (Walsingham), 7–8

Cleges (poem). See *Sir Cleges* (poem)

Cohen, Jeffrey Jerome, 18, 106, 110

commercial economy. *See* capitalism

community
  formed through gift giving, ix–x,
    86, 151n5, 168n29
  formed through noble giving, ix–x,
    119–20, 128–29, 146, 163n5
  formed through violence, 85–86,
    111, 140–41, 146, 149, 172n71
  logic of immunity in, 103–4
  role of chivalry in, viii, 87, 168n29

Complaint to His Purse (Chaucer), 65

Cooper, Helen, 16

Cowell, Andrew, 4, 8–10

Crane, Susan, 39–40

Derrida, Jacques, 45, 92, 108–9, 134,
    149, 151n5, 152n6, 154n38,
    163n16

Dryden, John, 160n11

Duby, Georges, 12

Edward III (king of England),
    165n41

Epstein, Robert, 74–75

Erec et Enide (Chrétien de Troyes),
    123–24

Esposito, Roberto, 85, 103, 148–49,
    151n5, 172n71

Essai sur le don (Mauss), 10–12

excess. *See* surplus

exchange. *See* gift giving; noble giving

Father's Instructions to His Son, A,
    43–44

feudalism
  chivalric violence in, 137–38
  in classic view of romance, viii
  coercion as base of, 27–29
  human surplus in, 56
  meaning of gifts in, 27–29, 92–93
  patronage system in, 65

  portrayed in Robin Hood ballads,
    133–34
  portrayed in *Sir Amadace*, 56,
    158n54

Floris and Blancheflour (poem)
  chess game scene, 24–26, 27–29
  cup's symbolism in, 26–27
  nostalgia in, x, 19
  paradoxical uses of violence in,
    23–29
  plot summary, 21–22
  self-awareness of, 19–21, 23

Fowler, David C., 167n18

Fradenburg, L. O. Aranye, ix, 5, 86

Franklin's Tale, The (Chaucer), 67–70,
    82

Galloway, Andrew, 22–23, 160n3

Gamelyn (poem). See *Tale of Gamelyn,
    The* (poem)

Ganim, John, 18

Garbaty, Thomas J., 125

Gasché, Rodolphe, 10

Gawain-romances
  dominance via submission in,
    111–12
  influences on, 166n60
  "nirt" removed from, 105–6
  reciprocity in, 117–18
  reimagining chivalry, xi
  transformation scenes in,
    116–17
  violence as a gift in, 89–90
  See also *Sir Gawain and the Carle
    of Carlisle* (poem); *Sir Gawain
    and the Green Knight* (poem)

Geoffrey of Monmouth, 50, 97

Gesta Herewardi, 124, 168n29

Gest of Robyn Hode, A (poem)
  chivalry's decline in, 132, 136–37,
    144–45
  chivalry's persistence in, xi,
    134–35, 145–46

debated classification of, 132, 148, 169n41
noble gift in, 133–46
reason for outlawry in, 171n64
romance reimagined in, xi, 132–33, 146–49
violence in, 133–39, 142–43, 146
wrestling match episode, 139–43, 170n57–58, 171n59
ghosts
in *Awntyrs*, 30–31, 36
as chivalry's return, 49–50, 53–54
early uses of, 158n42
in English romances, 61–62, 149–50
in *The Knight's Tale*, 78–79, 83
as return of violence, 59–60
in *Sir Amadace*, 49–50, 55, 59–60
in *Sir Launfal*, 49–50, 53–54
gift giving
anxiety in exchanges, 170n58
Bourdieu's work on, 13–15
in capitalist economies, 13–15, 22–23, 43–45
Chaucer's dependence on, 64–67
and chivalric desire, 23–29, 30, 93–96
and community, ix–x, 86, 151n5, 168n29
excesses of, 92, 112–13, 117
ghosts as return of, 50
impossibility of, 91–92, 154n38
instability of meaning, 96–106
measuring value of, 77–83
objectification in, 65–66, 73–74
obligation inherent in, 7, 11–12, 38–39, 43, 65–66
repressive function of, 94, 163n16
role of timing in, 143
romance as form of, 2–3, 18–19
social order structured by, 76, 93
symbolic power of, 5–6

as symbolic violence, viii–ix, 6–15, 88–89
See also noble giving
girdle (*Sir Gawain*), 88, 90, 92, 96, 104–5, 162
Grafton, William, 171n64
Gray, Douglas, 125, 135
Green, Richard Firth, 79, 121, 125
Green Knight (poem). See *Sir Gawain and the Green Knight* (poem)

Hahn, Thomas, 166n60
Harwood, Britton J., 5, 68, 91, 92, 101–2, 153n24, 163n11
Havelok the Dane (poem), 17, 41, 79, 81
Hawkwood, John, 160n22
Hazell, Dinah, 40, 156n18, 157n34
History of the Kings of Britain (Geoffrey of Monmouth), 50, 97
Holsinger, Bruce, 5, 152n13
Holt, J. C., 134–35
hospitality
coercive power of, 99–101, 110–12, 135, 164n27
community performed through, 128–29
inequality in, 100–103
possessive spirit of, 108–9, 111–12, 129
violent excess in, 109–12
House of Fame, The (Chaucer), 64, 65–66, 84
Hundred Years' War, 7, 39–40

immunity, 103–4, 111
"In Olde Times Paste" (poem), 126–27

Jameson, Fredric, 4, 45, 146
Johnston, Andrew James, 170n57
Jones, Timothy S., 123, 160n22

Kane, Stuart M., 120–21
Keen, Maurice, 139
Kelly, Kathleen Coyne, 22, 23
King Horn (poem), 2, 20–21
Kittell, Ellen, 170n55
Knight, Stephen, 156n20, 169n36,
    171n59
Knightly Tale of Gologras and Gawain,
    The (poem), 111–12
Knight's Tale, The (Chaucer), 160n22
    chivalry portrayed in, 58, 71, 73
    community formation in, 84–86
    cultural value of, xi, 75
    logic of commodification in,
        70–71
    measuring value in, 77–83
    noble giving in, 73–78
    romance's persistence in, 71, 83
    violence decentered in, x–xi, 85–86

Lacan, Jacques, 5–6, 152n13
Laskaya, Anne, 157n37
Lévi-Strauss, Claude, 5, 8
Libeaus Desconus (poem), 17
Lombardy, 52, 158n47
Louis (duke of Orléans), 6–8,
    153n17

Malory, Thomas, 147
Mann, Jill, 90, 103
Martin, Carl Grey, 34
Marx, Karl, 90, 94, 149
Massey, Jeff, 161n35
mastery
    and chivalric violence, 89–90
    "tappe" in *Sir Gawain* as, 95–96
    through hospitality, 109, 110–12
Mauss, Marcel, 2, 5–6, 10–12
McTaggart, Anne, 85
Medieval Warrior Aristocracy (Cowell),
    8–10
Mehl, Dieter, 39
mercantile economy. *See* capitalism

Meyer-Lee, Robert, 66
Miller, Mark, 94–95
Miller's Tale, The (Chaucer), 73
minstrels, 41–42, 46–48, 65–66,
    148, 157n37
Morte Darthur, Le (Malory), 50, 147
Muscatine, Charles, 41, 71, 90

Nerlich, Michael, 119
nobility. *See* aristocracy
noble giving
    and aristocracy, 153n24
    coercive power of, 25–29, 129–30
    cultural value of, 18, 67
    economizing of, 34–35, 45, 49,
        68–69
    excesses of, 71, 94–96
    forming community, ix–x, 119–20,
        128–29, 146, 163n5
    impossibility of, 108–9
    obligation inherent in, 55–59
    in outlaw ballads, 119–20, 127,
        133–46
    paradox of, 3–4, 49, 96, 137–38
    role in feudalism, 25–29
    scholarship on, 4–6, 10–12
    signifying chivalry's persistence,
        128–29, 134–35
    symbolic violence of, viii–ix, 3–4,
        6, 7–12, 18, 34–35, 74–75, 89,
        130
    violence of, 32–36, 74–77, 146
    See also chivalry; gift giving

Ohlgren, Thomas H., 134, 135,
    169n36, 171n59
Otter, Monika, 97
outlaw ballads
    chivalry's persistence in, 120
    confluence with romance, xi,
        119–28
    as post-medieval form, 167n18
    violence in, 120–22

See also *Gest of Robyn Hode, A*
(poem)
Outlaw's Song of Trailbaston, The
(poem), 121–22
overt violence, 13, 15, 147, 165n34.
See also symbolic violence;
violence

Parker, Martin, 133
patronage, 64–67, 97, 148, 164n21.
See also aristocracy
Piers Plowman (poem), 124–25
pledge drink, 101
Pollard, A. J., 168n23
potlatch, 10–12
psychoanalysis, 5–6
Putter, Ad, 39, 46, 159n60

Ramsey, Lee, 168n23
reciprocity
    inequality in, 111–12, 117–18
    maintaining hospitality, 109, 112
    obligation of, 11–13, 43, 99, 138
    role of timing in, 143
    violence of, 138–39
    See also gift giving
Richard II (king of England), 6–8,
    153n17
Riddy, Felicity, 91, 152n9, 154n50,
    163n5
Riverside Chaucer, The (Benson), 66
Robin Hood and His Crew of Souldiers
    (play), 133–34, 170n44
Robyn Hode (poem). See *Gest of Robyn
    Hode, A* (poem)
romance (genre)
    audience of, 86, 154n50
    Chaucer's impact on, 80–82, 84
    chivalric violence in, viii–x
    confluence with outlaw ballads,
        119–28
    cultural significance of, 16
    difficulties categorizing, 1–3

excess of violence in, 16–18
ghosts in, 50, 61–62
gift work in, 2–3, 18–19
impact on Chaucer, 67–72
persistence of, viii–x, 67, 71–73,
    83, 132–33
reimagining of, 146–49
retrospective reading of, vii–viii

sacrifice, 79, 81, 84–85
Sacrifice Your Love (Fradenburg), 5
Sahlins, Marshall, 12–13
Salisbury, Eve, 157n37
Schelp, Hanspeter, 156n20
Seminar VII, 5–6
Sheale, Richard, 148
Shipman's Tale, The (Chaucer), 69
Shoaf, R. A., 90
Shuffelton, George, 45
Simpson, James, 159n60
Sir Amadace (poem)
    biblical parallels in, 159n63
    chivalry's return envisioned in,
        49–50, 59–61
    commodities in, 159n60
    expectation of returns in, 55–59
    feudalism portrayed in, 158n54,
        158n56
    importance of secrecy in, 51,
        54–55
    plot summary, 54–55
    violence portrayed in, 56–61
Sir Cleges (poem)
    gift giving in, 38–39, 43–45
    issue of pride in, 156n20
    minstrels in, 41–42, 46–48, 148,
        157n22, 157n37
    miraculous cherries motif, 42–45,
        157n24
    plot summary, 38
    religious themes in, 38–39, 43–44
    violence in, 38, 45–49, 156n18
Sir Degaré (poem), 17

Sir Gawain and the Carle of Carlisle (poem)
  chivalric violence performed in, 113–16
  hospitality in, 108–12
  plot summary, 107
  power dynamic driving plot of, 100
  stag hunt episode, 107–8
  theological themes in, 101–2
  transformation motif, 106–7
  versions of, 106, 166n59
Sir Gawain and the Green Knight (poem)
  capitalism in, 90–91
  chivalry's persistence in, 86–87, 88–89, 163n11
  circularity in, 88–89
  community unification in, xi
  cultural value of, 89–90, 96
  gift giving addressed in, 91–94
  green girdle in, 88, 90, 92, 96, 104–5, 162
  hood game, 165n35
  hospitality in, 99–101, 164n27
  instability of gift's meaning in, 96–106
  sympathetic readings of, 164n31
  theological interpretations of, 91, 163n11
  violence as a gift in, xi, 89–90, 94–96
Sir Gowther (poem), 17, 115
Sir Launfal (poem), 49–54, 61
Skeat, Walter W., 168n23
Smith, D. Vance, 4–5, 52, 94, 166n55
social order
  accommodations between classes, 113–14
  in Brenner's thesis, 171n61
  outlaws in, 123
  role of giving in, 10–11, 76, 93

  role of violence in, viii, 6
  See also aristocracy; feudalism
Spearing, A. C., 33–34, 52
spendthrift romances
  Awntyrs off Arthur, 32–36
  chivalric violence in, x, 36–38
  Gest's inversion of, 145
  limits of giving in, 118
  Sir Amadace, 49–50, 54–61
  Sir Cleges, 38–49
  Sir Launfal, 49–54, 61
  and the total gift, 36–37
Squire's Tale, The (Chaucer), 72–73, 118, 166n63
Steel, Karl, 58
surplus
  ambivalence toward, 32–36
  in aristocracy, 79–80, 130–31
  in capitalism, 130–31
  chivalric forms of, 56–59, 71, 113–14, 138–39
  cultural value of, 22
  of the gift, 92, 94–96, 143–45
  in hospitality, 109–10
  minstrels benefiting from, 41–42
  of violence, 16–18
Sutherland, Keston, 149
symbolic violence
  Bourdieu's work on, 13–15, 165n34
  as a changing cultural phenomenon, 9, 149–50
  durability of, 146–47
  of the gift, viii–ix, 3–4, 6–15, 88–89, 139–42
  impossibility of, 154n38
  of noble giving, viii–ix, 3–4, 6, 10–12, 18, 34–35, 74–75, 89, 130
  in outlaw ballads, 120–21
  See also violence
symbolic violence theory, 6, 13–15

Tale of Gamelyn, The (poem), 121–22,
    124, 127–32, 170n57, 171n59
  classification of, 128, 168n23
  similarities to the *Gest*, 134, 139,
    140, 141, 142
Tale of Sir Thopas (Chaucer), 82, 125
Tardif, Richard, 135
Taylor, P. B., 90
Trinity Homilies, 158n42
Tristan and Iseult (poem), 123
Troilus and Ciseyde (poem), 161n35
True Tale of Robin Hood, The (Parker),
    133
Turke and Sir Gawain, The (poem),
    116–17, 166n61

violence
  changing forms of, viii–ix
  changing need for, 147
  and desire, 92–96
  establishing possession, 129–30
  excessiveness of, 16–18
  in *Floris*, 23–29
  forming community, 85–86,
    111–12, 140–41, 146, 149,
    172n71
  in *The Franklin's Tale*, 68–70
  of the gift, viii, 7–12, 32–36,
    89–90, 112–13, 146
  of hospitality, 110–12
  in *The Knight's Tale*, 70–71,
    74–77
  in outlaw ballads, 120–22,
    133–39, 142–43
  paradox of, 23–29
  role in aristocracy, 40, 97–99
  role in chivalry, 40, 45–49, 93,
    97–99, 107–8, 136–37
  as self-interested, 30–34
  in *Sir Amadace*, 56–61
  in *Sir Cleges*, 40, 45–49
  in *Sir Launfal*, 51–54
  as symbolic capital, 51–54
  transformation through, 106–7
  See also symbolic violence

Walsingham, Thomas, 7–8
Wars of Alexander, The (romance),
    16
Wife of Bath's Tale, The (Chaucer),
    72
women, 23–24, 26–27

Walter Wadiak is assistant professor of English at Lafayette College.

CPSIA information can be obtained
at www.ICGtesting.com
Printed in the USA
LVOW11*0526091216

516441LV00004B/10/P

9 780268 101183